Spirits of the Sacred Grove:

The World of a Druid Priestess

Spirits of the Sacred Grove:

The World of a Druid Priestess

Emma Restall Orr

Winchester, UK
Washington, USA

First published by Moon Books, 2014
Moon Books is an imprint of John Hunt Publishing Ltd., Laurel House, Station Approach,
Alresford, Hants, SO24 9JH, UK
office1@jhpbooks.net
www.johnhuntpublishing.com
www.moon-books.net

For distributor details and how to order please visit the 'Ordering' section on our website.

Text copyright: Emma Restall Orr 2013

ISBN: 978 1 78279 685 5

A CIP catalogue record for this book is available from the British Library.

Design: Stuart Davies
Cover image from a painting by Stuart Davies
www.stuartdaviesart.com

Printed and bound by CPI Group (UK) Ltd, Croydon, CR0 4YY

We operate a distinctive and ethical publishing philosophy in all
areas of our business, from our global network of authors to
production and worldwide distribution.

CONTENTS

Foreword to the New Edition   vii

Note   x

Preface   xii

Introduction   1

Chapter 1: NO-BODY   10
Samhain: The year begins in the dark north-west

Chapter 2: THE WOMB   32
Yule: The spirit affirmed in the depths of the north

Chapter 3: FIRST BREATH   65
Imbolc: Entering the world in the tender north-east

Chapter 4: NOTHING AND FREEDOM   98
The Spring Equinox: Finding inspiration in the freah
    air of the of the east

Chapter 5: SEX AND DRIVE   126
Beltane: Relationship in the richness of the south-east

Chapter 6: DOING WHAT   156
Midsummer: Understanding power in the heat of the south

Chapter 7: SAYING YES   189
Lughnasdh: Commitment in the wealth of the south-west

Chapter 8: TIDES AND CHANGE   218
The Autumn Equinox: Letting go in the twilight of the west

Chapter 9: EXQUISITE RELEASE   245
Samhain: In the darkness the cycle ends to begin again

Appendix: Glossary and terms   267

Foreword to the New Edition

A week ago the manuscript of this book arrived in my in-tray. In a twenty first century way, its arrival was almost silent but for the small soft bell that ushers in the inkless words of digital post. It should have landed heavily on the doormat, half a ream of paper, weighted with memories, for since its arrival I have felt its presence, acutely.

Published first in 1998 as *Spirits of the Sacred Grove*, a few years later its multinational corporate publisher re-titled it *Druid Priestess* and released it into the American market. Of course, any writer is grateful to have a book distributed more widely, but the new title was a little awkward: had they not read the note about 'Sexes', written for the first edition, and re-printed below? Each time I had to explain the contradiction, I laughed! It is with pleasure, then, that through Moon Books I offer this edition under its original title. That it is now published as a Classic makes me both chuckle and sigh, and wonder at the 17 years or so that have somehow trickled by.

While the heart of the book remains vibrant and valid, still reflecting many of the colours of my soul, some of the images and anecdotes may now feel dated. In some respects a good deal has changed over what is effectively nearly two decades. To start with, Druidry is far better understood and accepted within British society than it was in the late 1990s, and in turn that has facilitated its acceptance in other parts of the world.

Furthermore, books like this have made a significant impact on how Druidry has evolved, challenging the dominant male, middle-class, liberal attitudes that so pervaded the tradition when I was seeking it out a decade earlier. Others have followed me since, encouraging teachings that are wilder and freer, more female and fluid, presenting a practice of Druidry that could be seen as a 'shamanism' of Britain.

However, the other day I heard a respected speaker describe Druidry as a nice white wine. It was a wry and affectionate comment, but it provoked me to recall why I have always been a provocative voice in the tradition. Within every organisation or community there is a tendency towards conformity: to belong, we are guided to behave in a certain way, to agree with a certain set of beliefs. Even where such a pressure is not asserted or intended, there is still the risk that seekers may in some way acquiesce, compromising to fall in with the norm. And wherever such conformity exists, the result is bland and uninspiring. When I wrote this book, part of me was still exploring the territory of what was defined and delineated as Druidry, and in doing so I encountered a good deal of white wine.

In offering this book, I am pleased to be able to write a new foreword, not least because, in welcoming readers to these pages, I can emphasise the lack of need to conform. Indeed, I would hope that in my words, written so long ago, readers will find the inspiration to refuse the white wine wherever it is offered whenever they wish, without thinking that in doing so they are refusing Druidry. I hope readers will instead find streams of icy clear water to quench their thirst, and old flagons of rough homemade gin, and bitter dandelion root coffee, and the dripping juice of freshly picked apples, or whatever is the appropriate drop in each and every circumstance as it arises.

For if it can be defined at all, Druidry is surely about immediacy: the ability to adapt and honourably respond to each changing moment within nature as it rises before us on the paths of our lives. That is what nature teaches us, and being awake and willing to be taught by nature is the essential practice of this ancient British tradition.

I would like to thank Trevor Greenfield at Moon Books for typing the manuscript, and all those who have expressed delight at the prospect of it being re-published. Your encouragement is appreciated.

May you drink life in deeply.
Emma Restall Orr
Autumn Equinox 2013

Note

This is not a 'how to' book. It is my strongest advice to anyone wishing to know more or to follow the path of the Druid to find themselves a well respected teacher or training course. This can take time and patience. But it will also save time and potential confusion.

Before we know anything at all, we are free. When we have begun to discover, we each carry away with us for some time the burden of thinking we know everything. True magic is about empowerment. Empowerment is about personal creativity, not control. Competition is the game of the ego. A good teacher will never appear superior. It isn't a race for enlightenment; it is a journey towards balance and perfect peace.

There is no Holy Grail which holds all the answers. There is only our own freedom of spirit

Sexes

I don't like 'ess's. To me they make a word overly ornate. Always ensuring that when the ord 'priest' is used it is accompanied by the 'or priestess' (or vice versa) puffs out the text in an excessive way. The same applies to 'gods' or to 'godesses'. On the whole, I consider lurals such as 'gods' and 'priests' to signify either or both genders, though in the singular, if need be, I do differentiate with the horrible 'ess'. I never use the term 'Druidess', unless specifically to differentiate, considering 'Druid' to mean someone of either gender, as to 'Witch', 'Wiccan' or 'Christian', et al. I apologize if this is offensive to anybody.

Disclaimer

The characters portrayed in this book are partly fiction and partly taken from life. However, no one character is entirely based upon any one person; all are amalgamations of different people. In the same way, scenes other than those where I am alone are also a mixture of various events, different years, different places. The book was written in this way to allow me to write extensively and truthfully about the life of a priestess without worrying about misportraying any individual or situation.

I give thanks to every soul, every creature, every horizon, for their various inspirations.

PREFACE

In the course of my life, I have received some exquisite gifts. I have known love that melts your very bones, leaving the soul a shimmering pool of aching serenity. I have tasted death, I have seen its landscapes, and I have given birth. I have felt the pain that skids the mind in an endless crushing thrum; I have tumbled with the laughter of its release. I have known the warmth of my parents, the teachings of my blood line. I have worked with, prayed and danced with, some extraordinary people, priests of different gods, performers, healers and hermits. In so many ways I seem, in this lifetime of mine, to be forever landing in the most singular places, gazing about me amazed.

When this book was first published, as *Spirits of the Sacred Grove*, my motivation to write was the need to share the beauty of all that fuelled my life. Five years have since passed and, in that time, I have received that most luxuriant of gifts: appreciation. People speak of finding a sweet new sense of belonging, of acceptance, in a tradition which, I truly believe, is our natural spirituality. Druidry: it makes sense, for it is the very soul of the British and Gaelic people, the soul of their descendants now living all around the world.

My work in the priesthood has deepened over these years. As I say in the following pages, only the arrogant or ignorant would actively choose the life of a priest. In the priesthood we live with death about us, it seems, a good deal more than birth, with insanity and crisis delivered unwrapped to our door. Yet the role comes with significant gifts that, like the sleepy smile of an infant, makes the assault course worth its while. To witness the soul walking, lifting veils of anguish or apathy to see the beauty that surrounds them, is such an exquisite gift; to share moments of strength, of exuberant transformation, of dark pain and tenderness. For me, there is no choice but to walk the journey of my life entirely dedicated to my spirituality, a journey that takes me along the cutting edge of my soul, ever wakeful, ever learning, wonderstruck.

Five years is a long time. Public attitudes to Druidry have improved with more books published and, on the whole, a more intelligent attitude from the media. There is less fear and misinformation about the tradition, less blind bigotry born of ignorance. As a result, people increasingly feel able to share their Druidry with those outside it. Environmentalism, sexual equality, a growing respect for ancestral culture and individual creativity, all continue to add to the energy that will before long place the tradition where it should be, as an accepted part of the mainstream society, a source of teaching, celebration and community. The inner mysteries may remain hidden in the darkness of their very nature, but that is true of all religions.

During the years since *Spirits* was published, I have travelled a good deal, particularly around America where interest in Druidry is rich and strong, and especially in the Northern states where the climate is similar to that of the dark ancestral lands. Yet without the source landscapes beneath and around them, those studying Druidry in the US tend to focus on ancestral links and as a result the tradition often risks becoming an intellectual exercise. My hope is that these words inspire and emotional-physical interaction with the tradition where books and laws have until now held sway.

My journeys across Australia were a powerful gift of learning. Exploring the complex issues that exist when taking an ancient ancestral tradition not just from its native land and into a different climate, but also into a different hemisphere, I saw the flexibility of the tradition. As the quest for sacred relationships, for a bond between the people and the land, Druidry may have been inspired by the islands of Britain but it is a movable feast. If a priest or practitioner is competent and willing to detach entirely from the 'here and now', moving into an ancestral bubble, the circle can be worked as if it were in Britain. Otherwise the Druid's task is to listen and learn from that which hums around him, using his ancestral teachings as his perfect resource.

Indeed, only if we are able to open our souls to listen fully, to see without the blinkers of need, to touch the true reverence, can we begin to understand the art of living in a sacred way, inspired. Only then can we begin to live creatively. Beauty and freedom are not just a state of mind; they are a result of good relationship, spirit to spirit.

May your journey amidst these words be a marvellous adventure, sacred and free.

INTRODUCTION

It's a pub on the Oxford Road. The landlord has already called closing and occasionally he wanders into the doorway, wiping glasses with a sodden dishcloth, frowning, checking his watch, as he listens, curious, to the conversation. The reporter gives him a wide smile. 'Alright, Jack? Won't be long, mate. Ten minutes. Max.'

Through the window I watch a deep red maple leaf as it dances over the terracotta paving of the empty patio. In the eddies of the cold breeze it skips and twirls, almost laughing, barely touching the ground.

'Sorry. Where were we?' He pushes *Record*.

The gust moves on and the leaf is still. And in the warmth and gloom of the bar I smile. I'm listening to myself as I speak, aware of the quality of my voice, calm and quiet, the silence between myself and the microphone when my words come to an end, the chink of glasses. The look of frustration on the landlord's face, interplayed with such bemusement, keeps reminding me not to take myself too seriously.

The reporter slurps his coffee. He's young, eager to be what he wants to be, and he's polite, if barely listening to me, glancing at the flickering dials of his tape machine, scratching at his stubble, wondering how he's going to get what he really wants.

'I didn't realize women could be a part of these things.'

I laugh and shake my head. 'You're not getting this, are you?'

He smile too and shrugs and runs his fingers through his hair, embarrassed. 'Perhaps I'm not the best person they could've sent out. But at the same time how *could* I know anything about it, yeah? Secret societies and stuff.'

I realize why it is that he hasn't been listening. Time to try a different tack. 'This is not the occult.'

His eyes wake up and question me, an eyebrow raised, and I

laugh again, a tiny part of me hating to let the fellow down.

'It's an attitude, an understanding, an exquisitely simple and natural philosophy of living. For a great many it *is* a rich and ancient religion, a mystical spirituality. For others it's simply a guiding way of life. It is absolutely open and free for anyone to discover.'

'No funny handshakes, then?'

'No funny handshakes. No signs, no gurus, no great leaders, no sacred texts and commandments, no closed societies, no vows of allegiance signed and sealed in blood.' Yet as I say those last words, something stops me and I retreat for a flicker of an instant behind my smile, feeling the stillness of space rising deep inside, remembering in that split second the thousand ways I had dedicated myself to my gods. 'Sure,' I say softly, 'we retain a certain reticence about some of the things we do, but that's no different from the way in which you wouldn't talk openly about what happens between yourself and your therapist, or your accountant.'

He shrugs, in agreement if not in comprehension.

'What we do is very close to the soul. Much of it is about the deepest part of ourselves. What you tell of yourself to a lover or a counsellor is not what you'd tell to the media.'

'I can see that. But you don't help yourselves. What about these funny clothes?'

Again I'm laughing. 'You mean the long white sheets with pointy hoods?'

'It does give a pretty weird impression, a dozen blokes - OK, and ladies - dressed up like the Klu Klux Klan!'

I am used enough to these guys now to know that, despite the rolling tape between us, the questions he is asking will be edited out of the conversation, replaced by anything that will fit more succinctly with my answer.

'OK, some do wear robes when attending ceremonies. It's an important tool for shifting into a different frame of mind,

2

reminding us, affirming, that we are doing something special. But it's very seldom nowadays that they are pure white. Most wear natural cloth which is undyed and unbleached. Some wear tabards or overrobes which proclaim the grade of tradition that they are working in. These might be red or green or blue, even black, embroidered or simple. And some robes have hoods - they're another aid for focusing.'

'Like blinkers,' he says and I laugh.

'Yes, for a specific occasion and purpose. But most critically,' I tease him with my emphasis, 'the hood keeps out the wind and rain.' He smiles. I add, 'It isn't there so that we can cover our faces.'

'Yeah, OK,' he sighs, resigned. The landlord stomps back out to the saloon bar. 'Well, the point of the piece is this Hallowe'en fiasco.' He scratches at his face again, flicks through his notes and looks at me without concealing the measure of his disappointment. I'm quite aware that he had hoped the interview would be a good media stunt. A local evangelical Christian priest has put a great deal of energy into publicizing what he perceives to be the demonic nature of Hallowe'en and the radio station was hoping for an angry debate between two qually crazy people. I wonder if the vicar was as much of a let down for this ambitious lad, searching out fire and fanaticism. It's tempting to tease him with glimmer of what he wants, something he could misconstrue into the ridiculous or sensational. The story flickers through my mind of a friend, dark robed for her rite, opening the front door to a scruffy bunch of local trick o' treaters and crying, 'Marvellous! Just in time!' before calling back into the candlelit room, 'The sacrifice has arrived!' Of course, the young kids in their old sheets and ghoulish masks, cold fingers clutching onto their broomsticks and sweetie bags, all thought it was a great joke, if somewhat off the wall. Here was an adult Hallowe'en party, and somewhat outrageous at that. But to the young reporter I say nothing. I am tired, too tired to ensure that a joke

3

would be a joke. I've spent the past few nights working til the early hours, preparing for the festival, organizing class notes, dealing with the usual crises the time of year provokes.

But if he was trying for a last ditch attempt at throwing me, his next words nearly succeeded.

'What I heard is that you have a midnight ritual - and call up the dead?'

I go blank behind my smile. Grasping into the blankness I try to think of a response, positive and clear, while almost simultaneously it occurs to me that I never do think about how I will answer and so if I were to look through my mind I wouldn't know where to behind. Then I realize that's ridiculous. *Help!* I call.

The warmth of a hand sinks into my shoulder. A voice drifts into my mind.

Why didn't you ask before?

I thought I was doing fine. Wasn't I?

The flicker of his form moves around the table, tall and elegant, with the stature of a thousand years. *That depends on your perspective,* he whispers, dry as ever. He sits down on the tape recorder and the dials shiver.

'Hold on, the machine's playing up.'

The young reporter does his checks, forward and rewinds the tape, my beautiful friend in spirit standing up as the whirr of electricity tingles through him. I can't help but smile, and in my soul that smile stretches out so wide. I can barely remember a time when his shimmering presence didn't illuminate my life, filling my breath with laughter, when his eyes didn't show me the clearest way.

So what do I say, my Lord?

Tell him the truth?

But how? We do - have a ritual, at midnight. And we do invite our friends from beyond the veil to join in the feast. We do share and talk and dance with the dead...

I'm becoming aware of the reporter's voice. 'Do you believe in ghosts then? "Spirits at large and wandering the land..."

Have I been staring into apparently thin air? Seabhac lifts a finger and points at himself, then points at the man, questioning. I cough and swallow my giggles, sink my head into my hands. Breathe deeply.

'OK, let me explain. We call the festival Samhain. In terms of the cycle of natural growth the year is almost at its end and things are closing in, closing down. It's the time for formally honouring our ancestors. Death is all around us...'

I talk on, the words flowing, as Seabhac smiles and gazes around the room. I don't mention that our ceremonies are held at midnight, nor in the depths of an ancient forest.

'What about the trick o' treating?'

'That's a modern invention, but a reflection of the old Samhain, the time of chaos between the end of a cycle and the beginning of a -'

'It's one of Reverend O'Leary's main objections,' he interrupts, 'little children dressing up as devils and witches. Do you let your son go out knocking on doors?'

'He's a little young -'

'But would you?'

At last he thinks he's onto something. This time I give it to him.

'I'm not sure.'

'So you wouldn't either? Why not?'

'Perhaps it is a way of letting kids process all the fears about the culture's monsters, which is very important. But we do that another way, through a different attitude to life, and in sacred space instead of on the street, in a way which avoids the plastic commercialization of the festival - and rotten teeth - while not denying the point.'

'Which is?'

'The death and the dark are natural aspects of our world -

along with birth, growth, pain, change. We need to learn ways in which we can work within their natural constraints.'

My words seem to go straight over him. Or past him.

'Alright,' he grins, concluding, 'it sounds like we've got something there we can use.'

As ever, it all seems to be over before I've said anything and I feel at a loss, playing with my empty glass.

'I would've preferred to do it live, face to face with the Christian priest.'

'Yeah, well, he wasn't too keen. Bit nervous, I think.'

I smile, a little sad, suspecting his fear to be not only of the studio but also of me, of what he believes I am.

But then the young fellow looks up. 'One last thing. Maybe we could splice it in somewhere, or intro with it. I wonder if you'd tell me, you know, sum it up: what is Druidry exactly?'

* * *

The next day the radio broadcast a piece that was, for the listening public, a slurp of tinned soup – any potentially unfamiliar chunks either chopped too small or cooked to the brink of collapse to avoid any possible need for chewing. In my frustration I hoped that there was some nourishment left in it, that some hint of the beauty and joy was tasted by a few who had previously known nothing – those few who had ears to hear, who had the palate and sufficient hunger.

I had spoken about my role as I understand it, as I have been taught and guided and, as I always do with newcomers, with the media and with Great Auntie Maude, as a diplomat measuring how far my words could and would be understood, missing out anything that might be misconstrued. I had expressed my faith in a way that I felt would be acceptable, softening the brilliant primary hues, muffling the drums. I had started the job of chopping up the ingredients and thus played a part in the liquidizing and canning.

It wasn't that I wished I had said more, for it wouldn't have been viable. Certainly I hope that in the not too distant future the ways of the faith will be well known and accepted. But it was more than that. Rising in me was the sense that I had dishonoured my faith by the very act of containing it, even to the limited extent that I had. Summing up a spiritual philosophy to fit into the limitations of a radio current affairs soundbite is hard. If it were possible to do it with Druidry, I would have had it perfected long ago – only to *sum up* the philosophy would be painfully contradictory. For Druidry is simply a series of signposts that guide us though the landscape of our lives. It does not define the world that we see along the way. It has no distinct rules of practice or behaviour, no scripture. Like the little wooden marker posts we find in our managed forests, where many different symbols offer many different routes without any clues as to what one might find down any particular path. Druidry makes its quiet suggestions, encouraging us forward, and leaves us to be who we are, to see what we might see, to respond in our own way. It gently holds us on our experience and does not judge us for it, for it never constrains.

Perhaps it is my desire to release the feelings of frustration evoked by contradiction of wanting to – at times having to – answer that simple question, 'What is Druidry exactly?', yet not wishing to limit the incredible spectrum of its potential, that motivates me now to write as I do, to express the nature of the faith without losing its wild spirit, the mud and blood of its rich earthiness, or its diversity, in the dilution or the packaging.

No doubt also there's the wish to relieve the discomfort that so many of the tradition feel, the itchy ache that comes with not being able to express oneself fully, honestly and at any time without encountering the prejudice and intolerance which still rebound from a society that knows so little about the faith. My hope is perhaps my words will alleviate some of the fears that still exist.

So I wonder where to begin. If the process of describing Druidry definitively is barely possible without limiting it, and thereby invalidating its nature, then the act of committing it to paper is a worse task still. All I can hope to do is share my experience. And so I offer here a series of paintings, both portrait and landscape, in the colours and styles of what I have been taught, blended and detailed with the brushes of my own soul and this lifetime's personality. Each reveals a different moment in the daily application of a natural spirituality, together with ideas as to why it is so powerful a way of living.

When it needs a name, as a philosophy I call it 'Druidry'. As a practice it is 'Druidcraft', or simply 'the Craft'. It has been called 'the old religion' or 'the old ways'; it is the track of the old gods. Some aspects of it weave into modern Wicca and natural Witchcraft, the traditions of the Norse and what is now called the shamanism of the Native Americans and the Maori, and other ancient spiritual philosophies and practices. Some simply call it their own Paganism. It is the native spirituality of these Pretannic islands of Britain and Ireland, and of their people, some now spread across the globe. Its focus, its altar, is the natural world. Perhaps you will recognize it, perhaps already have your own name for it. Perhaps through my words you will sense some deeply familiar, though as yet unnamed, language of you own soul.

For many in my work I am a Druid priestess. Some of my teachers have been Druids, while as many again have been of other spiritual traditions. What I have absorbed of their wisdom has been woven into my Druid practice. It would be true to say that all the pictures hung here could be described as modern Pagan Druidry. But each one is painted through my own perspective and, though many may walk the same paths, we each experience the journey in a way that is entirely unique. Different trees, clouds and paw-prints in the mud catch our eye. We each find our own places to rest, to trip up and to dream.

If the journeys I take you along are to you pure fantasy and creative imagination, then it is so. If you run and dance with me, feeling and seeing what my pathway reveals, if for you it is a true world in existence, if not commonly perceived, then that is so too. For where I am, both views are necessary. Both realities exist and where they truly merge without need for reason, there is freedom.

But where to begin?

I

NO-BODY

SAMHAIN: THE YEAR BEGINS IN THE DARK NORTH-WEST

We begin at Samhain.

The first chill winds of Scorpio are howling in, blasting through the trees, tearing off the old leaves, bringing dead wood crashing to the forest floor. The first frosts of dawn are killing back the annuals, stripping herbs down to the mud, leaving stalks pale and bare. Everyone and everything that hopes to survive til spring is crawling into the warmth of the rotting leafmould, retreating to the roots, wrapping themselves up in layers of soft fat, in thick coats, gloves and scarves. There is no denying that winter is sliding in. Even when the sun shines between the clouds it's not warm. It's a time when we could slide too, into grey days and dark mornings shivering in the shower, clutching at hot coffee and dreams of summer nights.

But in Druidcraft that's not the way. We scrunch up our summer nostalgia and, throwing back our heads, howl back at the wind, calling out to the gods of the festival of Samhain, 'Hail!' Yes, winter is coming and with it that urge to curl up in our burrows and caves to hibernate. But we must wait just a little longer. Samhain is the last festival til the spring for which people will travel far to gather together and celebrate life, and the last great tales of the year must be told again, the wild songs of the summer camping-grounds must be sung one last time. Those whose harvest has been full will bring their excess for those in need as the bonds of peace and support are affirmed between tribes and allies, should they need to be called upon through the cold hard moons ahead.

For many in the Craft this is the most important of all the festivals, the most potent, the most essential. Ahead of us lie the unknown seasons of the future, but whilst our hands are still sticky with the experiences of the past year, the sweat and blood of our work, the tears and ecstasy of our creativity, we have no hope of fully grasping the potential of the next. So the Druids' rites and ceremonies are written and played out to focus on the chance to give thanks for the closing of another cycle before the winter covers the land. The past is addressed, honoured and put behind us.

Except that is a process which is not usually as easily accomplished as decided upon. Though the year ends, the new year is still in its conceptual state, still but a sparkle of anticipation, distant and intangible. Were it to step out into life right now, it would risk being crushed underfoot in the frozen mud. While secular modern society waits for that click which takes us from 23:59 to 00:00 on 31 December, the Druid knows that life does not work like that – there is no moment that marks the new year as having formally begun. There is a distinct gap between the ending of the old and the time when the new cycle is perceptibly underway.

At Samhain, then, untying ourselves from the structure of the old, dismantling the framework, we enter a period where there is no framework – and so no limitations already laid down which need to be contended with. The scope of our potential is once again opened out to its fullest extent. There is the possibility of the most poignant sensation of freedom. Suddenly anything can happen. And in the frenetic dancing of the Samhain rite and celebrations, exhilarated with the release and spinning round the fires, the night air is alive with this experience.

There is little thought for the trash.

But the mess of what we have taken apart is still strewn and liable to trip us unless we clear it up and out. Though some is consciously thrown into the ritual flames, much is left to be dealt with alone. The process has been started by the flames, but it is up to us to complete it in the privacy of our own journeys and meditations. And when the celebrations are over, heading into the long nights of winter, we are conscious that in the darkness we are not entirely in control; our vision is all but useless and our sensitivity is wildly intensified.

When the Christian Church set its ritual calendar, many of the local customs held around Samhain that could not be suppressed were addressed, contained and sanctified under the guise of All Hallows' Eve, followed by the liturgies for All Souls and All Saints. This time, the dusk of the year, when the fields are dark mud and the spirits of the trees sleepy, heavy, has always been when the boundaries between the living world and the lands across the river of death have been most open. But it isn't only our dead loved ones and guides who come to us at Hallowe'en; spectres of the past, the unresolved and unconcluded, the demons that scowl from the realms of our rage and denial, these too lurk in the corners of our minds, looming out of the darkness of the endless nights ahead.

So, before the land can even be prepared for the sowing of a new year's seeds, the trash of our denials and the residue of the previous year must cleared. So, in the chaos of Samhain, the Druid acknowledges the opportunity to walk into the dark, to look into the shadows and address the issues that have been swept to the back with the stiff brooms of denial. Not all will be cleared – but there are plenty more cycles ahead, after all.

There may be no framework within which to orient, but the Druid doesn't work unaided. She has her stag, her sacred circle and the musky scents of her ritual, her guides and allies in the worlds of spirit and of flesh, the tools of her understanding and, perhaps most importantly, her vision of reality. So she sets her intention, to live as she would wish, and she walks from the sleepy world of unconscious dreaming into the lucid dreamstate and from there steps over into conscious waking.

* * *

Leaving the young reporter in the pub that day, putting away his tape machine and chatting with landlord, I walk out into the scents of the late October air, bewildered. Bursts of rain are whirling in the breeze, gusts lifting the dry leaves into eddies of life, and down the city streets I hold on to the emptiness of my disconnection, concentrating on my driving, losing myself in the very action. The houses fall behind me, the roads become lanes and the energy around me begins to change, filling with a deep and exquisite hum. I stop a mile or into forest, turning off the engine and allowing the vibration to wash through my every pore. When I feel sufficiently calm I step out and breathe.

Calling to the guardian spirits of the forest, calling to the dryad, affirming the peace of my intention, I head down familiar paths amongst the trees. *O my Lady, may my every step be a blessing on your body.* Onto the deer tracks, slippy with mud and the glow of fallen leaves, overgrown with the bracken and bramble tangled, I weave and glide, ducking beneath low branches, breathing in the moist cool air.

It takes around 15 minutes to reach the gateway: five hawthorn trees grown thickly together, almost bare now of leaves and berries, in a swathe of holly that shimmers beneath beeches. I crouch down and whisper the words of the prayer. The faces hidden in the gnarled trunks acknowledge me and carefully I step into the mass of branches, spikes and thorns. Once I'm within and reopen my eyes, the way seems to open up and before long I am through and stretch into a new world. The skies seem higher, yet I can feel their touch and, as ever, my first reaction is a thick need to laugh, to release the sudden surge of energy that fills my chest, my stomach, bursting in my womb, my vulva, shrieking in my throat, expanding my cranium til I'm whirling with exhilaration. I throw my head back and, softly, strong deep notes roll out of me, yet from far within me it's as if the sound is that of the ground beneath my feet. And as I sing, I walk, feeling the weight and the give of every step, on through the oak and beech, through birch and ash, hazel wound around with honeysuckle and shining holly, so joyful to be at home once more, my hair free in the breeze.

The cry of a jay breaks through the trees.

Hello, brother, I whisper through my song.

And he yells, *Hey! Door's open! Watch out! Door's open!*

What door?

He laughs out raucously. I catch a flash of his black and white and blue as he flies off, leaving a floating silence. Have I left something open, somewhere? Is something wrong up ahead?

The bracken undergrowth is waist high and I am careful not to break the brittle stems and leave any kind of a path. Through the bank of holly, ducking under the branches of a great beech, at last I arrive, heart pounding. A gentle light is touching the ground. A grove of five oaks, all a few centuries old, creates a perfect circle some 30 feet across. Their branches interweave, bare against the sky but for dozen or so flittering dry leaves. Immediately before me lies the vast broken trunk of an oak long since struck by lightning. I bow, offering my greetings to the guardian spirits before entering the sacred space. *Hail in peace, Tyroshai. Blessed be as blessed is.*

I hadn't been aware of how cold I was until I feel the shift in temperature walking into the grove. My feet crunch on leaves and acorns, twigs torn from trees in the winds of the last week, as I slowly make my way around the inner edge of the circle, marked out as it is with chunks of flint, white and bluish grey, mossy and half hidden in the mud and leaves. As I walk the stones seem both to follow and draw me on and once again the space is mine, cast with my energy and devotion, provoking me to twirl and stretch and sing to the spirits of that place.

In my memory I see it as it was just a few days before – twists of ivy and flame-coloured flowers marking the points of the circle, lanterns flickering, wooden bowls of nuts and baskets of apples, squash and pumpkins, a gathering of friends come to celebrate the retirement of one amongst them, come to offer their acknowledgement, to respect the turning of his life, to drink to his past and honour the potential of his future, to allow the change and do so in a sacred manner. It was joyful and deeply moving day, so rich with laughter.

I scoop up a handful of russet and ochre leaves and throw them into the air, watching them dance and drift and settle as they will. *Hail, my Lady of this temple, to your beauty!*

There's a glint of blue and crouching down I find a tiny feather, a downy breast feather. Holding it in my fingers, breathing in the scent of its oil and freedom I look around for the jay.

Thank you. Beautiful Bird, shedding beauty. Remembering his words again, *Door's open! Watch out!*, I turn back to the gateway into the grove, the broken trunk to one side, the end of a candle from the last ceremony held here nuzzled into the crack on the inside. But the grove felt whole, not open at all.

I feel dreamy and the warmth of the circle makes me stretch and yawn. I have work to do and requests to look into and sick folk to attend to through the mists of the other worlds, but instead I snuggle up amongst the roots of an old oak. I am conscious of the sensation of being drawn up and out of my body, aware of the voice of Seabhac calling, as I slide…

But in reality it's not good trying to sleep. Just being in the forest is so wildly invigorating, fuelling me with such a vitality that it can't be more than five minutes before I give up, opening my eyes. The circle is gone but I don't notice. My body is itching with energy, rearing to go, and I grab my boots, pulling them on. They're so bright against the mud and soggy brown leaves on the ground and still so shiny from the shop. I stick my legs out straight and admire them. Bright red. (Mum tried to get me the green ones with bulgy crocodile eyes, but those are for babies and I'm seven and a quarter years old.)

I smudge off some mud with mittened fingers, jump up and I'm off into the undergrowth, picking up twigs and sticks, pulling at fallen branches to see what's dry enough for a fire. The ground beneath an area of young birch is littered with twigs that crack underfoot and *snap* when I bend them, and I gather up an armload, tugging at a big fallen branch to see whether it will move. And I play in the puddles of mug along the path, then run on to the open space where a few beeches have found enough room to spread out strongly. One has a lower branch that reaches close to the ground and I abandon my bundle to jump up and clamber through the branches, higher and higher, til I can shimmy up to the crook where two branches fork, making a perfect place to sit and survey the world. Over the tops of the birch and across the bare forest canopy I watch a couple of wood pigeons take to their winds in their flustered noisy way and settle again a little way off.

So far above the ground I feel like a squirrel snug in her drey. I could stay here for hours, just watching. The sky is thick with layers of cloud and way out to the horizon there is nothing but grey trees broken up here and there by patches of dark pine. In every direction there is nothing of my life.

Better than school any day…

Everything starts to swim a little in front of my eyes. Time to get down.

A squawking starts up behind me and when I turn, dizzy, holding on, I see a crowd of rooks perched up in the highest trees.

What's up? I call. *Isn't it just great up here?*

Yes, yes! One clamours, *but something must be done!*

Not again! Another yells, taking off, great black wings beating into the damp air.

That's enough! That's enough!

Another rook argument flares and dies down as I watch from

16

my treetop and laugh out aloud.

You're getting faint, whispers a voice. *Time to get down.*

I slide and step my way down to the lowest branch that bends down over the ground for a while, I lie, draped over it, half hugging tight, half relaxed.

Nearby a patch of greeny brown toadstools is growing in the tangle of the wood and dried up nettles beneath a long fallen beech. Some of the caps are as big as the palm of my hand and for a while I lie and watch the ants underneath. The beech trunk is covered in soft grey-green moss, its roots raised up in an enormous clump of mud and flint. A huge spider runs through the air, then I see its web stretched between the old twigs and I watch, quite captivated, as it sits very still, just waiting.

My breath is beginning to – *haaa* – get all misty. It must be getting late. I walk on to where the summertime wild raspberries grow, muddy puddles now, and scramble under a holly to where it's dark and enclosed for a while I wonder at nobody knowing where I am.

Except us, come little voices.

I know, I shrug at the glinting forms of the faeries, but then I shiver. *I'm going back to the rowan to make a fire. Get the camp sorted out for when the winter comes.*

And I crawl out and wander back, kicking at stones and gathering up a new load of sticks. The daylight is fading and now and then I have to wince and shake my head to see more clearly as the trees grow less distinct, obscured by curtains of floating grey. I start to stumble over roots and stones, my legs getting heavier. In my pockets I clutch at the conkers and the pits of the plums that mum gave me at lunch, but then I need hands to test the air as more and more I confuse the colours and shadows with the actual trees. I can hear my dad's voice in my head saying, 'Why are you so bloody clumsy?' and I trip over, scrambling back to my feet. But something's caught my coat.

Where are you going, little one?

Nowhere, I say firmly, gritting my teeth. *Get off me!*

We could have fun, princess.

I yank my coat back. *Go away!*

But the eyes are glinting through the mists of grey.

Come on, little one.

And then suddenly one of them is beside me, the dark form sharply clear yet almost sticky, and that whole side of my body starts to drag, the dreadful ache of its weight pulling me, and I'm screaming *No!* and running and stumbling and crying out aloud, 'No, no! Leave me alone!' and my voice in the empty forest is smaller than the squeaking of the mice under the mesh of the brambles.

When I crash through under the tangle of honeysuckle, skidding to the ground beneath the rowan, stars are spinning with the world before my eyes. I hold on to my head and determine everything to just *stop!*

The little figure calmly strolls through the undergrowth, as close as he can get, the magic of the rowan tree holding him back. *Remember?* He says, in that voice like grit and syrup.

No! I'm covering my eyes so tightly but still the horrid images slide into view. My heart is thumping in my throat, my face wet with that same old fear and the rage of my helplessness. *Help! Seabhac! Help!*

But Seabhac isn't there. And strangely it occurs to me that he wouldn't be there, because I didn't know him then. And a part of me awakes to see the child cowering in the half light of the old wood, clinging on to the rowan's silver trunk, stiff with fear. Her hair is a wild tangle of black rats' tails, her face streaked with dirt and tears, her clothes filthy. But it's the state of those clothes, the little red coat covered in mud, ripped at the shoulder that sends such a blast of emotion through me, through the me that is looking on, for I know that there is no way I can go home with my coat like that. Mummy will cry and it'll be all my fault again and when will she stop crying this time...?

Seabhac touches my face, very gently pushing up my chin.
Oh sweet salvation! I was dreaming, oh God –
I know, he says softly.

From his robe he brings out a silver flask which he offers to me
and, hands shaking, I drink the cold liquid, feeling it spread
through my body into every dusty corner, every part that is thick
with the sweat of fear. It takes a while before I can speak, before
words will pattern into any kind of sense.

Thank you. I breathe heavily the scented air of the grove. *Why?*
Come on. He moves to go.
Seabhac?

He turns to give me one of those looks as if to say, *Remember*
to think before you speak or how will you ever know what's yours?

We walk in silence through the half light, out of the grove and
along paths heading north-west, up the gentle incline through
the thickest part of the wood. I'm not quite sure who's leading
whom. Thoughts drift around me of my childhood isolation, the
ache of being ignored through my inability to communicate, of
holding my mother through the pain of her memories, her sense
of failure born of her own mother's.

My thoughts are still filling my vision when Seabhac's
response to the call of an owl draws me back into my present. I
realize we're stopped and I am gazing across the shining
darkness of a pool. The water is quite black in the twilight and
silent. Across the other side is a rock where I have sat before and
I make my way towards it, holding on to the thickest branches of
elder trees so as not to fall. But I misjudge a step and, grabbing
at the branch, reach into the blackthorn. I suck at the blood
oozing from my fingers and glare at the dryad. Flowing around
her wisps of energy like hair in the stillness.

Look into the water.
Seabhac?

He is watching me, questioning my hesitation. He is so old

and yet so beautiful at times I find it hard to know what it is about him that has aged. It is as if, were I to blink, his face would be soft and young.

I look to the water. In its sway my face, my body shift. Hooded and desolate I frown, then, childlike, dancing, a twisted old crone, silently screaming, laughing, unsure. The water draws me in, from the centre of my soul. I step in, my feet are slipping into the mud, my clothes picking up weight then the water removing it, its cold like an acid dissolving the scaffolding of my living. I let go. The icy darkness seeps deep into my body as a shadow emerges from the pool, rising up from the black water, looming for a moment in the night air above me. Memories of fear glide through me but none now stick and I continue to sink. And in my release, the pool's energy falls over me like silken rain, exquisitely cool, like a blade so sharp it gives no pain, and as I submerge it floods through my mind.

Deep in my grove, in the lap of the oak, something touches my face with the breath of a cool breeze. I am slipping back into my physical form. I stretch my fingers, yawn, breathing in vibrant air. A sleepiness falls off me like a veil as I glide to my feel and slowly I walk, running my fingers through the textures of the dusk, over the bark of the trees, touching, responding to everything around me. The layers of my dream journey are vague, playing around the edges of my waking mind, as if still being processed deep down where my active senses would interfere.

When the wood of my fire is sufficiently aflame, from a little box beneath the holly I fetch what I need. Lighting a charcoal block with a match, I watch it sparkle with saltpetre between finger and thumb before placing it in the darkened hollow of a large flint. I pour water into a conch shell, resting it in the earth. And I begin to walk the circle, around and around, an old chant humming in my mind, moving into my throat til it fills the air through which I walk, yet clinging to me like the moisture of the mist.

Raising the conch into the darkening sky, the firelight licking into the air, I call to the spirits and elementals. With my words, the shell tingles and suddenly I am dizzy, my head swirling til I acknowledge and focus the energy. With words sung in blessing, I scatter drops of the consecrated water as I once again walk the circle. I mark my own body with it, sip its coldness. From jars I take herbs and resins and, feeling the mixture charged with sacred energy, pulsing in my hand, let it fall onto the charcoal, and I dance in the richness of the smoky aroma, filling my lungs and my hair with its blessings, as it fills the circle beneath the trees.

From my neck I take a pendant, silver and pearls that I have worn for many years, and – barely knowing why – I place it on the altar stone beside the fire. I sink through my weaving dance to kneel in the leaves. 'For my mother.' I bow my head and tears roll into the emptiness. *For your pain. For the gift of your experience. For our life. I give you thanks.*

Into a pewter goblet I pour from a bottle of dark port, raising it in the name of my gods, bowing as I call to my ancestors, to all whose body and spirit have come before me to this world, to my heritage of blood, of womb and milk, of fighting and fear all that has taught and brought me to this place. *Hail in peace.* And onto the ground I pour my libation to my gods, to my ancestors and the gods of my ancestors, and into the flames that hiss with it. And as I drink the dark liquid it spreads through me like red fire, and with it come the memories of the black pool of my dreamtime.

My fingers are shaking with energy as in the same way I bless and offer the malted bread, crumbling it over the fallen leaves and the mud of the grove floor, dropping it into the glowing fire, tasting its sweetness. *Feast with me, oh blessed ones, the richness of our sacred earth –*

My energy surges again through my body, drawing me into

the dance as the sounds of chanting fill my head. *Mud and stone, blood and bone, all are one! All are one!*

I spin with my emotion and twirl and glide and stamp the circle cast, pushing my energy higher, faster, til my body and soul are so high with it that I must land or scream. Stumbling, reeling, I sink onto the flat stone by the fire, my breathing sharp like the drums in my soul, and slowly I grasp all that I have done, focusing, centring, stilling into silence. On the leafmould just beside the stone is a tiny blue feather. 'Jay,' I whisper, and smile. *You did warn me about an open door. I drifted right through.*

Looking up, I see Seabhac standing beneath the beech, the glow of his energy shimming in the darkness, the shining of his eyes.

You were tired.

I laugh aloud. For now I remember the end of my dreamtime. Emerging from the liquid darkness of the pool, brilliant, shivering with life, I had slipped back into clearer form, but not human form, not that of a woman. As a wild cat, as the bobcat in my soul, I had shaken the wetness from my fur and run through the woods, chasing rabbits, pouncing, rolling in the moss and leaves, batting at butterflies. And I had lain at his feet, panting, as he had rubbed the white fur on my tummy and under my chin.

Now, sitting on the stone, I'm aware of the purring inside me, the wonderful sense of release and freedom. I stretch my cat mouth in a yawn of pleasure and smile, opening my eyes and gently bowing to my friend in spirit.

Form my bag beside the stone I take out a bundle, unwrapping dark green linen to find the black-bound book inside. I smooth out a clean page, flickering white in the firelight, and allow my mind to open a door. Picking up the pen, I start write.

* * *

It is said that our fear of the dark is innate, rooted in an age when our most terrifying predator was the sabre-toothed cat. Nocturnal, on silent paws it leapt out of the darkness, its two extraordinarily elongated teeth slamming into the cranium. I rather doubt that the process took long enough to be painful, but if you should happen to be the observer the vision might well stay with you for some time. Perhaps ever lifetimes. And so it compacts with the weight of time, that fear, as the anticipation of what might be out there lurking in the shadows of the night, those dreadful fears, all that we just don't know and, the smaller one with sharper claws, all that we don't want to know.

As hunter and hunted, all the energy that is evoked surges through our bodies, instantly focused on the situation in hand. But few of us in our gently fertile land have been chased by wild and hungry carnivores of late, nor have we been shot at recently or spent days searching for food. We are relatively comfortable, comfortable enough to debate human rights, protest against road extensions, have depressions about lack of achievement and self-esteem, have crises over the ebb and flow of personal relation-ships, be worn down to exhaustion and physical illness over issues such as not being listened to or valued, to ponder our spirituality. Though for some such crises do reach life-threat-ening extremes, it is seldom so. Yet still the stress is there, the fear of what might happen.

Of course, even without the sharp-clawed and ravenous predators, there are great swathes of our planet where men fighting men have taken over the role of the terrifying beast. Yet even for those who have only seen the bloody and wasting edges of human life through the softening, distancing gaze of the television screen, the angst of the struggle is likely to be acute. The emotional adrenal response that would be needed to face the pack of wolves, the cat or bear, may now be directed at the government, the council, the boss, or may just be getting stuck and pumping up the blood pressure, but on some level the desperate need still remains to overcome the constant fear of not surviving, of starving, of painful death, being hunted, riddled with shrapnel or poisoned darts.

Somehow we believe that were we to have control over our environment, be it the family, the workplace, the neighbours or South East Asia, the strain of vigilance would disappear. Energy is poured into what we call our 'sense of security' and very little else is ever achieved.

In evolutionary terms, this seems rather a small step from frenetic survival. Perhaps we have moved from the ancient reptilian part of our brain, where there is no sense of self, up into the limbic, paleomammalian parts, where our emotions are played out, our mothering issues expressed and explored. In terms of the etheric body, we have climbed from the root chakra to the sacrum, but we are essentially still focused on safety. I wonder, as I walk my own pathways, how much is it from that need, where the limbic brain connects way down with the sacrum, into the womb, that our spiritual search is motivated?

Searching through our heritage, it is easy to see just how frightening nature as a whole would have been to our ancestors. Without the understanding and rationales offered us by science, or the ability to conceptualize so clearly, the unpredictability of the land upon which they relied, hand to mouth, would have been daunting beyond what we can imagine, with or without the wild bloodthirsty cats. The savagery of nature, with its glistening teeth and torrential storms, was 10 days' walk through the great forest from village to village, was the quicksand and the howling of the wolves. Out of that fear, with increasing self-awareness, would arise, perhaps, the possibility that someone or thing was making the big decisions as to when the spring returned and where the lightning hit. And so, through a need to reach and interact and plead with this controlling force, the gods were first invoked.

These gods were not battered by the storms and the cold, nor ever lost in the forest to be eaten by bears. They resided in a safe space. The impulse to stretch and stretch to this space has gripped us down the millennia. Of course, through the logic and revelations that science has given us, our prayers may be a little different from those cast over the hills and into the skies by the Druid priests of our ancestors. Yet our ability to control nature is not that proficient. Droughts and flood, viruses and hurricanes batter even these temperate isles. It only takes one experience of the ground shaking beneath one's feet to know just how beyond our control the nature of this Earth is. Yet we crave control, afraid of the darkness of what we don't know and haunted by what we don't want to admit.

Some, through their religious philosophy, declare a human superiority over nature which somehow widens the gap between the civilized conscious self and the alarmingly wild unpredictability of nature, both within and all around. Many spiritual traditions take it to the extreme of denying the physical any value at all, either focusing on their own spirit or reaching out to a spiritual force above, either way eager to transcend the body of flesh and red blood. Yet such beliefs require a constant watch over the physical, with tight restrictions that affirm its baseness or prevent expression of its instincts, of the ebb and flow of its energy. Then, because the physical can give us such pleasure, pleasure is next to be denied. Meanwhile the transcendent force, now perhaps given form and name along with full responsibility for the oppressive rules, promises a blissful salvation that is little more than the release from the chains of suffering that it itself has imposed.

Religious and spiritual paths like these are found everywhere. The great force is called by many names, beseeched in times of need, placated with offerings and the sacrifice of self and others. Contrary to what many like to think, these are not necessarily monotheistic nor all patriarchal paths. That configuration may be the most powerful in terms of an awe-inspiring authoritarian system, but I've come across equally dictatorial spiritual systems practised today right across the board, from Christianity into the New Age healing group culture. Wherever there is someone who craves control and other susceptible to being dominated, these ideas seem to spread and flourish.

Within Druidry, transcending the physical is a very different idea. Where there is an acceptance that the gods reside in everything, that every cell is vibrant with the spirit of the creative force, where every movement is both a prayer and an expression of deity, there can be no denial of our animal nature. Our instincts and passions, our sexuality and laughter, our hungers and revulsions are all part of the dance of life that creates our world in all its beauty. It is nature – and to deny any part of nature would take away our ability to perceive its wholeness, its completeness. And through that judgement we would be separated from it, cutting the connections that feed us.

The concept of dominating nature is anathema to Druidry. For although nature is wild and dark, filled with the shadows of the unknown, it is also the physical expression of the gods. The Druid responds to nature with a poignant reverence, always open to its beauty with wonder and awe. This love of the natural world is perhaps a pivotal part of the Druidic attitude.

Many times I've been asked why we feel it necessary to make a spirituality out of what might simply be seen as a deep respect for nature. Why complicate it with all these rites and rituals? I can answer only that for those of us who do walk the paths of Druidcraft, there was no crossroads or choice to be made. The step into 'religion' was not conscious. Indeed, many barely notice the moment it happens.

At some point in our lives, most of us have felt the exquisite touch of peace, that sense of connectedness which is so deeply nourishing, perhaps within the embrace of relationship, in the garden tending plants, watching a sunset, or the moon on the ocean, seeing a smile or feeling the sleepy head of one's tiny child snuggling up. It may have only been a glimpse, but for some that is enough. For others it is not. They are driven to search for a way to experience that feeling with more frequency, more certainty, to know our natural state, which is our joy, the ecstasy of clear flowing energy though our body, sweet interaction with another, with the rest of creation.

For a Druid, that feeling is the touch of the gods. Exchanging energy with that force, be it a goddess, or a god, a being beyond polarity, an elemental spirit or deva of the sacred land, brings with it the experience of wholeness, a flood of absolute peace.

When the gods do touch, they touch the spirit within us, the energy which created and sustains our life, and which will bring it to its close. When this happens our focus is brought directly into that supernal power of energy and with that comes a sense of its extraordinary invulnerability. When I am held in the arms of my Lady or am dancing with my Lord through the streaming rain, there is no doubt, no fear, no craving for security. There is neither place nor need for any denial and the darkness of the unknown becomes sweet adventure through which I am always well guided.

So the search that is Druidcraft is for that direct interaction with the gods. It is a guiding hand into the experience, an experience which without guidance can be both terrifying and disorienting. Yet without reaching the gods, the search is simply philosophy and any realizations are but mental satisfactions. When we achieve that interaction, the purpose of the search becomes quite evident: it is freedom. We find safety.

The last cars have driven away. It's 2.30 in the morning. I turn out the lights and walk back into the sitting room, where the swirling energy of 30 people is gently settling, like cottontree seeds floating to the grass, as the room clears, darkens and slowly becomes quiet. I think of my lover's warm body in the bed upstairs but know that I need to clear my head before I am ready to sleep. A jack o'lantern on the window sill is still glowing though its toothy smirk and wide eyes with the last of its candle. I pick it up, with a few mugs which I leave the kitchen on the way out.

The grass is thick with rain and freezing around my bare feet. I shiver and the cold tension stabs pain into my back. I breathe deeply and focus on my internal fire as I have been taught, spreading the energy and warmth through my body til the muscles relax. The wet ground is soft underneath my toes. I look up and feel the presence of the star that always draws me, look around and feel the beauty of the garden in the darkness, and I wander over to the elder tree, sitting down on the log stool beneath its branches, setting the pumpkin beside me.

After the intensity of my private rites and celebration, alone in the forest and later with my priest and partner, the more open rituals with a group always feel gentle and warm. This gathering, called the Grove of the Golden Owl, meets at every festival and tonight my role, as ever, was to guide. And it had been fun. Nobody had noticed that Jade had slipped away on the long walk through the forest under the moonless sky and when she entered the circle in the middle of the ritual, black and veiled and floating in the aura of the goddess with whom she had meditated in the darkness of the undergrowth, there was horror and confusion on more than a few faces. Intensely serene, she had walked the circle and I smiled, watching recognition break over various faces as she began her dance, suddenly chaotic, confronting each soul and screeching her challenge, demanding their offerings, symbols of what they would release after the long year, ideas and hopes that would not survive the cold moontides of winter. As Grove priestess, I psychically followed her in her guise as the veiled Cailleach, winter goddess, silently encouraging each person she challenged, holding the energy of the circle strong and safe. Quiet tears were shed and there were nods of determination and whispered prayers as the owls called through the huge oak trees.

When she came to me we smiled our covert satisfaction that the surprise had worked, before I closed my eyes and called through my soul, handing over the wand of elder which was my own offering, ogham marked as it was with oils of myrrh and cypress, and with it letting go of another chunk of self-negation.

As Jade danced and cried out the words of the goddess whose winds strip the drying ochre leaves from the trees, whose icy touch kills back the last of the season's growing, sending the creatures scurrying off to their winter's sleep, I felt the energy of the Grove as a director might look at his players on the stage. As Jade hurled her store into the flames, I laughed inside at the beauty and the melodrama. And Tyroshai, my grove guardian, put his hand on my arm and together we watched the fire momentarily blaze with its fuel of hopes and fears.

As the flames burned lower the four who had invoked the cardinal directions of north, south, east and west stepped forward. Two were in robes of calico and linen, two in jeans and waterproof jackets. As they spoke, their lanterns shedding light over their ritual scripts, a vixen barked through the trees.

Hello, sister.

She was here last night, murmured Tyroshai.

I thought I smelled her.

I held his hand and strengthened the circle boundary as the four knelt down and, using trowels and bare hands, smothered the fire with mud and sodden leafmould. They walked back to their places and the last of the lanterns was extinguished. For a moment it was utterly black.

Slowly, as eyes adjusted and apprehension eased around the circle, I stopped grasping his hand so tightly and, leaving him to continue holding the energy, let myself drift into the silence and emptiness.

Now, sitting under the elder at the edge of my garden, I remember my fear of the dark as a child. In the depths of every cupboard, every passageway and dusty recess lurked black elves and demons that sniggered and snarled. And when they leapt out at me, tripping me up, when the bowl I was carrying had smashed at my feet and they were dancing their horrid dance, my fear was still drawn to the darkness of the corner where I knew the spirit who was contriving my destruction still stood. Or so I believed.

I look up at the window of the room where my son is sleeping, probably snug in his daddy's arms where he has fallen asleep, putting the little lad to bed, and I wonder what he is dreaming.

Now the darkness is deeply nourishing to me. Used to the different balance of spirit and body energy, able to use the cat inside me to see and to feel when my human senses fail, the darkness is rich to me and beautifully rewarding. In the Grove a few hours ago, I was loathe to come out of my sweet meditation but, though we had to put out the fires of the year, time had kept passing and Tyroshai nudged me. Into the silence I'd spoken of the dark, aware that the circle cast was so strong that my voice was held within the space, as if the trees and the undergrowth that surrounded us were the walls of a room, and into that contained space slowly people's attention returned. I could feel them listening. I wanted to break it, to scream the chaos of the moment, but the stillness was perfect. The single candle was lit, flickering in its lantern, the spirit light that remains deep within the dark. And not long after that we were calling in the seed thought of the new year that loomed out over the far horizon, and with the jingle of the tiny bells had come the soft rain. As we called out the *Awen* chant, it was coming down in buckets, and I laughed and threw back my head, for the chaos of nature had shattered our gentle hold on the darkness, and any amongst us who were thinking of staying dry had soon given themselves up to the torrent of water that poured out of the sky. Our laughter led to hugs and wet grins as we questioned our sanity in the middle of the night, utterly exhilarated and drenched right through.

I breathe in the night and rich wet earth.

From under the hedge leaps a form, 18 inches tall and all in black. He snarls, *Hello, Princess.*

Oh please! I laugh. *Piss off!*

II

THE WOMB

YULE: THE SPIRIT AFFIRMED IN THE DEPTHS OF THE NORTH

One of the most powerful images of my childhood, as part of a family without roots or a clear concept of home, was in my contact with the native peoples wherever we went: the peasant farmers in the hills of Franco's impoverished Spain, the people of the desert plains and the rainforests of Venezuela, the old folks in the mountain villages of rural Japan. As I remember those faces, expressed through such a different cultures, rich and dusty colours, there is a quality which each and every one of them holds. It is a quality which to me is almost more beautiful and precious than anything in humanity and as such I have found it hard to describe in words that do it justice. To the vagrant civilized races, tied to their houses and possessions, it looks like pride. To the insecure of those vagrants, it appears as a groundless arrogance. As a child I saw it as a regal and extraordinary grace, and treated such people with awe and reverence, as if they were great kinds and dignitaries. They appeared to own barely anything at all, legally not even the land that lay beneath their leathered feet. Yet I believed they knew it was theirs.

When I myself was getting a clearer idea of what I was searching for, I found that same light in some of the Native Americans I met, and in Rastafarians in England and in the Caribbean. I became aware of what happens to that dignity when first the land is taken away but, more critically, when a soul's ancient bond with the land is broken. And I realized why I had held that grace in such high regard: in seeing the subsequent and extraordinary grief, I felt something deep within me which resounded as if from many, many lifetimes, a grief which to me seemed beyond any that could be felt over a parting with another soul. When I consider that native pride now, it shines out as a primary motivation for why my own pathways have taken me into the sacred rites of Druidry.

When I started my search, in my teens, I was looking for my roots, believing that if I could simply find where I came from I would be able to access that pride and certainty of being. I would discover who I was. Gazing out of the car at the suburban maisonette where I'd arrived into the world I was bewildered at the total lack of familiarity of place and culture. I was further frustrated to discover that my grandparents, wandering Europeans like my own parent, were equally unrooted. Then I met a woman. She was born a century before, almost to the day. She had died in her fifties, but when I met her, sitting on the porch of a thick stone white-washed house, in long black skirts and black crocheted shawl, she was humming with life. I was the spirit travelling into her reality.

As a child who had naturally drifted through 'daydreams', most of which were more real than the incomprehensible world around me, as a child for whom spirit presences were not alarming or unusual, to slip through the framework of time and space into another landscape was not something strange. Beside me was a soul, someone I was able to trust more than any person in body in the uncertain world around me, and (perhaps naively) I never questioned where he led me, through the woods and meadows of my inner landscape, to find the doorways through which we could slide into different realities.

Some call these other dimensions 'the inner world' or 'the inner plane'. For some it is all simply the imagination, a place where memory and expectation are rearranged, a part of the subconscious mind. For me the attitude, the childish freedom of seeing all realities as equally valid was never constrained; the inner worlds I shared with spirits and faeries were as existent in their own right as the other world of agreed reality, itself filled with mystery and illusion. The powerful physicality of those other worlds affirmed this for me, such as the lady I was led to meet. I could *smell* the musky oils of her dusty hair, thick and black as my own.

She was olive skinned, as I am, and her lips were chapped in the dryness of the wind. Her voice was deep and hoarse from the dust and, though I understood her words, the language she spoke was thick with the guttural inflections and melodies of an eastern European people. When she saw us first she gesticulated a greeting with a shrug, as if to say, *Hey, what is this? Are you looking at what you see?*

I bowed a little, vaguely thinking through my usual greeting.

So what do you want?

I'm not sure, I whispered. I wanted to say *Certainty?*

Ha! She barked, and she shouted something behind her. Young children were running around near the house, yelling their games in the wind. One little girl, in a ragged dress, was sitting on the ground where horses were pulling at the dry grass.

I want to know where I come from. I want to belong.

Yes, but to what? Really, hey?

She saw me watching the girl and laughed.

Yes, you are like her! She is my daughter, your great-grand-mother. You can see it in her eyes, mourning, mourning for something she doesn't not know. Mourning for her Mother.

She clenched her fist against her heart and I realized she meant something much bigger than herself. And this woman knew my thoughts.

Yes, it does not occur to her to reach out to me, just as you could not reach your own mother. Look how she lies on the Earth and she sings to her Mother, who dies of this thirst.

She spoke melodramatically, lifted a handful of soil, crumbling it into dust that disappeared in the wind.

Then she laughed a laugh which shook my very being so that,

needing stability, I found myself sinking to my knees, aware that in doing so I showed the extent of my weakness, aware that I wanted to hide, to curl up and weep the pain I could barely understand. I stared into emptiness.

Child, she said, after a while. *There is no need. We cannot change the ways of the wind. Nor should we wish to. Listen to the song. Always listen.*

The little girl lifted her hand to the muzzle of horse that was closest to her and a smile broke across her face that utterly astonished me.

See? She learns. As you will learn too. Hey! Why do you think we are here?

As I looked up and into her eyes, I saw what seemed to me the very richness of the earth, the darkness of the forest, the rage of the bear and the softness of the doe, out there in the wide open drought of the steppes, all held within those dark eyes and I knew that she was priestess of the Earth, and I realized that my search had been misdirected: I had been looking for sense of possession.

In that meeting, in all she gave me through her eyes, in the ease with which she welcomed me as a spirit searching through time and space, my ancestor showed me the links that held us together, she and I. And before me she threw down many other answers, to questions I could then barely even verbalize. She showed me my pain, and those answers were like clues which I knew would relieve it, raindrops in the dirt, guiding me on along a path, the path I have been striving to walk since that day.

* * *

So many reach out towards spirituality from a broken sense of belonging. Having found no common perspectives with their own people, their ability to relate often in tatters, they have lived with a feeling of being utterly adrift. Though a few manage truly to thrive entirely alone, as a species in our essence we are animals, who work in packs, flocks, prides: tribes. To be or to believe one has been rejected by one's tribe is a process which eats away at the instinctive soul, gnawing at wounds that made of intensified by experiences of shattered homes, fractured communities, no employment opportunities, tortured by drug abuse and the pressure laid on by those who are coping or even succeeding. The ability to trust is severely battered, if not destroyed, as the fears of the vulnerable solitary creature kick in with the aggression and self-destruction of the permanently defensive.

That sense of alienation exists within a spectrum. Not all who cry out when they feel their roots are cut or withering are living outside society. Very many more continue to exist within worlds that do not nourish them, ever glancing between the silhouettes of those around them for that freedom they know is a reality somewhere. Yet when the fear strikes, the quick instinctive reaction is to run for cover, find safety, and in that instant it doesn't matter if it it's a retrograde step. So our patterns repeat, using up creative energy and fixing the status quo. Again and again, progress made out into the fields of self-expression is voided by our legging it back to the safety of the old just as soon as the anticipated threat looms too large. The side-effect of shattered trust is a poverty of confidence and gradually we grow convinced that we're doomed to failure. Apathy sets in, the poison of our culture.

If the craving to belong is actually addressed, it's the desire to belong truly within a tribe that is often the primary issue. And to leap from one society into another is the easiest way to move, particularly when energy is low and the first has already shifted you out to its borderlands. So it is that many spiritualities open their arms to these wounded souls. Christianity, as a fine example, has the billboard outside letting passersby know that within its embrace is the warm and unconditional love of their saviour.

I worked with a young man a decade ago as he came through rehabilitation from heroin and alcohol addiction. Not interested in the enfolding philosophies of the NA and AA therapy, yet accepting his need for some place where he would feel securely held, he told me he thought his options were to become a born-again Christian or find a Wiccan coven. He chose the former (Wiccans were more likely to drink). Perhaps this was a strange way to choose a spiritual path, but it showed a certain understanding of what both offered. Another told me clearly that he had chosen to become a Wiccan because he could relate to a tradition which had been persecuted. He felt that Wicca, with its strong group bonds, still operating in the darkness and out of the public eye, contained something that would hold his sense of social alienation in a tender clasp. (This was his personal view of Wicca and not necessarily the modern reality.) Both men were looking for deep healing."

While Druidry does openly offer a resolution of this crisis of not belonging, it offers neither the promise of unconditional love nor the affirmation of ostracization. Though some of its rites are practised in the darkness of privacy and the privacy of darkness, its strong and supportive community joyfully celebrates appropriate rituals openly in public. An essential tenet of the faith is that it celebrates the inspiration of the natural world, of our heritage and our land, and as such there is no separation from the people that the land sustains. There are no corners of Druidcraft in which to hide and snarl at our culture, other than those which we have backed into and must at some point give up, laughing at our pride.

The tradition is rooted, however, in this search for belonging, laying it as a foundation for holistic growth. In finding our connection and our identity within time, through the history of our culture, our heritage and the land, we find the inspiration to live appropriately in the present, within the environment and its culture. While that doesn't mean we must agree with the government or with conventional society, any sense of alienation is gently dissolved.

So it is we address that conflict which is so prevalent: that *in order to feel safe, I must hold myself in, though in order to be happy, I must have the freedom to be myself.* Choosing the safe option exacerbates the dilemma, for we know that we can never be true ourselves as long as we do so. In holding back our self-expression, our relationships remain superficial and there is little hope of any true sense of belonging anywhere. Druidry addresses this conflict by starting the search for belonging with a deepening understanding of who we are.

The search is pivoted around the concept of the ancestors and in Druid practice this begins with our own bloodline. We work to discover who were the souls who gave us our genetic inheritance, our strengths and weaknesses, our hips and noses, our freckles and our tendencies to limp in our dotage, gaze at the moon and sneeze at the cat. We find out a little more of who we are by understanding a little more of what created us. And we give thanks – yet to do so with sincerity requires an acceptance of who we are. It is easier to contemplate our great-grandpapa, to meditate with him by the fireside alone, to understand his brutality or infidelity wrapped as it is the veils of time, than to accept the reality of our own parents' shortcomings. Yet when we consider ancestors, and we give offerings and reverence, in doing so we honour all those in whose veins the colours of our blood have run, those long dead who stand behind us in spirit and those still around to yell down the phone.

As we come to honour our blood ancestors sincerely – though respect may take many year and true acceptance even longer – we turn our attention in Druidcraft to the earth beneath our feet, to the soil that is made up of the bodies of all that has lived before us. We acknowledge the physical flesh and blood and bones, the bodies of the animals and plants that have compacted into the stones rotted into the humus. We explore the world around us and we honour the work, the sweat and tears, of all who have given their energy to create the environment that we live in – and on and with and through. We see their mistakes, we accept their gifts.

And in our rites, we give of ourselves, consciously aware of our part in the ongoing process of creation.

By finding our place in time, in the genetic chain that links our ancestors and our descendants, and finding our place on the ground, within creation, using all that exists around us as a four-dimensional map, we locate ourselves. And in doing so there comes a sense of mutual acceptance between the soul and reality, the self and the Earth.

Yet there is a third level of work with the ancestors used in Druidcraft, the one which brings us specifically into the tradition and cements that state of belonging which we crave. This is the acknowledgement of our spiritual heritage. It is our reverence for those who have taught us, and it is understood in Druidry that many of our greatest teachers exist only within the inner planes. They are guides and devic energies, they are people now in spirit who bring wisdom from the past (or elsewhere), they are parts of our own soul. They are a source of our inspiration and the holders of the ancient's stories of the land and its people.

Those who carry our spiritual heritage may not be of our own bloodline, but they are honoured as our ancestors. They are the ones whose life energy, whose emotion, love and rage, passion and inspiration, still shimmers in the air that we are now breathing. It is their music which rolls through the valleys. They are amongst the spirits of place, and by honouring them, by opening ourselves to listen to their teachings, their songs and tales, we open out our perspective and discover the beauty and wisdom that automatically follow such a scope of vision.

So it is that in Druidry we honour our gods, we honour our ancestors, we honour the land on which we live, and we blend these in our honouring of the gods of our ancestors and the gods of the land through the spirits of place, we blend the mud and the blood and the spirit, allowing all to continue their natural course, with the currents of the rivers and the gusts of the wind that blow the year: the passage of time.

Samhain is long past. The gales have brought us into the depths of winter, the trees bare and sleepy, their energy withdrawn to their core and their source, down in the dark earth. And with the snow playing in the icy air outside, it is by the hearth, in arm of our family, in our solitude, in the flickering light of the fire, where there are so few distractions, that the shadows of our ancestors appear. Through the longest nights we look to our roots, to the earth that nourishes us. We explore who we are.

Yet, in digging into the physical, it loses its density. In searching into our existence, we face our insignificance. As we work with our ancestors, we work with our own death.

* * *

'Are you alright?'

I realize I've been staring into the fire a little too long. I put down the papers I've been holding, supposedly reading. He's sitting on the sofa, a coloured pencil raised, three more in his other hand, his expression sharp with thinking, the very edges a little softened with his concern. He seems to me to be three fields away.

'Could I have done more?'

'For whom?'

Though I spoke from my thoughts, he knows who I mean. His question is specific: for the girlfriend, the dying man or for myself? Shit.

'Go and work it out,' he whispers.

'I said that I'd help you, that we'd do this together.'

'Screw that.'

He smiles. I guess I haven't been much help. I gaze at his paperwork, at class notes and mind maps strewn in front of the hearth. My mind is blank.

'Go on,' he urges.

Up the stairs, I leave my slippers at the door. It's the 'red light' of my 'dark room', the sign that I'm not to be disturbed. I drift into my temple room, kneeling down at the altar in the gloom, allowing myself to slip through the blankness into the calm of the space.

In time, I lean over and open a chest, feeling my way for matches, lighting the candle beneath the goddess of yew and jet. The flickering light dances through the leaves of plants that stretch around the windows, through feathers and wood sculptures. A bundle of herbs, tied with horse hair and hemp, lie in a clam shell. I roll the end in the candle's flame until it ignites and rising to my feet I move through the room, leaving a trail of pungent smoke. Before the altar I slowly sweep it through my own aura. It leaves me clear in my sinuses and lungs, but heady too, energetic and dreamy. I kneel again and call softly to my Lady.

She comes to me through the form of an old Druid wise woman known to me as Nathair de Danaan. As I undress and light the candles that mark the cardinal directions, she speaks to me of the darkness of the places of denial, of how we turn away and the old cobwebs of time drift down onto us, barely noticed, til we are hidden, weighed down by the accumulated blanket. How over time it takes more and more energy to move at all. And she takes me into the cold night of my inner grove, where we walk beneath the sleeping trees, our footfalls crunching on the frosty leaves.

With my back leaning against the old yew, my fingers in the flakes and ridges of its bark, I gaze out into the darkness of the forest. A little face is looking at me through the leaves of the holly, head on one side, sparkling eyes, questioning my thoughts.

Well, could I have done more? I shrug.

How much do you want to give? The sprite says with more than a hint of cynicism. *Martyrdom? Again, priestess?*

Another face, pouting. *Didn't you work very hard?*

Then the wild jingling of the laughter that is so infuriatingly infectious. This is all I need – pixies take the mick.

I'm trying to think!

Close your eyes. Nathair's words.

I do, and I recall crawling along some motorway in a five-mile tailback, eventually reaching the cause of the jam where three cars and a truck were mashed together, blackened with smoke. Firemen had cut through the metal to free drivers and passengers. Ambulances were crawling away. As I passed I saw a women, wandering amongst the wreckage, dazed, trying to understand what was going on. She was looking for herself. Torn but needing to drive on, with nowhere to stop, I called out to my goddess to be with that woman whose tears I was crying, again and again chanting the word of the prayer, *Be with that soul, whoever she may be, show her the way, by the power of three, oh my Lady of sweet serenity, be with that soul...*

That night in my circle, a stranger came to me. Her image drifted but her voice was distinct, if exquisitely soft, and she thanked me. She had died as her car was crushed beneath the truck, as had her child. She gazed around at the paraphernalia of my temple, the candles burning, stones painted with symbols, incense rising into the darkness. She was bewildered, not knowing who I was, not understanding what I did, but she thanked me for my guidance that had helped her see the way.

All I did was express my own sorrow –

Nathair nodded. *And so it is that we relate.*

And I call to where I know there is comfort.

Your knowing was her light.

I understand, but am also aware of how hard it is for me to

accept that I was of value.

Can my own belief really make that much difference?

Not belief. It is the knowing.

But my knowing is not fact. Just my own perspective, experience...

Your knowing was her light.

As I gaze into the dark forest, I remember journeys of my training in the Craft, walking out of the warmth of my grove at night, under the canopy of the old yew, drawn on in my search for that knowing, heading north, downhill, into the darkness of the forest that I barely knew. The holly is black and, replaying a memory, recrafting it, I stumble through the undergrowth and low branches of the trees as the chill creeps into my clothes. Fear rises up as I realize I am more than lost, just hearing the voice that calls from up in the bare branches of the trees, the voice of the owl, *Follow! Follow!* The ground underfoot has been muddy and I've been sliding through puddles that come over my boots, but now it's changing to rocks, suddenly hard. I'm straining to see through the blackness, trying to avoid the invisible branches that whip my face, and I start to feel a soft wetness, realizing it's snow. I am overwhelmed by a feeling that I am running away. I am getting so very tired and so confused. All I want to do is stop and curl into a ball in the hollow of a tree.

The dryness of Seabhac's voice slides into me: *Back to womb position.*

I want to scream at him, but my flailing arms break through into emptiness. I am standing in a clearing. Above me, one star, in a break in the clouds.

Beneath the yew of my grove, Nathair speaks.

You see the fear of death.

I look up.

We fear what we do not know. And darkness is the land that lies beyond the light, beyond the bounds our consciousness. We forget that it is a land that is rich with potential, a land just waiting to be discovered.

I light the candle in front of my goddess and it flickers for a moment, touching the quiet of my room.

A man lay dying today, while his partner howled. He had reached the place of calm, where life's hand holds and precious gems held no more importance. There was nothing left to do. There was no course for turning back. The light of his conscious soul had already partly made the journey and he could sense that it was not one heading into some dreadful darkness. But for Julie it was black as hell.

Over the weeks he and I had spoken of death and life and love, and now, while Julie saw to the children, we affirmed those conversations with our eyes and the touch of hands, and I chanted to soften the changing of the room. Though I could go a little of the way with him, it was not a journey that Julie could make. Of her path all she could see was the edge, the drop into an apocalyptic void. And when the dying man slipped into periods of unconsciousness, she squealed her pain and her anticipation of her emptiness through a caustic fear of his parents' demands for a Christian's burial. It had been arranged, there had been time, so that all who had loved him would have a way to say goodbye, both in his mother's church and also by the ash on the brow of the hill where he himself had celebrated his rites in the moonlight. But in her rage Julie could only see her need to fight, for herself and for him, he who had accomplished so few of his beautiful dreams, never having broken the dread of his father. He was so young.

And so she wept and we lit candles and I walked in the garden while she sat with him alone, the wind outside bitterly cold and dry. The flowerbeds were bare, the soil frozen hard, rose bushes cut back, grey thorns sticking out. I crouched to touch the earth and listen to the hum of life breathing, sleeping, dreaming, deep within it.

Some part of me so wanted to pacify, to calm her, mother her. To stop the noise.

When her anguish was out, she softened. And when he had squeezed her hand and died, his soul rising into its freedom, she laid lilies on his chest and I held her as the tears flowed, sharing my strength as she let him go. And she held me in my confusion, in my knowing that was released in peace, yet aware that the emptiness of his leaving was also what she wanted me take away.

Back in my temple room, my cat purrs against me. I light the candle in a white holder reserved for those who have journeyed on and called through my guides for news of the young man. I sense that he is busy, talking with old friends, laughing, watching in wonder the processes of his own existence. I move away, finding the centre point to come back into my room, when suddenly the air is thick and dark and he is before me, no longer scarred by the violence of the cancer, but vibrant and glowing.

Tell her, he grins, a deep softness in his eyes.

You tell her.

How?

You'll find a way.

* * *

Death and the beliefs that we hold about it so distinctly colour our attitude towards life. Death gives a culture, a religion, its most prominent texture. It is so much of the essential flavour, composing the strength and force of its underlying fears, its motivations and rewards.

Believing in an afterlife, a heaven – be that a place beyond need or desire, a garden of beauty or a hall of raucous and perpetual feasting – can certainly ease the anticipated blow of dying, particularly if what is ending is one's only bash at life on Earth. Many who hold such a belief, however, also maintain that entry into such a glorious place is conditional. What's more, those conditions can be pretty damn tough. Paradise lies through the gateway of judgement and the fear of being judged provokes excesses of bravado or resignation that increase with the perceived power of the judge himself. We know we haven't kept *all* the rules. We hide and lie, we deny and compensate. We give up and reject the whole wretched notion, or we build up our defences, finding scapegoats, asserting our own righteousness. We are scared. If there is an afterdeath existence and we haven't made the grade for heaven, what is the alternative?

In Druidry there are no such politics, largely because of the lack of judgemental deity. There is no hell, but also no reward of heaven. Nothing in nature is that cut and dried. The understanding the most clearly guides the Druidic attitude to death is that the soul simply continues its existence on another plane of consciousness. Life carries on.

Druids work on a range of different levels, according to their own strengths and experience. In most tribal cultures, it was understood that the shamans or medicine men did not themselves make the choice to follow the path but were chosen by the spirits through some near death experience that took them out of the normal perspectives of mundane society, leaving them with a different vision of life and death. This experience might have been a severe illness, chronic pain or disability, an almost fatal accident or period of insanity. I like to imagine that it was the same for the Druid priests of our ancestors.

In our culture now, however, many make an active choice to follow the paths into mysticism, healing and priesthood. However, the degree to which they themselves have moved into the worlds of spirit dictates very distinctly how deeply they are able to work in their own spiritual journeys or with others. At the same time, Druids are called upon to perform very different tasks. Some people want the priest to take them or travel for them deep into the dark places of death and beyond, while others don't want or need to go so far.

Through my own experience of long-term pain, the effects of which have more than a few times taken me out to the edges of life, it was not only natural but almost inevitable that I should begin my adult life working with the dying and those who had passed through to the other worlds. Working as an exorcist, the first people I helped with healing were those who had died catatonic with rage, grief or terror. There was never a point where I had to decide whether or not I believed life did continue after death.

While not all Druids work so closely with death or have experience of the worlds within which we exist before or after life, the vast majority of Druids do hold a belief in reincarnation.

Having memories myself of more than a dozen previous lifetimes that are as clear as the memories of the childhood of this one, with images of some that are clearer than last week, I am quite sure that we live many lives. As my role as a priestess developed from working solely with the dead and dying to include those seeking healing, body and soul, many who have come for help have very often spontaneously regressed to pre-birth states and to lifetimes in the whole spectrum of eras and cultures. For someone who was previously sceptical, such an experience can instantly shift their belief system and thereby change their attitudes towards all of life.

It may be of course that such 'memories' are all merely visions from our imagination. Certainly, while some of the images that I've been shown by clients from their semi-trance state are incredibly specific in details that have later been verified, others are wildly fantastical. I've seen the confusion of thinking that an experience was one's own, from some previous incarnation, and finding out it was an old movie. I've watched regressions dissolve into Disney fairytale. But in healing, as long as the client knows that what they are seeing are scenarios given them by their subconscious which may as easily be symbolic as actual memory, these pictures are still wonder tools for the process, expressing their sources of pain and confusion in the terminology and determination of their own psyche.

All our memories are subjective and shift and change with every recalling, translating themselves into current language to be processed. We know that we only recall the initial incident once, afterwards recalling its memory instead. That a memory is badly interpreted or fantastical in places need not takeaway all of its possible actuality. It certainly doesn't invalidate its being in the psyche, for which there must be a reason.

To complicate the matter further, it doesn't appear that we necessarily reincarnate chronologically, but might come into body in any era, past or future. Existence is understood to be a humming connectedness of all spirit energy clear across time and space, linking every moment to every other moment simply by virtue of being, rather than because of any linear or syllogistic process – the causal being a tool of our perception. Memories that do surface tend only to be those that relate to the present, but not always. Memories of the future don't arise very often and are at risk of total misinterpretation, particularly where there are concepts and objects that are not yet a part of current reality, leaving it hard to believe they are anything but fantasy or science fiction.

As a tool well used, memory is an excellent medium for searching through the psyche. As a fact, it offers even more. Not least, if we learn to use it well, it gives us sources of our own direct prior learning, experiences to recall and use, all of which can help us avoid repeating mistakes as well as saving time in the journeys of our soul, in our search for information and sources of inspiration.

It also offers us more time. For we begin to learn the art of dreaming, planning, creating, on a soul level, not constrained by the all too quickly passing four score and ten. Our vision begins to extend across centuries, through lifetimes, calming that crisis of the need to achieve.

There is time too for truly long-term relationship; we've all met people whom we feel we've known forever. We've been to new places which evoke an extraordinary sense of ease or foreboding. Knowing that these feelings come from contact in previous lives affirms the relationship, allowing a deeper connection or a quicker release. And knowing that our interactions last beyond one life span encourages us to think more clearly about our actions, our commitments, the amount of energy we are putting into things. Folks talk about the inheritance we leave to our children, especially in terms of global health and resources, but knowing that we shall ourselves rebirth into that reality provokes a heart/gut response that inspires more action than the intellectual acknowledgement of our responsibility.

Far from the clean slate that many believe we are born with, we come into our lifetime with a poignant responsibility that slowly dawns on us. We are carrying the burden of previous unresolved traumas, our lacks and weaknesses, along with the lessons learnt, our joys and strengths. We bring with us the need for certain issues to be overcome.

From Druid's view, perhaps the most crucial point is the way we address fear – and fear of death is paramount. Working with people in regressions, I found that the first fear is usually of the associated pain, and the last moments of any lifetime are often the most powerful. Just as when seed pods are fit to burst, the aerial parts of a herb dying back into the earth, so it is that those final thoughts and decisions of life, made upon the whole lifetime's experience, are the seeds of the next. Dying in pain, be it physical, emotional or spiritual, stays with us, impacted into our soul memories. Apart from anything else, I guess we rather hope we avoid doing it again. Coming to understand that this is only the memory of a pain which may not reoccur, and certainly isn't requisite for dying, helps to dislodge the fear.

Perhaps it is our base animal instinct to survive that stops us from easily releasing the body, despite any pain that may be making it unbearable. Yet animals die with a good deal less struggle, in many cases anticipating and preparing for the journey, and embarking on it with significantly more dignity, as indeed do those people of cultures where the connectedness with the earth - that soul belonging - still persists.

The more primitive and profound fear of death emerges from within and beneath this; having achieved a consciousness of self, individual and separate, the soul cannot tolerate either its annihilation or the disappearance of the manifest world on which it depends, as a mirror, to know its own existence. It's the realization that the reality of dying contains neither of these that brings the extraordinary freedom which Druids and other mystics speak of. And an intellectual decision will never be enough: the realization must come through the living experience that takes us from 'belief' into that place of subjective 'knowing'.

No shifting the fear of death can eliminate the essential tension, though. It flickers scalding hot and icy cold, brilliant light and utter darkness, holding us taut between the drive to live and awareness of death (which some might go further and describe as the drive to die). The animal instinct to survive dances around the human craving for release.

Deep in Druidcraft this is a tension which is mined as a potent source of change and inner growth. Druids who work shamanically within the worlds of spirit use the momentum of its stress to journey through fears, through the darkest realms of unknowing, either for themselves or those they are working for. Working with our ancestors on this level of consciousness takes us into the shimmering and precarious balance between life and death, between the freedom of formless existence and the lightning spark that is conception for rebirth, between energy and matter.

Unlike points of conflict that are based in negative emotion and are therefore inherently solvable, natural polarity offers states of sustainable tension which, within time and space, are never going to go away. If a priest is able to work clearly, they offer an infinite source of energy that is potentially pure, neutral and can be used for whatever he wishes. Where there are fears still present, with careful guidance and support, the energy of the tension can be a trigger for healing that reaches deep into the cold depths.

As ever in Druidry, the images and symbols of our psyche are correlated with the flow of the seasons of our year. Far from rejecting death, the Druid accepts its reality, just as we accept the inevitability of the winter's freeze. While throughout the year death is never so very far away, coming and going, as midwinter approaches it lingers close, becoming a constant presence. Walking on ground that doesn't give, frozen hard as stone, the smell of death is pungent in the cold clear air. What wasn't likely to survive should have been thrown into the Samhain fires, for now it is faltering, collapsing. We know it will die. We know we must conserve our own energy, focusing carefully on all that we determine will last through til the land begins to warm. There is no growth (or none that can be seen). At times there is very little evidence of life at all, as the days get shorter and there is less and less light. We are almost sure that, with the blessings of the gods, the warmth will return. But to be certain we give our offerings and our devotions to the altars of the land, to our Mother Earth, on whose generosity we are so wholly dependent. As the nights get longer, our prayers get louder...

Til the turning of the year does come. And three days after the solstice has passed it becomes evident that the darkness has reached its peak and within the arms of our family, our clan and tribe, we celebrate Yule and all that affirms the continuation of life. Evergreen trees, whose eerie songs still drift through the sleepy forest, are covered with faerie lights, and boughs brought inside decorated with little shiny paper pendants of rich chocolate and marzipan. We call to the spirits of the festival and we give of ourselves – to our loved ones and to the Earth – and we share the joy of receiving the gifts of life and love.

The days ahead will now start to get longer. We know hard times are still to come, but the currents at least are now flowing in the right direction. The eternal spirit that was affirmed in the candle lit in the darkness of Samhain has taken us out of the spiral of dying. Though we have believed that we were still spinning in the cauldron of chaos, we have been in the womb of the mother goddess. We have been saved! And we celebrate, all our attention suddenly held on this newly birthed light, still tender and tiny, so bright with the promise of new life, this our gentle saviour, the sun or Son, the highest light, who will take us into a new cycle of life and opportunity (our local *star*). Jesus, Arthur, Robin, all the knights in shining armour that fight the good fight against the tyranny of darkness, are hailed with the mead horns by the hearth fires of Yule.

Away from the noise of the songs, and the thrust and swing of the Bard's voice as he tells his winter tales, out in the calm of the night, we acknowledge that this too is the very depths of the darkness. And into the vibrancy of the Mother's energy that is both bright and dark, the Druid walks.

She has given birth and the Druid kneels at her altar.

* * *

The candle gently flickers in the stillness of the air. Its glow falls over the frozen earth but the earth absorbs none of it. Even the darkness of the air seems to push against it, giving way only as much as it must. Yet half hidden by the tree roots and tangle of ivy, the figure holds a pool of it, golden, in the breach between her belly and thighs. She is all curves and satisfaction, eyes closed, her head tilted a little up towards the starry sky, yet all her energy spreads out from beneath where she sits. She amazes me.

And when I move, from the plate in my hand I take the conse-crated bread, the cobnuts and the sticky paleness of dried apples, putting them down on the earth before her, whispering my thanks. I bow and open myself to her as that energy of warmth and such unmovable certainty washes through me, filling me as if I were a chalice til then empty. For a while I hold that feeling, and within it I offer the image of where I am headed, of all I wish to have achieved as this cycle now beginning comes to its close. I am aware of what feels like shards of light falling around me, settling into the ground, til again it is dark.

Time to go back, priestess.

Slowly I open my eyes, as if after a deep sleep, focusing the energy that suddenly spins me dizzy, sliding fully back into my body.

Thank you, Nathair.

Again I bow to the figure of clay and earth beneath the tree, and she seems to soak up my closing prayers in the same way that she holds the light. My heart is full, sated and calm, and I want to stay, comfortable as I am, kneeling in the grass, absorbed by my Lady, but a little way behind me I hear the door opening. A rush of noise escapes over the garden before it clicks shut. A few footsteps on the patio.

I hold a moment of quiet, gathering myself together, bidding *Fare thee well in peace!* to those in spirit who had shared with me, while aware of someone waiting. When eventually I turn, Jenny is gazing up at the stars. There's something about her that makes me wonder and I get to my feet and pad silently across the grass towards her.

Blessings of the sabbat.

'Hi', she whispers softly. Her smile is coy and she bites her bottom lip.

I raise my eyebrows. *Well?*

She nods, her face breaking into a shining smile that's quickly mixed with tears. We hug really tightly in one of those precious moments of understanding and support, and I call to my Lady for blessings, gently aware of Jenny's feet touching the ground with a little more stability as from the kitchen comes the sound of Suzi yelling to someone, 'It wouldn't bother me!' We grin and laugh.

'Can we tell everyone?'

'In the ceremony? Would it be appropriate?'

'Of course!'

We walk back into the deep aroma of juices mulling with herbs, simmering on the stove, the warmth of chatter drifting through the house. Suzi is laughing as she sees us.

'Hey, Bobcat, Jenny! How're you doing? Aren't the stars great? Tony?' She's off into the other room, squeezing past Rosy, who struggles in holding two enormous flasks.

'I've got some of my own brew,' she grins. 'It's been steeping for a *week!*'

She's wearing little silver earrings of Witches on broomsticks, rings on every finger and bangles that jingle.

Tony walks in, throwing his jacket on a chair. 'Hi Bobcat. D'you see the cake Suzi brought?'

'No! Hey, let *me* show her!' Suzi hollers, bounding back through the door and pulling off the cloth that had hidden it. She presents it with great majesty to Jenny and me.

'Why, it's a perfect Christmas cake,' I laugh.

'Quite so,' she says. Proudly, as if introducing it to the rest of the feast, she starts to reorganize so as to find it a place.

Every surface is filled, salads of every kind and colour configuration, loaves of bread, buns and rolls, cairns of mushrooms, baby tomatoes, bowls of nuts and dried fruits, platters of vegetables and pudding basins of houmous. There are apples and bananas and satsumas, grapes overflowing all over the place, a huge box of cookies, and balloons in bunches hanging from the lightshades, the musky smell of the spiced juice on the stove warming everything, washing it with a saturating burgundy red. I shift a plate heavy with some kind of a beanloaf to put down the food I've just been handed, while Jenny still looks awestruck at the cake.

'Did you do it?'

'Hey, what's all this?' Pete has come in, putting two cartons of juice down by the stove.

Andy and Skye have followed him in, together with someone I don't know. Skye yells after Suzi, 'Is this from your mum? Wow! Look, everybody! Isn't she great!'

Pete leans over her shoulder. The cake is decorated exquisitely, with sugarcraft holly, oak and mistletoe. Around the bottom is a sweeping script in red icing.

'What are the words?'

Pete reads, 'Blessed Alban Arthan!'

'Damn, I wish I had a mum like that,' says Skye.

'Your mum did it?' It's the guy I don't know.

'Suzi's,' I smile. 'I don't know your name?'

Pete introduces us. 'I'm sorry, Bobcat. This is Michael.'

He smiles, a gentle smile. 'It's good to meet you. I've seen you at the Avebury Gorsedd festivals. It's really great to be here.'

'Aha, another Bard of Caer Abiri. Sabbat blessings. You're very welcome. Have you seen a copy of the ceremony we'll be doing?'

We walk together back into the sitting-room. About 20 people have come, some of the Grove of the Golden Owl, together with a few close friends and family who wouldn't normally join in. Being Christmas Eve, many have obligations they can't slip out of or wouldn't wish to. It's a time for family. With so little of my own blood kin, I look around and smile at the closeness of the Grove, the gentle ease with which people are relating, new faces and old.

And arm comes around my waist. It's Andy. He's a designer in his late thirties, a Druid who weaves his faith with his Christianity. He's survey the room. 'Where's Jim?'

I laugh. 'Ah, Jim sends his apologies. He was invited to a party he just had to go too.'

While most are used to the Grove's no drugs policy, including alcohol and marijuana, tonight is the kind of night when some would prefer a different sort of wild night out – drink and warmth instead of mud and balefires.

'I see,' Andy nods, distracted. 'And Carole?'

'Over there.'

He adjusts his hair and steps over people and around chairs to the girl of his dreams. Sitting down with a hot glass of the mulled juice, I watch. Those who have speaking parts in the ceremony are reading through their scripts, and seeing me there they occasionally call out with questions and wisecracks. My son is in a corner reading a story to one of my apprentices. My partner is standing by the window, tall and so urbane, talking to someone's brother, laughing, listening. A group with another small child are hanging things on the Yule tree. Everybody's talking. I close my eyes and feel the energy of the festival dancing through us, centring us perfectly in the moment, midwinter.

When the ones too young to stay up are in bed and tucked up, and all those who are leading the ceremony are sufficiently confident and geared up, I take one of my Bards, Accolon, and head on out to prepare the temple grove. It's bitterly cold with a clear black sky, and out on the edge of the forest we stop and gaze at the stars. From where we are standing the far horizon is some 60 miles distant. There are houses in amongst the trees, but their lights are hidden, and clear across to the horizon there is darkness. The Gemini twins are bright, as is Orion, with his dog chasing his heels, Sirius, rising above the misty sulphur glow of a far-off town. Taurus and the Pleiades cluster.

We hold hands and I'm dizzy for a moment. I breathe deeply, then I'm off, out and flying over the fields of frozen mud and flint, down across the leafless treetops on silent wings. The darkness takes shape and holds me, directs me, in that ecstasy of freedom. Then, utterly exhilarated, I'm swooping back to where Accolon stands strong and sure, meeting him hard. He holds me tight.

'Hey,' he says, softly. *Careful.*

I'm OK. Very OK. We smile a deep if not conscious knowing.

It takes a half hour to reach the grove, walking through the wood at night without any light. We say very little, for when I walk on cat paws my vision is better. Occasionally I turn to him and see his bright eyes shining. As cat I perceive him as fox and there's an intangible excitement in our trotting along the deer tracks together, yet a vague confusion as to why. When I talk aloud everything changes as I slide back into human form, clasping my staff and blind to everything below a foot from the ground. There is much less distinction between the trees and their energy, the shadows and the spirits, and I must concentrate on my focus in order not to be thrown.

The Old Faith has always been known for its priesthood working with animals as allies and 'familiars'. Learning to talk to other creatures, to learn the languages that exist across the web and the ways in which others will respond, what they are interested in, how they can help and how to motivate them to help, is an important part of Druidcraft. Learning to see through the eyes of a different creature is a wonderful experience. Where the human body is limited, there are creatures that can fly or squeeze or run to reach our goals for us. Where human mentality is limited by self-consciousness, by the experience and the expectations that bind us into time attachments and cripple our ability to be absolutely present, there are animals whose perceptions and attitudes towards any situation can be awesomely clear. Where human emotion is overwhelming, there are animals whose simplicity refreshes us. Where we are trapped and blocked, there are creatures whose natural instinct can find us a path straight through. There are animals that just know how to stretch in the sunshine better than humans. So, to use these skills and the freedom they bring, the Druid learns how to shape-shift.

There are two basic ways of shape-shifting, but both are based in the mind. The first way is simply the releasing of the physical human form, letting the astral or the soul rise of out the body, and shifting into another form. Some shifts work with actual creatures that are around locally, pets or wild folk, with whom they have a relationship, merging with these animals to use their abilities. It might be called possession, but any shifter will know that merging with a creature who doesn't want you there is not only exhausting but ultimately dangerous. Most shifters don't work with another physical body, but shift their mind set into another form and work on a soul level. It's about easy transport most of the time, getting somewhere quickly, flying high or silent, swimming or running fast. It is also often used for freeing ourselves, living life a little more to the full. Someone who is sensitive to energetic forms will be able to pick up the subtle presence of the shifter in their altered form, should they come into their vision, and communicate with them as they might with any spirit.

The second way of shifting is when we release not only our human form but also our human perception. The usefulness of this is purely to experience a situation from an altered viewpoint. It is deeply teaching. In this kind of shifting, we have taken our minds into the belief that, temporarily but absolutely, we are another creature. With training and practice, we pick up the frequencies and vibrations that are the energy of another creature. We then shift in order to experience that other state. During these times the human physical body is relieved of any intense energy which it is finding hard to bear. When the shifter is out there in another form they are able to move instinctively according to whatever are their most basic needs in order to find a state of satisfaction and equilibrium. Through the process of returning into the human consciousness, not everything is lost: the memory shifts, translating itself, into the human mind, and the more clearly this happens the more profound is the experience and its teaching. When or why the shifter does return varies. Sometimes the human body is disturbed by something external or by pain or discomfort. Often the turn is a natural flow from the point of satisfaction. It is possible, at times, to be shifted for too long. The usual result is an incredibly sore human frame, with muscles and even bones pushed out of shape by the power of the mind. The longer one is out, the harder it can be to slide back into a normal human mentality.

It's the kind of thing, rather like past-life memories, that is either declared to be utterly ridiculous or is considered intellectually and held a little sceptically as reasonable belief or possibility until is it experienced.

It is true that many natural shape-shifters – people who don't need much training other than a little guidance and direction – are those with physical problems, weaknesses which don't allow them to lead an active or physically fulfilling life. My hypersensitivity limits me in terms of what I can achieve with my body, but working with other animal forms allows me to do what I want without overstressing or hurting my body.

So it is that the bobcat and the fox, stealing through the trees, stopping now and then to listen to the owls, make their way to bank of pine, where, slipping between the spiky bare lower branches, they come out into the clearing that is the grove.

Moving silently to the west, holding my staff firmly before me, I move my consciousness up from the cat's sight, centring myself once more in human form, rising up through the branches, the tall straight pine, the shining holly underneath the bare oak, out into the dark night and the shining stars, then slipping down through the staff and into the rich leafmould, the flint and clay beneath my feet.

I walk into the circle and move to the east, greeting my grove guardian. *Tyroshai! Hail and blessings of the night!*

He comes to me through the dark pine trees, robed in white, holding a staff ornate with carvings of a ram's skull and horns. He is ageless, but older than I, and he nods his greeting, his acceptance of our presence. I tell him of our plan for the evening and who will be coming. He looks across my shoulder to where Accolon is building a log pile in the grove centre, starting to lay the fire in the light of his lantern.

With your permission, my Lord.

With your care.

I bow and am aware of his energy flooding around the circle.

I kneel beside Accolon. 'Bank it well. The earth is so dry.'

When the fire is lit, I start to walk the circle, preparing mentally for the ceremony that is to come and simply feeling the joy of the place. Accolon stands in the firelight and starts to play his mandolin, quietly singing his ballad of the forest. As I am filled with the energy of the grove, I hear that his words are about us and the way that we are together, and the energy rises and I start to dance. Swirling around the fire, I call out to my Lady of the Forest and his rhythms get faster as I chant and whirl around him. We're utterly linking and each movement of mine pulls on him, and each rhythm of his music pushes me on. Our eyes are connected, and as I move we are like snakes, writhing entwined, yet we never touch. For he is my Bard and not my lover and he plays for me as we create the magical temple together in the power of that cohesion. And when he sings again, he sings of the spirit of the forest, of the Lady in Green herself, and I laugh as I dance, for I can feel the little people dancing with me and I can hear the laughter of the elfish folk, the hum of the Earth.

The music lulls and then builds, and again it lulls, and with each surge of energy we wash the grove through with a different layer of colour. I gaze at Accolon in one such lull with his brush of blond hair and his deep eyes sparkling, enjoying the sensation of this partnership, this love that is a love of the forest, a love expressed between us only within the bounds of the sacred circle.

All too soon through the forest come the owl calls of the first of the Grove. Accolon grimaces and I laugh, knowing now how we both crave to spend the whole night dancing our faith around the fire, to whirl and intensify the energy, to find the climax, the scent of which already evokes a deep longing between us. But it is time to give over what we've created to others.

By the time the circle has been cast and consecrated, and some 20 souls are standing, each with a candle flickering, beneath the canopy of the sleepy oak, within the circle of pine and holly, and the flow of the ritual has begun, I am able to glance across at him and smile with thanks. The smell of the incense drifts through me and I breathe in deeply. The grove begins to fill with the hidden company, spirits who are drawn to the high energy of peace and devotion. Many are devas, spirits of the wild, of nature, the trees. Beside one young Bard stands her father, a man with gentle eyes who passed on some five years ago He is usually there, loving her, supporting her, and we nod to each other a silent greeting as the ceremony begins to get under way. Most of it is being performed by others and I'm able to settle back and listen, feel.

'Since the changing moon of Samhain have we been reaching for the light that will give us our security, that will help us to know who and where we are. But it is dark and in that darkness there is chaos...'

It is my third Yule ceremony of this cycle. The first was with some 70 people in an old barn as the sleet froze the air outside, and we shivered as an old mythic tale was played out by the fire's light. The second was just Silverwolf and me in the midwinter dawn. This one was written by an apprentice and we've been over it three or four times, perhaps more. I know it sufficiently for the words to take me easily into glimmers of thoughts that are barely formed. I glide into their mist and drift down into the earth where I am held in the soft and sure embrace of the Mother...

'In the centre, there is stillness...'

...where there is no need to move, no urge to strain or push against her embrace. I no longer feel her body, just know she is all around me and, for a moment, there is such rich and nourishing contentment. But I am aware that I am growing with the food of her love and feel awe at my being changing...

'...yet the life force is strong and craves expression!'

And in the deep earth, in the womb of the goddess, I stretch and suddenly feel the rush of my own life energy, aware that I am growing, that I am becoming. Someone steps forward, out of a chanting, to place the Yule log into the fire.

'From the womb of the night, comes forth new life and light!'

'The Oak King is born!'

Back in the grove, I am watching the log. Someone's obviously washed it with liquor and flames leap up around it as drums start pounding and folks call their welcome to the returning king. Rather jerked out of my private meditation, it takes me a little while to join in. With so much happening in my life, any opportunity to integrate and to ground, to honour my roots and the source of my nourishment, is well taken. I pick up my drum and call out my welcome to the newborn child, while in my heart I bow low to the mother, adding to the rhythms as people dance, chanting their thanks and celebration.

Stilling the movement, Pete steps forward in his robe of green and white. He walks the circle, addressing the spirits and dryads of the forest, then looks up and through the trees to the point where the midwinter sun will rise.

'Reborn in the wide skies, you bring us hope of new life, shining clear and bright upon and through us. By the power of the gods, the blessings of the goddess, may we too have that great courage to take the leap of faith through the void, to allow the light to be rebirthed within our hearts and minds, within our souls, rebirthed without the limitations of our fear, without the restrictions of our expectations of form.

'*May we be rebirthed in beauty!*'

And everyone calls, 'That we may know the beauty of all creation!'

'And reborn in freedom, let us resolve to share that freedom with all around us, letting go our need for Mother Earth, our brothers and sisters, the stones and crystals, the flowers and trees, all the creatures of land, sky and sea, let us resolve to learn how to love.'

A vixen barks somewhere in the forest and I look to Accolon. His eyes are closed and he smiles.

It is my part of the rite and for a moment I still myself, centring, feeling the energy of the circle and all who are present. Jenny has walked to the altar stone where, taking up the branch of mistletoe, she raises it for the blessings of the gods. There is a beautiful stillness, even amongst the forest folk who watch from the undergrowth. I walk forward, as does a Druid from across the circle. His inner name is Luis, Gaelic for 'rowan tree', and he is an occasional visitor to our Grove. We meet at the altar and hold the mistletoe together, both attuning to its magical energy. Our eyes meet and we smile.

'This sacred plant is a symbol of the moment of infinity.'

'Of absolute fertility.'

His voice is soft, but fills the grove.

'As such let it be distributed to all.'

As we move around the circle, Luis breaks off a sprig and I embrace each person, whispering, 'Blessings of new life!' By halfway round, Jenny's eyes are filled with tears. When we return to our places I step again into the circle.

'So it is that we celebrate the birth of the sun, rebirthed once more into our reality, the sun that will stay wrapped in the arms of his mother through the long nights and dark days that still lie ahead until the season of Imbolc, when, as a child, he will come out [well, now and then, between the rain and snow]. Slowly, as he grows, he will once more touch the land with warmth, quickening the seeds, waking the trees.

'May we keep these soft white seeds of mistletoe as a token, a symbol of the light within us that waits for the higher light to draw it out and into the manifest world. In the silent depths of our being, we each hold the spark of the new Sun Child that will grow as the year progresses. May we touch its truest wisdom that we may shine with love and joy.'

My Lady, may it be so.

'One amongst us holds the Sun Child within her spirit too. A soul has come to her and asked that, through her, it may rebirth as her child, coming again into body, another Earth adventure, a new incarnation within its soul family. As a Grove, as a fellowship, as a tribe of friends and families, let us welcome this spirit upon its journey.'

There are an exquisite few moments of silence, as all around the circle hearts and minds flow out to the new spirit. Quietly, a few offer their blessings of love and welcome. Then Pete steps forward, demanding, 'So who's the blessed mother?'

I laugh and turn to bow. 'Jennifer Grant, this is your life!'

The Grove is about to yell and cheer, but Pete takes the attention, walking over to Jenny and, kneeling at her feet, he addresses her belly.

'Sweet courage, little friend. You've a fine woman here!'

Then through laughter and howls and whoops and great applause, a few others go to her, women with hugs and congratulations, sisterhood blessings from mothers to the new mother-to-be, gifts of awe and thanks from Andy and Jon. The drums start to roll, this time pipes too, tin flutes and bells. And Accolon playing his mandolin and the music is wild and rich as the dancing begins.

III

FIRST BREATH

IMBOLC: ENTERING THE WORLD IN THE TENDER NORTH-EAST

The period between Yule and Imbolc is seldom quite as quiet as I would like it to be. The weeks of Capricorn are always a struggle – cold, hard and immovable. For a solitary cat, brought up under warmer skies, these are the weeks when I wish most to do nothing but curl up by the hearth and sleep. It is very likely that anyone who comes close will be greeted with a snarl. To those brave enough to reach out and stroke me it is made absolutely clear that, at this time of the year, it is more likely that they do it for themselves than for my pleasure and an instant too long will be shortened by a sharp claw. It's a time for thinking, thinking so deeply it's hardly thinking at all.

Yet, as Imbolc rises, the energy changes. The snowdrops are flowering, the crocuses elbowing their way through the soil. Though the nights are still long and the air is even colder, we know the tides of the year have turned. The sun is rising nearer to the east, there are lambs in the fields on wobbly legs, shaking their tails. If not yet inspired to clean out the kitchen cupboards and repaint the skirting, we are starting to formulate, to create from those plans that have been gently cooking deep inside. It's time to consider making tentative first steps.

People often tell me this is crazy. 'I can't have thinking time! I've got deadlines to meet!' In that daily battle of priorities, the urgent and unimportant tasks often win out over the real stuff, what's important but not critical now. We're exhausted and seldom satisfied with what we do actually manage to achieve.

In Druidcraft, as we watch the ways of nature, a process

begins of working within those tides and currents. It isn't a struggle. There's no sense of *Hey, I must get this set up, but I can't yet because I must wait until the daffodils are in bloom.* It's an easy rhythm, understanding and accepting that our bodies do more effectively work in tune with the climate and seasonal changes. Many people notice that their most prolific time is early in the summer; for some this is chaotic, for others productive, but either way the energy is strong and high. Yet as the harvest starts to roll in, a heaviness of growth slows us down, and the Leo energy encourages us to find that shady spot and lie down for a fat tummy snooze. For many the period between Christmas and New Year is a write off which stretches, yawning, through a good part of January. Yet this is a time when we are supposed to leap into action and lay down a sound foundation, securing wonderful omens for the coming year. Screw that. By the end of the month, folks are tired, having worked too hard, left home before it's light, returned after dusk, and carried the guilt and stress for not managing to get it all done. For these people, February is but a little lighter and holds no real relief. Winter continues and the energizing days of spring seem to be aeons away.

For those who flow with the tides of nature, the dark days of winter are a perfect opportunity to get done all those long and profound tasks on the agenda for which there is no time, no quiet space, during the wild growth and creativity of the summer months. If something *must* be grown through the winter moons, we know that it will need more care, it will take more resources, artificial light and warmth. If an idea must be found during the height of summer, one is best to hide away. Ideas conceived in the bright sunshine of May and June are likely to be parched or munched up, or overwhelmed by those that were born in the early spring. A good deal more energy is required to protect them.

This doesn't only refer to the big things. Our attitudes towards the daily processes of life, our eating and communicating, our making love, are wholly affected. Perhaps it's an obvious statement, but it's one which lies as a foundation of Druidic belief. Finding a synchronicity with the currents around us, we access an appropriate energy which is more potent than if we were struggling against the tide. It's in the struggle that apathy kicks in.

In Druidcraft, the winter is seen as the realm of earth. It is the darkness of the womb, the cauldron of the magical brew from which come the drops of perfect inspiration. It is the cave of our hibernation. Though the old ways are taught through many different methods, it was into the realms of earth that I was first taken and it is into its dark recesses that I head my own students as they begin their own journey. As we study this element, our focus is drawn downwards. We look to our feet, becoming aware of where we are and the forces that keep us there. We look at our stability, our sources of nourishment. Our state of being is encircled, observed and pondered. We scream and deny what we see, making to run but not able to move, turning away from ourselves into masks that stand strong and untrue. We curse at the earth for holding us back, tying us down and restricting our soul flight. We begin to learn that the earth only holds us so that we might grow, allowing us the roots that are the umbilical cord of our connection to nature, the cord that feeds us, assuring us our security, safety. And through the silence of the connection comes the gradual acceptance of ourselves and our present. The chains of the mundane become the arms of the mother.

With our feet more firmly on the ground, we journey on with a surety around the wheel of the year. From Yule, when deep within the womb life is affirmed, through the Capricorn days of holding the newborn close to the breast, still wrapped in the initiatory veils of the magical birth, we move on step by step, day by day, towards the time when the child is revealed. Growing strong and plump and joyful in its mother's arms, its play brings it now into the open world. Soft and innocent, hiding and watching and gently investigating, the Sun Child touches the earth. So it is that our first spring festival comes. It is Imbolc, Candlemas, celebrated at the beginning of February or the full moon of Aquarius, and as its energy creeps through me, I am drawn away from the fireside and into the gentle ponderings of what to do with my winter's dreams. Slowly I begin to put out feelers, to check the air, the mood, the wind. I gaze out of the window over the snowy garden. I'm not ready to break through or open any leaves. But my focus is heading upwards. My energy is rising. Quietly, so that no one might see me and bite off the tender shoots, I stretch up. I breathe.

Imbolc is a festival of thanksgiving for that abundance of sweet breastmilk that nurtures and nourishes us. For me it is the gentlest of the festivals, the most feminine, and veiled in crisp and misty white. It is a ceremony of quiet joy, of poetry and sweet laughter, little children and dawn's rosy glow. We have emerged from the womb of sanctuary, dark and rich with placental blood. The profound mysteries of birth have been left behind and the cool air flows softly around us, awakening our nervous system to the sensation of our skin, of our form. We breathe and through the emptiness of clear air we smell the rich warmth of the breast, the white milk. We open our eyes into the soft sunlight.

And we see where the Sun Child has reached out and touched the earth, warming the soil with its fingers. There the snowdrops have flowered.

* * *

There is a stillness around us, a sense of pause and purpose, as if we were sitting on a plank of wood just a little above the ground, patiently, biding our time, knowing the moment will come when we will land on the grass, knowing there's nothing in the world we can do but wait. A mist is faintly visible over the forest beneath us, a wash of pale grey between the black of the trees and that of the distant fields. Yet above us the sky is an indigo blue, almost too light now for the stars to be clear, a blue that seems to colour the darkness of the air.

It must be an hour yet before first light. She sniffs and I breathe, as if the noise has reminded me to. Her face is glowing. 'How are you doing?' I murmur.

She closes her eyes for a moment. Little pipistrelles appear, diving free through the air. I lose them in the darkness beneath the horizon, but watch as they swoop low against the paleness of the mist, then up into the indigo sky. When she looks up she smiles, as if the little creatures reflect perfectly the dance of her thoughts.

'Relieved.' She clears her throat and the bats disappear. She touches a finger to her lips, suddenly aware of her body. For a moment we watch the noise being absorbed into the night air. Then she looks at me, uncertain, whispers, 'Isn't that dreadful? I should be feeling ...' She shakes her head. 'But I'm relieved.' Her voice drifts formless into the darkness around us, as if the sound were making no impression at all. Her words are spoken to herself and the quiet dark world knows it and doesn't respond. 'It's over. I did it. I didn't chicken out.'

Her car has stalled on the way to the forest, taking 10 minutes and serious thought before it would snarl back into life. She'd arrived with crippling stomach ache. She'd almost cancelled twice. 'it's normal' I whisper.

'My resistance?'

I nod and she smiles inside, her aura washed with clear blue. There is the flicker of a question, *It didn't happen last time,* but she doesn't say it out aloud and I respond in thought, *But last time you were only determining to take the first step.*

She turns to me and through the dark I can just see the mist of her breath. 'How many do we go through?'

I grin. 'Til when?'

She shrugs and smiles.

'It isn't a course you can graduate from.' My voice lingers in the air. 'We begin with our first dedications, those that take us into the tradition, as you did. And when we move through the barriers of our fears, finding deeper levels of trust, we open ourselves on those levels, committing ourselves with our vows, to ourselves, to the gods that we work with. And we mark our journey, when we're called to do so by our gods and guides, with rites of initiation.'

Her smile spreads and she breathes deeply. When we are once again gazing out into the night, she whispers, 'I would've understood your words before tonight but now I can really feel them. I feel ... excited. But I'm not sure I know quite how I'd reach that energy, it's so deep inside me. Inspired, I feel inspired! But *literally*, as if I've been breathed by the spirit of this place, in and out, and I feel honoured. I feel honoured.'

So do I.

I close my eyes and a yawn rises up with a rush of tiredness, but the priestess in me suppresses it, pushing at my jaw. It's been a long night. The cold is seeping into me, the heat of the rite wearing off. I shift my bum on the frozen earth and find myself stiff with cold. The grass is crisp with ice. The forest grove where we did the rite was white with hoarfrost, sparkling in the candle-light, as if all life were paused within that silence. I wonder if the field that we're sitting in would be white in the sunlight. I slide more fully into my body and concentrate my inner heat, spreading it out again through my limbs, willing my muscles to relax into its warmth. As heat pours through my aura, it spreads into hers. She breathes in and sighs, closing her eyes.

'I now understand why so many initiations are made at Imbolc.' Nodding with a surety, she turns to me. 'It's like being able to breathe in a totally different way, taking the first breath again. It kind of hurts, but it's a new life.'

And the Mother, I ponder, *at Imbolc, is still with us, protecting,*

holding us through the process of change. There are times when the
steps we take through our fears must be taken alone. But, yes, we begin
again at Imbolc, rebirthed from the darkness. And we return to the
Mother again and again.

'And I feel ... enthused. But literally again: *en-theo.* I feel as if
I've drawn the gods into me, in as much as I can understand that
right now, that perfect spirit of place, that divine energy I found,
I've drawn that deep down into my soul. And ... and it makes
everything seem strangely right. Perfect time. Perfect place.'

I remember where she has stood in the middle of the grove,
shivering in her robe. Into the plait of her hair she'd slipped
feathers of the wood pigeons that roost in the trees outside her
bedroom window, waking her each dawn with their velvety *croo-*
ooo. Her face was pink and wet with tears as she'd pulled at her
fingers and again I'd whispered, *Centre.*

The rite was almost over. But shaking her head she'd sobbed,
'I can't *hear.*'

'What do you want to hear?'

'I don't know. I want to say that I'm forgiven, but that's my
childhood speaking-'

Gently I'd laughed. 'Wrong religion, honey, but that's OK.'

Through her tears, she'd half giggled, which let the tears flow
more freely.

'I just want to know that it's *real,* that what I've said has been
accepted.'

'By whom?'

She'd nodded, realizing how much her expectations were
limiting her vision.

'Stop trying. Let go,' I whispered, 'You know the process
now.'

And I'd closed my eyes and slipped into the trees, calling
upon my Lady, *Nemetona, be with me, hold this space, simple, clear,*
and I had reached out to her, through her, as her, through the
mists to the threads of life.

Then, from the edge of the clearing that glistened with frost, I'd opened my eyes. She was no longer trembling. She looked like a fawn, newly born and immensely vulnerable, yet radiating an extraordinary hope. My spirit had made no noise on the frozen leaves and twigs, but slipping back into my body I'd shifted my feet, crunching on the ground, making myself jump. Across the grove Nathair moved, her black robes sharp against the candlelit frost, and I'd smiled broadly. The circle's boundary was aglow. *It's lile a bloody electric fence!*

She raised an eyebrow.

I emptied, disappeared and watched the woman in the grove, careful to remain just outside her focus, a step away from her energy. There were devas in the shadows, and the birch whose flaking bark shone bright in the flickering of the candles seemed to open a sleepy eye and reach out a hand of acknowledgement. When she faltered, I'd whispered, *centre,* urging her on. *This is your space. Use it! Remember why you are here.* Slowly but surely her energy had filled the grove. (And the rest is her story.)

It was a poignant rite. It was not about finding a profound and brilliant power, but about finding a centre point and, opening in trust, claiming one's own space. For that woman, as for so many, its pivot was on trust, *perfect trust,* out of which emerges a genuine empowerment.

The sky is growing lighter; it's almost a royal blue. Just the morning star shines now, like a diamond floating in a queerly calm sea. An owl flies low, skirting the edge of the field below us, gliding through the air that is darker than the sky on a last excursion before the dawn. I start to gather myself together, physically and spiritually, so as to make a move. I am starting to think of home when a figure emerges out of the darkness, walking towards us. For a moment I assume it's Nathair, but as the shadow draws closer I see that's not.

Sister. I bow.

Priestess, she says. She is tall, with a Roman nose. Her mouth is set, though her eyes seem to twinkle. *I am come of the bloodline.* She gestures with a sureness of hand towards the new initiate. Sitting beside me she's quite unaware of the presence of her ancestor, but snuggles deeper into her coat when the spirit comes closer. She's gazing out over the forest and I see the same hook of her nose.

A priestess I was of Brighit, the spirit continues. *I am used to work between the worlds.*

I bow my respect. *Blessed be, priestess of Brighit. Are you bid to guide this woman who is of your own blood?*

I am, along the paths of her journey. It is known that you do so on this side of the mists.

As long as she wishes.

She nods and looks around her. *This is a blessed country. It is new to me but strong. She lives close.*

Down through the valley there. Sister, her vision is yet cloudy and she does not see you. Would you wish that I make your presence known to her now?

The time will come.

The air is broken by the sound of a voice and we both turn to the woman, who is saying aloud, 'I'm sure you didn't mean me to answer this with a thousand different ideas, but ... it's as if I feel like I've become aware of myself for the first time, I feel ... as if I'm not alone.'

I have to close my eyes to hold back the giggles.

'In fact,' and a little hesitantly she laughs, 'I almost feel crowded. I know it's really inside, but it feels as if it's outside me, as if there's this crowd of women standing behind me, around me. I'm not sure I want to turn around.'

I collapse into laughter, and confused and relieved, she begins to laugh too, until giggles quite take hold of her. The spirit smiles, shimmering into the brightening air with a colour of deep fuchsia pink, and I shrug at her as, beside me, grasping her tummy, shaking with the laughter that tumbles out of her, such infectious laughter, our tenderfoot charge falls back and into the grass.

I am suddenly struck with the presence of the moment.

The plank I thought would land has upturned and we've fallen off.

'Oh dear,' she sniffs. 'Have you got other mad people to work with today?'

'Well, after I've found all the parts of me which I've lost from frostbite, I'm going to a child's blessing.

'Ah,' she giggles, 'I do wish you all the best. Is the child any younger than me?'

* * *

In Druidry there is no initiatory rite of endurance which has to be passed in order that a person might enter into the tradition. Though such rites do happen in branches of the occult, they seem to me to be merely a way of perversely massaging the insecurity of those who hide within the covers of their secrecy. Modern druids, no longer under siege from a conquering religion, are not practising in secret. There need be no test to discover who can be trusted to keep silent under duress. We swear no oaths of exclusivity or secrecy. There are no vows to be made but those we make to ourselves.

Initiation within some Druidic Orders is a matter of completing a set number of tasks or years and progressing by initiation through a series of grades in the same way that we might make our way through a school system, only without examinations to test our ability or understanding. Most Druids will agree that this is not in itself spiritual initiation. Initiation is an experience which is ongoing from the first time we dedicate ourselves to a tradition. As we make our way through the barriers of fear and distrust which have constrained our natural freedom and joy, and we find ourselves able to open into different levels of being, of fully living, in our awe and thanks we make offerings to ourselves, to our gods and guides in the context of formal ritual.

Further into Druidcraft, rites of initiation are carried out that actively push at the boundaries of our abilities and capabilities, provoking fears and challenging our dedication and commitment.

Initiations are rites of spiritual passage marking the points of our journey according to our own progress, our healing and clarity. These moments of our lives are considered to be pivotal in Druidry, as are the other points of transition in our mundane and physical lives which are also marked by ritual and celebration. In secular society there are rites for marriage and death, while in Druidry rites are offered for the marker points such as the falling of the first baby tooth, for puberty and the first menstrual period, the first sexual experience, new homes, pregnancy, and many more through to death and even beyond. While there are times in life when we need to experience such events privately and alone, there are others when the open acknowledgment, the acceptance, support and respect of our family or community, a parent or an unrelated elder, is a powerful affirmation of our having reached that point, with all its associated achievement. And in doing so we are better able to transit through, finding the new beginning which lies beyond.

There is a gentle understanding in Druidcraft, however, that all new beginnings are formed and coloured by the beliefs we hold, conscious and subconscious, positive and self-negating, beliefs that are our base foundations. While an initiation may mark a transition from an old perspective or attitude to one that is less constraining, underlying beliefs might still remain that hold us down. Our talking-self chatters. Conscious of its independent individuality, it babbles away, making sense of the constant waves of input, justifying and rationalizing, making choices and asserting boundaries, ordering its world. From our first experiences of life, the talking-self starts to make decisions about our environment, guiding us as to where to find comfort and nourishment, where to avoid being hurt. And through the noise of its commentary, our limitations and our basic expectations are prescribed.

The Druidcraft belief that the soul is cognizant between lives extends to an understanding that we are highly aware throughout the process of coming into the body. The personality's consciousness takes time to develop, nurtured within the new environment, but the soul takes on board the experiences of every moment of its existence, responding, learning, communicating or just flinching. On some psychic level then our conception and our entire gestation and birth, as well as those first few vague years of infancy and toddlerhood, are held within us in their every detail.

During the process of birthing and the moments that directly follow the most powerful reactive decisions are made. Far from being dull and without feelings, the birthing infant is at its most acutely impressionable stage. More decisions are made during our first years of life, with most defensive barricades becoming firmly established in the psyche by the time our baby teeth are regularly falling around the ages of six or seven. While most of these decisions create the positive framework within which we survive, each one of us holds a great many more which are utterly misconceived, which snatch us back into safety when we could otherwise have moved through a situation, creatively learning. Furthermore, we hold just one or two which are entirely pivotal.

But beneath the talking-self exists the child-self, the part of our psyche that isn't held back by the criticism, crises and didactics of self-consciousness. Not aware of being separate from its environment, the healthy child plays and sleeps within the aura of the mother, still trusting to the embracing safety that her being confers. The child-self is free to express itself as itself. It hasn't yet picked up the masks, crafted and adorned as they are with the colours of those primary protective decisions, the masks of our inhibitions which both protect us from and deny us the joy of interacting intimately.

Many mystical spiritual practices guide us directly from the talking-self to the higher self, to that wonderful concept of 'enlightenment', or to the realms of the gods, by actively using the mind to release ourselves from self-consciousness, facilitating a glide from devoted concentration or concentrated devotion into a state of emptiness, and perhaps from there into the experience of divine inner peace. Druidcraft takes another route, by first searching out the child-self.

It begins with the creation of special space, sacred, set apart, safe. There the physical and subtle body senses are gently encouraged to awaken, to become vitally aware of the energy spinning and weaving our worlds, that we might start to feel life as it flows and bubbles through us. In the process of creating that space, and as we listen to our body, to the earth beneath us, the skies through which we are ever moving, the talking-self becomes quiet. Almost before we know it we have slipped into the child-self, not just inspired to express the flow of energy but *needing* to. And through our creativity, our loving, laughing, our walking and working, our very living, our whole body is brought into play.

Play is the crucial word. Exploring, discovering, lifting up logs and watching the stars, all alone or with whomsoever, through a state of awe we open ourselves. We hurl off the masks and smile with dirty faces, relating with an honesty and without inhibition. We trust.

Where as a child perhaps I would've dragged branches to make a camp in the undergrowth of the forest, hidden away and safe from the demands and conventions of the adult world I could not understand, now I cast a circle which delineates the Druid temple that is my special place. Instead of torn and muddy clothes, now in a robe washed and dried softly in the breeze I consecrate with sacred tools, saining with cleansing herbs grown and dried in my own garden, aware of my devotion to the beauty of the forest, to the power of the land and the force of its currents, aware that my adult mind does not allow me to take any of it for granted.

'In some ways,' I said to one woman, 'Druidcraft might be described as the spirituality of the uninhibited child expressed through the mentality of the responsible adult. It's about finding the freedom to feel pure joy, which I believe is our essential state, the natural-'

'So it's a good excuse to have fun then.'

'Well, yes!'

Then I realized she was talking with a patronizing cynicism. It isn't an unusual response, though one that's derogatory tone always stuns me.

'But not an *excuse*. It's a potent and effective way of finding how it is we *can* have fun'.

Across the table a friend of hers laughed, raising his glass, 'We know how to have fun, eh?'

She shrugged. 'It isn't just the booze – it's being with friends that matters, and in the *real* world. The point is, we don't need some religious philosophy to tell us how we can have a good time.'

'Sure,' I had to agree. 'Except –'

'It just sounds like escapism to me'.

I wondered how, without myself being patronizing, I could explain about the exhilaration that shivers through every cell, the sense of freedom and certainty that comes without a drop of alcohol. How, instead of escaping from the 'real' world, it gives a way of experiencing its beauty and its reality more intensely, of tapping into its extraordinary wells of inspiration. I wanted to talk about relationships, about connecting without the masks and inhibitions of our protective decisions, about reaching out for the gods and the spirits of the land, reaching out to our loved ones as our true self, in honesty. About being unchained.

But across the table at a party just isn't the right time.

* * *

You didn't ask me for help.

I've been dreaming, waiting for dawn, gazing into the fire and feeling its warmth playing with the cold where my skin is bare. Her voice slides into me like dye through still water. For that first moment as ever all I feel is the bliss of her formless presence, such exquisite relief, and when I open my eyes the grove is brilliant with her energy, a light that is darkness too, a richness of colour and vitality that is absolute clarity. I am overwhelmed by the peacefulness.

You didn't ask me for help

For a minute I just stare. She is unconcerned but waiting.

I bow my head and stammer, *Y-you are right, my Lady.*

Did you think you could do it alone?

I don't think I thought.

Do you think you went through it alone?

It felt that way. I frown, turn away. *Nathair was there, at some point. But she disappeared.*

To you.

To me, she disappeared.

Her silence fills the grove, as if ending the conversation.

I look down at the altar stone, firelight dancing on the chalice.

The charcoal and herbs on the flint are now a heap of soft grey ash.

A little handful of snowdrops lies there and the wing of the blackbird found in my garden, perfect feathers interleaved, the bone that joined the shoulder clean and bare. I run my fingertips over the feathers, allowing the strength of the bird once again to flood through me, that magical song lifting my breath.

Yet in my rite of thanks, calling to the spirit of the bird, I had been thrown. Oh, I have worked with eagle and with raven, with owl and cormorant, and my blinkered arrogance had such clear expectations of the energy and wisdom I might be able to access of the gentle and sweetly singing blackbird of our ancient lands. I had followed its enchanting call and meditated deeply, I had listened to its teachings and found an understanding of all that I was clear enough to see. I knew of the myths, had heard the tales of its power to heal and to guide us through the changing times of dawn and dusk. I thought I knew the blackbird, which the Irish call the Druid Dhubh. But never had I worked with one specific bird, never held it in my hands. And in my rite the bony wing had fleshed out, warm and round with breast feathers soft, and so close to my face its song had shattered the icy air between us.

And my Lady, we flew. Not like that wide, open, high glide of broader wings, but like flying on music, on breath itself.

And then? It was Nathair who spoke. She was standing behind me.

Then I lost it. Hit by doubt. *I guess it was simply my expectations breaking up.* It was like hitting a wall, then finding I could burst right through, almost crashing, so as to wake up. Yet, while a part of me did wake, it awoke to the dustbins. *It was hard, I was shattered. And there, in a heap, in this bright new world I'd broken through to, the doubts just mobbed me.*

Again, the silence is almost tangible. I turn to Nathair, but she's gone. The grove, though still strong with that energy of my Lady, seems empty. For a moment I feel lost and the memory of one of my old teachers comes to me, how she would simply touch my arm and close her eyes. Now I close mine. The words seem to fall out of me: *There is nobody to help me.*

And in that instant I understand. I want to laugh and cry. It seems ridiculous and critical, as if a crowd has been trying to explain a joke and I've only just got it. I'm embarrassed at my stupidity and I want to yell with sweet relief, remembering my lady's words when I said that Nathair has disappeared: *To you.* To me, she had disappeared.

There is nobody to help me. How much of my life has been guided by that principle.

I open my eyes to tiny snowflakes falling, landing on my skin, melting like kisses, and see perched on the altar stone the blackbird watching me, his head to one side as if listening to the painful chugs and clucks of my brain in action. I start to half chuckle, the weight of the realization very slowly shifting with the effort and with the need to express it, to release it. The force of Nemetona's energy once more breaks over me.

Where are you?

I gaze around me at my grove. It is an island of warmth, the fire flickering gold in the soft blue-grey of the dawn between the trees, a dark circle of swept earth within the white sleep of the wood. Glistening white spiders' webs hang between branches in the stillness, hoarfrost lies crisp under a layer of snow quiet suspended through miles of forest that surrounded my sacred grove, quiet but for the occasional twig snapping under little creatures' paws, the flurry of a wood pigeon.

I smile as beneath the trees that encircle the grove I see my guardians, the wolves lying still, licking at snowflakes that land on a nose or paw, the crows now and then shuffling in the branches above. My bobcat mate stretches, front legs, then back legs, and strolls unconcerned towards me through the snow. We touch noses, share misty breath and he growls his assurance, pushing my shoulder with a paw.

Not now, I whisper, though a part of me is so longing to curl up with him, sated, utterly present. I glimpse the black eyes of the little people that shine from darker shadows, the movement of the winter devas, and my embarrassment deepens. How could I think I was alone?

Nathair stands beside an oak. *Look up sister,* she whispers.

I do and go blank, breathless in the energy of my goddess. She seems to flow with a deep forest green that shimmers violet yet is no colour at all.

Where are you? She asks again.

I want to justify myself and explain, but she overwhelms me with simplicity and I stammer, *H-here. Now.*

She smiles, and her smile fills me. Yet it also triggers tears which rise so quickly they almost choke me. When they roll down my cheeks, they take with them that weight I seem to have carried forever, for though it feels like the grief, this is release, the sweet relief of actually having let go, knowing I am not alone. So easily I could just surrender, lie back and bathe in the ocean of my Lady. But she would shift to make me listen, a rage of wind would chill me through. I stagger to my feet and walk the circle round. When I'm standing before her I breathe deeply and open my soul, making the signs I have been taught.

My lady.

Priestess.

I am here. This is my home. As I talk everything slips into its perfect place. *This is your temple. Here I am never alone. Here I am heard, in my pain and my ecstasy. Here I am free, in my trust and my honesty. Here I live within your energy, within your aura, your circle. Here I dance my life to your music. Here I rest, in your arms.*

Yet?

Yet this space, this circle is me.

And so it is ever with you.

As are you.

For I am your grove. And, like the air that you breathe, I am ever within you and ever surrounding you.

My Lady, I forget.

Though you are marked.

And I learn.

Then let it be so.

* * *

O Lady of beauty, of life vibrant with joy! Spirit of my sanctuary.

Very little is written about the goddess with whom I work so often, Nemetona. Her name is found on various epigraphs and little more. The Celtic word *nemeton* is most often thought to denote 'sacred grove' and in modern Druidry Nemetona is most usually associated with the groves – in woodland, parks and gardens – that are many of the temples of faith. Whether the Druids of Celtic Britain actually did practise their faith in woodland groves or whether it was Roman suppression that forced them out of their temples and into the seclusion of the forests that then covered much of the land, we have no clear evidence. We do know that trees were of great religious and spiritual importance, the felling of certain trees in some parts of the Celtic world would being a capital offence.

However; *nemeton* would better be translated as simply 'sacred place', and in essence to me, Nemetona is the goddess of the sanctuary. Her arms enfold us within the sacred circle. She holds the temple that we might find the release to be soul naked and true, and to focus effectively.

Each person's most sacred place is an individual issue. It may be a gully on the mountain across the lake or a spot by the pond in the park or the dark little room at the back of the house. More important is the sense that one has found a place where the soul can be free.

The forest is the heartland of my soul and the grove is my holy temple, the ceiling of sky and floor of earth and walls of living wood, every aspect in a constant state of change – the clouds above, the wind in the trees, growth and decay, night and day. At times it is all enclosed by the forest canopy, sunlight flickering through the leaves, and at times it is bare branches, silver and black in the frost night. Yet it is always filled with certainty.

Starting out on the path of Druidcraft, the first steps take us in search of our own sacred place, somewhere to work. In the beginning, unless one is lucky enough to live near or to own an area of woodland or wilderness, or have a garden that is not overlooked by the curious or concerned, for many that first space is indoors. Sacred circles are cast by clambering over beds and chairs. Once the kids are asleep, the toys put away, a sacred rug is laid down and the circle is scribed. I once worked with an urban priestess whose indoor sacred place was her bathroom. It was the 'only room in our bloody chaos where one can disappear and lock the door!' It was a good-sized bathroom, so I don't believe the loo was regularly scribed in and consecrated, though it's a nice idea which could have had interesting effects.

Working in that first circle is important as a way of committing to the work as well as a way of dedicating time and sacred place to oneself. It is from the cast and sanctified outer circle that we travel into the inner planes, assured of no disturbance or distraction, letting ourselves journey deep within. Here we find our inner grove. For each person it is utterly different, in a different location, with differing trees. For some it is deep in a vast temperate forest, humming with life from butterflies to bears. For others, whose fear of the dark wood is too great, the grove must be but a circle of trees on the edge of a meadow or on top of a hill. Wherever and however it appears – and for a while it may waver and change – it is decreed a safe place within.

While for many people the only perceived threat to their order is from outside, others know immediately that the greater chaos is within. The mind itself is a fanfare of noise and distraction. Any therapist will confirm the mayhem of the average psyche, crowded as it is within different facets of persona, characters, memories, fears and cravings. Deeper, in the unconscious, lie the shadows of all that we have denied, where the nefarious and the guilty lurk, Christian devils and shamanic demons and the spirits of those who are squatting in our souls. We have to either be extremely well balanced or extremely good at denying the shadow if, while travelling the inner worlds, we come across no scary monsters. I tend to presume this is true, having never yet met anyone who can rightfully claim never to have encountered dangers. For some it takes seven years of wild hiking, while others are leapt upon on their first excursion. Yet however close the demons are to the surface of the subconscious, the inner grove is a safe place. It is a place which is discovered or created with that very intention, and each time it is blessed and conse-crated that intention underlies the action and is strengthened.

Whereas the shamanic or psychotherapeutic journey into the lower levels of the mind can be unnerving, even in the competent hands of a guide, in Druidcraft this is a journey that is taken perhaps every day and alone. Consciously, we have taken possession of a small area, a base camp, over which we have all control in terms of who and what can enter.

A student called me once in a fluster. Arriving at her inner grove she'd found it crowded with creatures and devas. Still unsure of herself, she'd sloped off to do her work in another part of the wood, just over the stream.

'Well, I didn't like to disturb them. Come on, Bobcat, stop laughing. What was I supposed to do?'

'Tell them to shut up or get out!'

She had cast her circle, affirming the grove, with the clear instruction that nothing should or could enter but that which came in love and peace. Certainly the little fork who had been picnicing in the sunny glade of the grove were laughing and dancing and chatting. There was plenty of love there and not a whisper of conflict. She thought about the conditions that she had laid on the circle. Next time she went back in, she sneaked up and watched through the trees. There were squirrels, rabbits and chaffinches, and elfin folk fluting and dancing their jigs, and her resolve to kick them out disappeared. They taught her about playfulness.

'I couldn't believe how they just accepted me.'

'You know how to be accepted. And besides, they kind of knew you – they'd been dancing in your energy for over a week!'

Finally, whenever they got on her nerves or she wanted quiet, she asked them to leave.

'I only wish the kids were so co-operative!'

It can take some time for the inner grove to become firm. Trees change, swap places, suddenly appear and disappear. At first this is an indication of uncertainty and a lack of confidence. Later, the sudden shift of a tree can have a more profound explanation. But as confidence grows, the inner grove gains clarity. We move from observing ourselves within it to being there with every sense alert.

The nourishment that is gained in such a place is extraordinary. For many Druids just thinking of their principle grove in passing brings a smile and a dreamy expression, followed by a *thwack* of wonderful energy.

It isn't that long before the concept of practising the faith beneath any roof becomes anathema and if an outside grove has not yet been found, the search begins for an outer counterpart to the inner haven.

Life has its crises and, however established our special place may be, a shock to the psyche can disrupt it completely, along with our belief in it is as a sacred sanctuary, just at a time when we most need it. Such a shock needn't be extreme or obvious, as overt as a car smash or the death of a loved one. A collision of souls in an argument might be sufficient. Essentially, if one of those primary and protective decisions is shaken, the repercussions may hit the grove. So it is that we call upon someone to act as a caretaker: the grove guardian.

Some guardians are keepers of a single grove. They remain in the energy of that temple, often emerging out of the environment or the spirit of that place, and they will not or cannot move.

An old stone circle is likely to have its own guardians who have always been there and always will be. In my vision, they

usually present themselves as earth energy partly anthropomor-
phized or holding some of the human qualities and priorities
that were presumably those of the ancient cultures who built and
used them. Having said that, I have been to some stone circles,
such as those out on moors which are seldom visited, and found
them to be guarded by the little people and devas, spirits who
are far from willing to compromise or negotiate with a member
of the human race. They have been out of use for so long that the
spirits seem to have forgotten (or dismissed) the energy of the
humans who originally laid the stones.

Some guardians are mobile and stay with a certain priest or
practitioner, holding the energy and protecting the temple space
for that person, regardless of where it is that the circle is cast.
These guardians tend to present themselves in a human or
animal form and work very much like guides to the person,
amplifying their energy for the purpose of their rite. Animal
allies, like the wolves and crows in my grove, often hang out
around the edge, giving the grove its particular colour, smell and
atmosphere, and affecting the temple's priest in just the same
way.

Some guardians are deities outright or in disguise.

But what is a Druid deity?

This is an impossible question, yet essentially simple. Druidry
cannot be defined by the gods which Druids might revere, for
there are too many, and likewise no gods can be defined by the
nature of their priests. In a Druid's search for his sources of
perfect inspiration, he may reach into a culture, a landscape, an
era, a pantheon or an aspect of nature, and there he might come
face to face with that tremendous surge of energy that he might
deem to be deity. But just as our sources of inspiration differ
enormously, so do our deities.

Though it's dependent on semantics, it could be said that
most Druids are to varying degrees both pantheistic and
polytheistic. Although many would define themselves as clearly

pantheistic, believing that deity exists within everything as everything, they would also acknowledge the existence of many gods. Some may focus their devotions on just one or two, but there is an understanding that these are merely the gods that they have chosen (or who have chosen them) out of the many. As a basic tenet of the tradition there is acceptance of the existence of many pantheons, including those that Druids themselves have no experience or understanding of.

Seeing this tolerance in practice is tremendously inspiring. Being in a sacred circle of some 300 people, such as gathers at the big Gorsedd festivals, and knowing that within that circle there are probably at least 30 named gods invoked in the hearts and minds of the people there, and many more that are unnamed, is a glorious realization of the faith at work. Beside a priest of Saxon Woden stands a devotee of Mercury, who in turn stands beside a lover of the Wiccan Cernunnos, perhaps with her coven, and they beside a hearth of Odin and then a priestess of Roman Diana, a hierophant of Isis and a Druid of Danu, a Bard of Cerridwen beside a novitiate of Arianrhod and so it goes on, all around the circle. At these gatherings, we had many Christians, as well as Ba'hai, Buddhists and Hindus, and when the oath of spiritual kinship is called, hand in hand, each one swears their absolute acceptance of each other. In a world of religious intolerance, it's a sight which is both moving and educating.

Our culture, however, is one that has a craving for monism. Though our apparently monotheistic state religion has a fairly low practising congregation, it seems that its reflex into secular society is strong. As a society we look for one reason, one person to blame. We look to the discipline and values of one career, one lover, one marriage, one thing at a time. Meanwhile, millions are spent by scientists searching for the one basic building block of life.

So it is that within the belief in the existence of many gods, some still crave a oneness. One entity or energy form must have created the omniverse. All gods are one god, all goddesses are one goddess. All deities are one deity, though invoked by many different names, worshipped in temples of brick and stone and wood and sand, in many different ritual forms and languages. Some, from that point of view, even name the one deity as the mother or father of all the gods.

To a radical or true polytheist such as myself, this is a bizarre concept. The gods are to me as separate and individual as you and I. Monism seems to be reductionism to a lowest common denominator and to do this to the gods is anathema, if not high sacrilege. But to the monist, this is the opposite of what they wish to do. They hold the concept of a higher deity, a unifying force beyond limitations. For many Druids this would simply be the life force.

The pantheist believes that manifest creation, which incorporates all that we perceive and also those worlds that lie both beyond and within, is both deity and an expression of deity. As Nemetona said, and indeed she expresses it in many ways, *I am ever within you and ever surrounding you.* But as a polytheist I know she is not All. She is one colour of the spectrum, one note in the perfume of my experience of being. At this time in my life, what she expresses is my motivating ideal.

The difficulty with polypantheism is the tendency to order, to classify. If all creation and beyond is an expression of the gods, then what is what and which bit is which? Nature seems to be a jumble of a jigsaw, puzzling the ordered human mind. For me, though, this is self-defeating, for to impose any kind of order only results in limiting our vision of the deities. When we do that, we limit our potential interaction for learning and for joy.

Some deities are very clearly associated with or expressed through a particular aspect of creation. There are the gods of the winds, of the rain and the thunder, the gods of oceans, wells and streams, gods of the mountains, the moors and the forests, gods of the stones and gems, gods of the stars, the moon and sun.

While some Druids would call these deities, some would refer to and honour them as elementals and spirits of place. Even to those who don't practise the faith, the concept is not unfamiliar. We revere the spirits of place in tending our gardens, in gazing in awe at the beauty of the countryside, in caring for our neighbourhood.

The Earth itself is usually considered to be a deity or the expression of a deity and in Druidry she is most often referred to as the mother goddess. In balance, the father is seen as the sky or the sun, and the qualities attributed to the two tend to attune to the stereotypical but ideal mother and father roles in our culture. She is nurturing, apparently stable, and it is in the folds of her body that we sleep. He is transient, guiding, more distant. In more tribal cultures, it is the grandparents who take on the task of teaching and rearing the children while the parents are busy working, and so we hear the terms 'Grandmother Earth' and 'Grandfather Sky'. Our families here are more disintegrated and the grandparents are seldom honoured as the teachers, in many cases seldom present. Meanwhile, the parents are still busy as squirrels at nut fall and in our naming the gods as such it is the parents that we are reclaiming. We search for a mother who can give abundantly and not smotheringly, we look to the archetype in our healing. We search for a father who is present or omnipresent, who is reliable, sharing his strength and wisdom.

For many of the tradition, to honour these spirits in their natural form is not enough. We crave a better understanding with nature and ask that these spirits appear in a human or animal shape with which we can interact and converse more clearly. Some do and some don't. Certainly one can understand that it may well be easier to communicate with a god who presents himself as a great Celtic warrior on a magnificent horse than with a bank of black clouds and a roll of thunder. It is difficult for us to imagine, other than through genetic or past-life recall, just what it was like before science was able to explain the more violent processes of nature – what the thunder was, the earth-quakes, the hurricanes and hailstorms. Wanting to find safety, most would run and hide. The strongest, the warriors, the strange, perhaps those who had been through extraordinary experiences of near death or toxification, would be out there, crying out to the tempest, awaking the gods to the trauma of the people. *Why do you torture us with your rage? What must we do to appease your anger?* Perhaps those with the freest vision or imagi-nation were able to hear the gods' response, and hearing it, understanding it, would indicate that there was a human aspect to the gods. To anthropomorphize nature is a natural response to the need to control our environment in order to release that constant tension of survival. We can't fight the wind – perhaps we can talk to it. Maybe this was how the priesthood was born, and in the same way the heroes and deities of myth and legend.

I use the word 'creation' and have been questioned about it. The debate as to whether the world, the omniverse, came into existence in one tremendous swoop of divine creativity or developed slowly through some kind of evolution seems from a pantheistic viewpoint fairly irrelevant. We can see how the gods are a part of the continuing, evolving process of creation: they are the vitalizing, creative force, the sustainers and the destroyers, integral with the forces of nature, its flows and currents.

Yet within nature there is also humanity, and perhaps it is the whirlwind and blizzards of our own minds that are most scary. Further to the gods of the outer environment there are those of the inner. They are the gods who caricature moments of being. Some declare a specific emotion, such as love or ecstasy, but some associate themselves or are associated with occupations and actions. Yet it is the controlling, directing, focusing of the emotions, those internal storms of energy, that the gods guide us through, from denial and rage to exhilaration, as they work with us in our actions, be they healing, thinking, sex, poetry, war, craftsmanship, writing, giving birth, teaching and the rest.

Perhaps the great difference between the two, the gods of nature and the gods of humanity, is that those of nature are *definitively* non-judgemental. Not only do they not interact in that way, but they have no understanding of judgement. The questions screamed at the storm about the gods' rage are nowadays recognized as invalid. A modern day Druid priest might scream, sodden to his underpants in the middle of nowhere, *Help me to see why this is a part of my life!* Or *Let me know the joy of this because right now I'm having a bloody awful time!* He may address the spirits of place to guide him to find shelter. He may even howl *Give me a fucking break!* – but not because he believes that he is being punished.

Whether the gods of humanity do work judgementally is a matter of opinion. I would doubt whether any Druid, working centred and within their clarity, would take seriously a deity who presented on that level.

This expresses another principle element of Druid deity: that we do not subjugate or sublimate ourselves to the gods. It's all about relationship and sharing energy.

There are many gods, then. To ask why or whether we need so many is a question which reveals the questioner's belief that the gods are created by us. Declaring that the gods are 'real' evokes endless debate and in terms of agreed perception, of absolute and indisputable, tangible evidence it must be said that they are not. *They are not?!* Again, it is semantics, here of what is 'reality'. I define 'real' as merely a tool that we employ in order to grasp and hold some object, to make it sufficiently solid to be usable within a world that is all illusion, where everything is simply a reflection within a dream. It isn't entirely black and white, but a spectrum, from the stable and apparently unchanging to the swirling mists of illusion and potentiality.

The gods are of the higher worlds, where the boundaries of limitation are more than hazy, and this is certainly a large part of their charm. Most Druids will admit that whatever we ask of our goddess, it is not *her* lack of resources or ability which might keep it from us. Where the gods reside, everything is possible. Either they do indeed offer you what you have asked for, the miracle in its very sweetness, or else they make quite clear why you are unable to see, hear or grasp its manifestation through your own limitations. Some gods will leave you stranded, bewildered. Many a goddess will make it clear that if you were to come a little closer into the warmth of her arms, the softness of her breast, yet more of your heavy constraints and limitations would fall from you like chains. You would get just what you want. Indeed, each time you lie with her, she takes you a little further out of your body-focused consciousness into an understanding of spirit, of pure potentiality, diving into the very essence of creation, into the shining silver threads that weave the fabric of living.

The gods, then, are more of an illusion than reality. In many ways I say that they are *perfect* illusion. Yet in saying so I don't deny in any measure their full existence. I know beyond doubt that my deities exist, both to me and to the Druids with whom I celebrate my rites, as they do to many souls more.

As self-conscious creatures we are able not only to feel our needs but also to dispute and analyse them, and work out various ways of satisfying them, and fantasizing about them and their reliefs. If the gods' state of being were purely as a concept in the human psyche, if indeed we are no more than animals on a little planet somewhere in the outer reaches of the galaxy, to me it would make no difference. If my Lady of the Grove were wholly within me or wholly outside of me, I would still crave that relationship. I would still need her. Why?

Any dedicate will confirm that their gods have their needs, their demands, of time, attention, energy. And, hell, if you don't heed those demands, if you aren't paying sufficient attention, a gentle whisper, like the breeze through the willow, will fast turn into a kick in the groin. But unlike within a human relationship, where needs are also strong and can touch us deeply, contact with gods is never draining of one's soul energy, purely because they are perfect illusion.

Everything we perceive, be it outside us or within us, is taken as an affirmation of who we are, of our value and achievement. Our inspiration explodes into thoughts, which slide through our emotions, settling into manifestation, often as a sorry reflection of that primary vision and usually so distant from it we have forgotten our motivation. The 'real' world is slow and usually a long way behind our growth and mentality. Yet we look to the state of things and consider what we see to be valid criticism of our current internal workings.

It is hard for us, as a race, as a species, to acknowledge our own value. Genuine appreciation tends either to boost defensive confidence (the ego base) or fly way over our heads uncaught. But, little by little, we begin to find our self-worth, our self-esteem. And in a world where we are usually surrounded by people who either feel so insecure they must openly attack or try to undermine our confidence in order that they might feel safe, or people who do not know how to appreciate, for they have never been appreciated themselves, it is a tortuously slow process. Yet, though it may be subtle behaviour, not overt and obvious, it is there, through our mundane and daily environment and experience, affirming to us our lack of worth.

The perfect woman, shining, gazes at you across the room, through the crap, until you realize she's looking at you and the strength of her look throws its weight into your soul. You're almost too embarrassed to look back. She is rich with energy and her own power. She knows exactly who she is. She knows precisely where she is headed and why. She knows just what she needs and what she wants from you.

Being with a women who is this strong can be devastating, especially for a man (or an attracted woman). Were we to reverse the picture, replacing her with a perfect man, in beautiful proportions of strength and sensuality, focusing his gaze directly upon your soul, the same would be true and would be equally difficult for the opposite or attracted sex, poignantly revealing our sense of personal inadequacy and how far we have yet to go. Yet it could also be extraordinarily inspiring, if only we were to allow that powerful presence to reflect the highest potential within ourselves.

To be with such an extraordinary woman who is not quite real, who is a fantasy, an archetype, a heroine, can be distinctly easier to deal with than such a force in flesh and blood. After all, the fantasy is there just for us. Nobody else is there threatening to charm her away, taking her attention. She wants to be with us and brings with her sweet relief for all our needs in their exact proportions: it's special catering, physical, emotional and all the rest. She is a glorious and ancient dreamtime fantasy.

Yet for some she is more than that, she is a goddess. And in his silk shirt or rough Saxon weave, he is a god. Again without any way implying that she does not exist outside the human psyche or collective consciousness, by raising the perfect human to the state of deification, we give ourselves the reassurance that she is more than just our own creation, formed out of our deepest need for love and safety. We affix on the illusion the label of real: real goddess.

And as Druids we cast our sacred circles, we enter into those places where we feel sufficiently safe to strip off to our naked souls, held within the energy of the grove spirits and the temple guardians, the ancestors and the beauty of nature. As such we are given the opportunity to reveal our truest selves, and in the loneliness of glimpsing who we are, we call out to our gods.

My Lady holds out her hand, exquisite mother to the child within me, who runs into the wealth of her arms, opening laughing, crying, to be flooded with perfect love, mama's love, ever there, ever guiding, heedless of mistakes and failings. She holds out her hands, most respected teacher, that in my confusion I might be shown through the chaos of those long and tangled silver threads that, lost and scared, I might be guided, that in my stupidity I might be thrown smack back into my senses and in my dying be led to the eternal flame.

Not all the gods are beautiful. The hag, the dark hunter, the crippled gods of sacrifice teach us of different aspects of life. They may be seen as manifestations of our greatest fears and the fears associated with our underlying cravings. In whatever form they appear, they fulfil our needs. The closer we can get to them, the more strength we have to surrender utterly – and the more those needs are filled and disappear.

Surrender is a difficult word. In surrendering to our gods, though, we don't abandon who we are, nor do we give up our will, our life force or purpose. We don't relinquish our rights or our choices; as I said before, we don't subjugate ourselves, kneeling before them like wolves low down in the pack's hierarchy bearing their throats to the boss. Except in some way that is exactly what we do. In order to find our true power, we must know perfect trust. We must understand what it is to be without threat. Constant defence is extremely energy consuming and living, as we do, with animal instincts alert and cautious, conscious of our safety, emotional and physical, the act of letting go is hard. Yet surrender can be a deeply initiatory experience. It is a powerful ecstatic – just as when we are tickled, when our vulnerable spots are stimulated by another person whom we trust is not going to hurt us, it makes us laugh, sometimes hysterically. But without perfect trust, being tickled can get us wildly angry.

Are they real, these gods to whom we reveal ourselves in our pink nakedness? If our need for reality is a measure of our need for stability, then my Lady teaches of the beauty of change, of adaptability, and potentiality – of illusion. The cycles come and the cycles go, growth, decay, spring and fall.

My Lady Nemetona. Are you Real?

A breeze shivers through my studio, the flames of the candles on my desk dance momentarily then stretch up and are still. I am struck by an irrepressible need to giggle.

Perhaps I don't need to know.

She laughs and our eyes meet, as she whispers, *Neither do I.*

IV

NOTHING AND FREEDOM

THE SPRING EQUINOX: FINDING INSPIRATION IN THE FRESH AIR OF THE EAST

And so the cycle rolls. We have studied earth and learnt to surrender our adult selves to the warmth of the womb, returning to the seed form enveloped by the rich soil of the great Mother. We have journeyed to and through the transition of the Imbolc moon, anticipating, reaching up and stretching through the confines, breaking through the soil and taking our first breath, then our first steps. Still moving within the aura of the Mother, we have begun to venture out, to discover, to play, each expedition taking us a little further from her, out into the wide world as dawn has quietly been brightening the air.

The path has taken us to the edge of the forest. Meadows lie before us, the mist hanging in the valley below. Over the hills slips the golden curve of the sun and for a moment all we can do is watch, captivated. So gradually it rises, and knowing its strength and the power it holds over us, we can for these few minutes hold our breath and look directly into its face, feeling both that power yet also the momentary gentleness. We touch every instant, knowing it to be precious, for when the last part of the circle clears the horizon, the full force breaks over us. Then we must avert our eyes. We look down.

We have walked into the east of our sacred circle. This is the realm of air, when, having fought for that first breath, and felt our way through our play and curiosity out of the soft dark of the forest, the safety of our mother's skirts, we find ourselves suddenly caught under a brilliant light. Panic. Racing screaming back through the forest to mother, to earth, we fling ourselves back into her arms. *Who was that? Help, mama, hide me!*

It reminds me of when I learnt to fly. Like many small children I flew in my dreams but somehow the habit disappeared. As a young adult it happened again, but erratically, and when first I was studying the ways of nature and the gods it was something I determined to be able to do by choice.

I was out before dawn, loving the cold cloak of the darkness around me, walking high along the Ridgeway, that ancient track which runs some 40 miles through Wiltshire to the Thames in the east, sliding in and out of its past, feeling, recalling, envisioning my heritage, my bloodline, acknowledging souls of distant times and those of yesterday, each one expressing the great journeys of life, the determination of the track, the focus of the pilgrimage. Through the rich colours and scents that flooded across time and memories, in the glow of the indigo sky, I became aware of someone walking beside me. It was an old teacher in spirit whom I know as Fearn. He's not the easiest of people.

Where are you?

Feeling how this place used to be.

Breathe.

I do and the present floods back through me. In the half light I can see the first signs of the landscape that flows down from either side of the ridge, the wide open spaces of the ploughed and sown fields, darker patches of woodland. Beneath my feet the track, made mostly of chalk and flint, seems almost to glow. The air is cold and as I breathe my lungs open, as does my body, opening to the air around me.

Come, he beckons, and guides me off the track, through a gap on the leafless mesh of elder and blackthorn, to the edge of a field. A little way off I can just see the mound of the nearest hill fort, across the meadows and fields which, like the swell of a great ocean, roll and rise in every direction. Fearn glides, barely touching the ground. I am aware how firmly my every footstep judges and holds the earth as we make our way along the frozen ruts of the ploughed field. Gusts of wind push me, pull my hair from my scarves, tangling it across my face. Every time I look up and out over to the horizon, every time I start to think, he whispers through the wind, *Breathe*.

Dawn is spreading fast when we stop. It's at a round barrow, an ancient burial mound, and the slope is steep from there down to the plains below. Giving my greeting, offerings to the dead, I follow Fearn to the top, where his robes are billowing in the wind. I sit down a little way from him, my coat wrapped around me, my chin on my knees, and try to relax, determined to ignore him for a while and just watch the sun rising. That half hour of waking day, the first smell of dawn, with skies gently lightening and pink clouds turning gold, is a haven of calm through which I float wonderfully, without a thought. And when the sun appears, silently slipping over the horizon, then bursting into fullness, I bury my face in my knees. My heart is filled. Only when Fearn speaks do I remember that it was he who brought me here. I shudder in the cold golden light, in the gusts of the wind and the pale blue sky.

Limelight, he says.

Sitting just off the Ridgeway, in the middle of nowhere.

Alone, he says, without a trace of emotion.

Yet in my solitude I fell intensely revealed. All that I am is displayed around me in the light of day, papers in the wind, the unbound catalogue of my achievements.

Walk into the light and see who you are.

Words seem to drift around me, floating in the wind, the lilting soft voices of the sylphs, lifting, gliding, shimmering, whispering, *The pointing finger of our Lord of the Rising Sun watches you...*

I see my thoughts, who I am, blowing away in the wind.

I'm losing myself... I get to my feet

What do you want?

To know...

To know what?

I thought I had an understanding of who I was, who I am, but I'm losing it... in the wind... I need to know, to see, what I am in the crowd of creation. All I am... right now... I know all I am is here but how do I know myself? I need... to be recognized. But by whom?

Dancing around me in the wind, the sylphs are still singing, *The pointing finger of our Lord of the Rising Sun accuses you...*

I need something to hold on to. Some kind of certainty.

Certainty?

Acknowledgement –

The pointing finger of our Lord of the Rising Sun knows it's you...

Something to hold on to? Asks Fearn, he seems the only thing which is still, firm on the solidity of the earth, yet beyond reach. *What can you hold on to?*

Standing facing east, the wind is shifting my balance all the time. I am conscious of air, run my fingers through its emptiness. Yet it is filled with sounds, with the music of the sylphs and the spirits of the wind, with light and my visions, but they, like thoughts, slip from my grasp. I can sense the voices, the breath and the tales of those who have been here before, who have reached out into the elements craving understanding, but I feel nothing with the physicality of my need. I realize I'm trying to find hand holds in emptiness. I sink, crouching down, taking myself out of the full force of the wind, my hands flat on the mud and damp grass of the earth.

Grounded now. But held, he says softly.

And a voice whisper, *Back to Mother.* My bid for independence has failed.

Come on.

Where? I murmur

Come on.

But I'm stuck. *I know where I am.*

I thought the issue was who.

I just want to be, I cry.

Always in the dark?

The voices in the wind drift around me again, *The pointing finger of our Lord of the Rising Sun accuses you...*

I look up and start to breathe again.

I just want to be me. I'm sounding like a child, the therapist kicks in and takes note. How old am I? What happened then? Is this the point of my critical repression? But the adult sweeps her out.

I don't want to lose this!

What is stopping you? he asks

Me. Me. I struggle to my feet. *My body.*

Is that all you are?

I know, that's the great bloody excuse. *My mind.*

So what do you need, to know who you are, to be you?

Freedom!

Take it.

And in that moment, that strange moment in which I was utterly trusting of Fearn, had giving my direction to his knowing, and was both deep enough within my subconscious in my communicating with him and intensely aware of my physical environment, I let go. The wind was no longer a force of nothingness. It pushed me and, turning, I found that it guided me. With such a need, I didn't need even to jump, but merely to let go my grasp of the mud and rock, to be caught up its currents and flow. And in scrambling to stay upright I discovered that my slightest movement adjusted my course within the flow, that I could turn and rise. I could glide face into the wind, with the rush of it over my body I could dive.

I could fly.

So it is with our thoughts.

Held down by our need for security, for confirmation from the manifest, from others around us, we wholly fail to catch the thermal. We stay grounded, not accepting the freedom that is waiting, in the very oxygen, all around us.

For some, the journey through earth is a dreadful struggle and, if badly taught, they can launch (back) into the air, into their freedom, footloose, never having properly learnt to ground. Although for many of those I have worked with earth is hard to come to terms with, the majority find a deeper fear in air. Even those who have naturally flown all their lives now discover that part of their freedom has been the denial of the earth below, and those rocks which they have now acknowledged are a distinctly sharp hazard and hard to avoid.

When the gales are not blowing, many never even try. At least we can feel the wind, whereas the touch of still air on our bodies and minds is something we've grown numb to. There is so much of our environment that we are no longer conscious of, so much of our belief systems that we don't sense at all. Yet within that blindspot are the weights and sandbags that restrict our flight. Learning to fly without the aid of the conscious force, propelling us, motivating, is a process of awakening to the touch of the air on skin, on feathers.

As Druids, a sacred circle is not only a place in which we can play in exquisite safety, but also one in which we can investigate all the dark and dusty corners of our mind. It could be said that the edges of the circle are the limits of our knowing, both conscious and beneath. So it is that when the priestess casts the circle, describing it with her wand or sacred dagger, or the tip of her finger, she is delineating the boundaries of knowing, both for the physical world, including the others working with her and those beyond, and for the subconscious, the inner environment and the patterns of belief.

Sometimes priests will cast the circle using energy, leaving a little barrier of whatever colour vibration they deem to be appropriate or is required by their tradition. This may be strengthened by a specific intent. I was taught further, that the colour or energy left as the priestess describes the circle is a result of what she is doing, rather than the sole action. Understanding creation to be a web of spirits, whose energies are woven together by the sticky threads of thought, emotion and physical contact, when a circle is cast, the work of the priestess is that of cutting through the web.

The purpose of this is primarily that it protects the circle space from any energy that might intrude upon the ceremony, including both psychic (other souls?) interference and any physical disturbance from people who might wander upon the place, unknowingly attracted to the high energy buzzing along the threads of the web. So protected, the circle is a place of safety sufficient for us to express ourselves from our soul's depth, through what we fear to be – our babysoft vulnerability. Further, by cutting the web, we are protecting the outer world from us, from what may be the chaos and tangle of discovery and ecstasy in its higher vibrations, from the powerful emotions evoked and the spirits and deities invoked. Just as nature isn't particularly nice and gentle and tidy, neither are the other realms where the bounds of the physical are not existent to hold matter in. As the ritual workings are concluded, that high and perhaps wild energy is very clearly directed, either to be utilized immediately within the circle, poured into some element for cleansing or neutralizing transformation, or designated for some objective outside. The priestess walks the circle in the opposite direction from the way in which she cast, and as she goes she reweaves, reconnecting with the outer world, and in doing so allowing the energy to flow out as charged and intended.

The cast circle is sacred, set aside for religious or spiritual work, and detaching it by breaking the threads shifts the space in its entirety. We call it 'a place that is no place in a time that is no time'. A space, however, that is completely separate has lost much of its usefulness – at least with regard to anything that might later need to relate back into the mundane.

The circle is a haven; it holds the scope of our knowing. Into it we deposit the contents of our soul, our memories, our beliefs, our understandings, our confusion, our complete experience and observation upon our existence, externalizing what til now has been hidden within. The circle is our shifting aura – the electrical field which flinches and stretches in response to the world around – made stable. It is an actual location, at the same time physical and non-physical, in which we can settle.

How then do we begin to arrange ourselves in the circle? Well, essentially we don't. We simply land as if from a great height. It can be messy. But to use the circle as a space that's intended for healing, for magical and transformational work, at some point as a sanctuary of peace and calm, we need to understand what is happening in that space and where to find things. We need clues to help our dusty clogged brains, signposts to make for a little speed in the jumble. So far from total consciousness, we need some measure of order.

The first thing we do, as we sail along in our magical balloon, is sling out the ropes – four ropes, each weighted sufficiently to hold us in place, like guy ropes. They don't restrict our travelling yet they give us a basic connection to the earth and to our present. These are the four cardinal directions of north, east, south and west. They are the underpinning markers of our circle.

On top of that foundation, we lay every other aspect of our existence, by a system of subjective and very personal associations and correspondences. Yet it is the cardinal points that characterize the nature of each quarter. For every person each of the points is slightly different, but within a culture some basics are shared.

For example, in the south and south-west of England, where I have spent most of my last 10 years, my understanding of north is that it is cold. The northerly winds are the most chilling, and geographically there isn't a great deal between our islands and the North Pole. These things I share with my local culture.

Furthermore, personally, I think of freezing my socks off in the Highlands of Scotland, the winter I spent in a derelict castle in Caithness, and driving over the Pennines and losing my toes on endless hikes in the sleet over rocks with sheep looking at my huddled sodden being as if I were completely mad. I think of the cold and suspicious stares from the old and silent locals in pubs way out in the Yorkshire Dales. I recall the snowy woods of my childhood home in Denmark.

Turning to face the west, letting the images flow in, immediately as an Englishwoman, I think of the ocean, of rainy days in Ireland, of the wet south-westerly winds, of beaches in Devon. And I think of the years of my life spent in the States and South America, of my family who still live there, and my ancestors in blood and spirit for whom that land was so sacred. I think of the grief that is evoked by my connections with the native people of those lands, the tears that flow and those which are too painful to express, the sun setting shimmering over the deep waters, bringing the day to an end.

In the south is Spain and all the rich and wild memories of my life and heritage from the golden land. It is long days of joyful adventure, chasing grasshoppers and watching the lizards doze. It is summer heat and making love on warm nights beneath the fullness of the moon in fields of ripe barley. It is the rich primary colours of Africa.

Then, turning to the east, I am immediately aware of a mass of people. It is my years in Japan, the emptiness of pink plastic and the dreadful mistakes of adolescent relationships mixed up with the memories of school, of endless exams, underscored with the random melodies of the windchimes on my balcony. It is the stillness of the *tatami* rooms, the silence of the shrines.

Yet for somebody living on the east coast of America, the water is in the east. To the west there are 3,000 miles of land. Unless the spiritual heritage they'd brought with them from another land were to overwhelm the experience of the environment, their associations would differ considerably from my own. To someone in Perth the south is cold, the west is ocean, the north is heat, the east is empty desert. In Tokyo, the ocean is east. In LA, it is west. I have never lived in the middle of a vast land mass, but the signs would be equally strong for those living in Idaho and Berlin. There are the prevailing winds and which winds bring which weather. There are rivers, the water of which might be the lifeline of a community.

In many traditions and myths, there are also spirits of the environment, spirits of place, which fight for supremacy, some benevolent and some aggressive towards the human population. Where the spirits are strong, these will also affect the circle worker's spread of natural images.

We begin then with four words, out of which spring quite naturally bubbling streams of associations. When we create our dedicated outer sacred space, positioning it, decorating it, we do so through the way in which we relate to the cardinal directions. When we discover our inner grove, it is through these basic ideas that we can understand why it is how it is. Even for those who begin knowing nothing about trees and plant life, there is an association in our culture between water and certain trees such as willow, between the north and the high pine forests, the great oak or dark groves of yew, the east and perhaps the poplars that gossip in the breeze, the south and the flame trees or acers, or the beech woods of southern England. Of course, most inner groves are not arboretums of specimen trees, existing more usually as they might do in nature, perhaps being all of beech or oak or ash. Yet even in such a uniform grove, the quality of light, the undergrowth, the sense of what lies beyond the trees that encircle the glade, the wild flowers and streams, meadows, vales and rocky climbs, are affected by those deep connections held about the directions.

Slowly, we start to note down the correspondences. It is enough at first that we understand those primary points through which all our work will develop. To rush would mean intellectualizing the process and mistaking another's view for our own. So we begin to establish the basis of our magical and spiritual practice. Furthermore, by studying our perspectives of life, beginning to map it out, together with our dedication to our own growth and learning, we clarify and intensify our experience of daily living as it unfurls outside the sacred circle. The process starts to snowball. We come to a point where we can no longer deny to ourselves what is important.

* * *

She is just beautiful. Every face around the circle, eyes sparkling, every little smile, glows with it. She more than glows, she shines with a passionate pride, walking, as slowly as she wishes her heart were pounding, hardly making a whisper of a footfall, around the circle, eyes down, too excited to bear to catch anyone's gaze. She stops before one of the quarter gates, each one an arbour of withies decorated with flowers, facing east in the way that I'd told her. Holding up the daffodils, she gazes out across the meadow and makes her own call for the first time: 'O spirits of spring, of the pretty flowers and the beautiful baby animals, spirits of the land where we live near London, I thank you all for all that I have and all that I am.'

Her hands, long slender fingers, are tightly clasped around the flower stems – 39 blooms. I'm not sure that I could hold so many, but it was her choice. 'Three for every year of my life,' she'd said. 'I'll weave ribbon around them so that they're all joined together, if that's OK – oh, but what colour ribbon?'

I had smiled, raised an eyebrow, and she's laughed at her own constant questioning, answering herself, with a decisive determination that was soft with dreams, 'Red.'

So, painstakingly, she had woven the ribbons around the stems. There was more of the same ribbon tied into her hair. I'd watched two of the women helping her as dawn broke, giggling and chatting down on the terrace steps, breathing deep the vibrant stillness of the valley that enfolded us. The same women, her aunt and her mother's best friend, had checked her ritual dress and sown in the flowers while we all drank tea in the kitchen around the long oak table, the smell of toast around us, and now and then one of us would turn from the laughter and organizations to gaze out of the window to where she was walking in the garden, barefoot in the dew, in jeans and a jumper, picking up feathers and singing to herself, her blonde hair so beautifully plaited, the red ribbons fluttering in the breeze. A few of us remembered our own menarche rites, but for most the whole process was a healing of which the first step was the reopening of the wound. Tears often rose into these women's eyes and we held hands and hugged, knowing and not needing to say all those words which could only be screeched in pain.

Last night, after Melanie had gone to bed and we were sitting around the fire, some with whisky and others with coffee, stories flooded out, as often they do. We had two days here, away from the menfolk, away from the distractions and crises of everyday life, away from work and the kids: five friends, a priestess and a daughter upstairs who was sleeping her last night as a child. The next evening would be the feasting. That night six women told tales of the worst, of appalling lovers, of chauvinists and bastards, of passions and lust and glorious amoralities, of those tender-heated men they had truly loved, of the pains and the anguish of childbirth and motherhood, of the courage of the grandmothers, the beauty of their own mothers and the poignancy of their failings. And each told of her own experience of the first bloods. Sometimes we laughed, rich belly laughs which brought snorts and farts and sometimes we sat in silence and honoured the pain. Before each woman drifted off to her bed to dream in the warmth of friendship, each left on the table in the dancing candlelight a symbol of what she had brought to the valley.

In the early hours alone by the fire, I thought of my own life, and I tranced recalling past lives and my mother's own pain of being unmothered that had led me to adulthood too soon. On the floor before the table I sat and wept, feeling the fear of having no mother to hold on to, feeling the strength after the healing, feeling the joy of this gathering of friends. Amongst the crystals and cookies, the tulips, the needlepoint and the juggling balls that were each woman's sense of her own value, I placed my pentacle stone, giving thanks to my Lady for this work in her name that had once again brought me into such a blessed and precious gathering.

In the morning, no one spoke of the night before. Melanie's anticipation, the grace of her respect for what was to happen, focused the minds of the women who in the firelight had spread their energy like hippos in the mud. They got on with their tasks, kneading dough, slicing carrots, mixing dyes, filling baskets, putting the last touches to this and that while I prepared for the rite and went to find Melanie.

I wasn't sure how she'd take the next stage of the day's rites. It is a policy in all the Pagan groups that I know of not to accept anyone under the age of 18 for training, though children and teenagers are welcome at most open ceremonies. Indeed it is often the case at public celebrations of sabbat festivals that small kids and dogs meander in and out, with only the noisy and disruptive being guided to stillness or controlled. At private ceremonies, only the children of adult members are admitted, only those who have been brought up within the faith. One of the reasons for this is the dregs of public misunderstanding about the craft and the responsibilities that such a situation puts upon those who allow others' children into their midst. But a more distinct and positive reason is that the very nature of ritual – our actions, our dance, our sensory input – weaves our mind, deeply affecting the subconscious. For children brought up within it, the energy is home. For others it can be confusing, in the same way that a young son of a Druid friend refuses to enter a church – the weight of the energy scares him, a very deep fear which has since been compounded by visions of sacrifice, of flesh and blood consumed, ideas that are taken as normal by Christian children.

One of the wonderful aspects of my life as a priestess is that so many of the rites I am asked to perform are not for Druids or Pagans but for people whose spirituality doesn't have any structure, specific language or tradition. Here are many for whom Christianity is an alien and political institution. Even if no longer overtly patriarchal, it is still felt to be both overly male and human-centric. From a Christian mystical point of view, it could be said that this is not a view which reflects true Christianity, painting images more reminiscent of primary school RE lessons. None the less, among those who have rejected the monotheistic and Middle Eastern faiths, there are some who practise a quiet spirituality, without specific deity yet with clarity of respect. It is these folks who often ask the Druid priesthood to perform their ceremonies and rites of passage.

Melanie and her mother were from that mould. They'd been to a few non-specific Pagan-type ceremonies, the kind without a trained priest to focus, yet where the energy is free and bright. They wanted more for this special time and had asked a friend who attended an open coven. She was here too. She'd been at a wedding where I had been the celebrant.

A few at a time, we made our way down to the stream, beneath a wide blue sky in soft sunlight. We were sitting on the rocks, chattering like the water, when Katy, the youngest of us, brought Melanie through the trees, and with silent smiles and nods we greeted her. A couple of crows screeched *Pretty maiden* and a magpie chuckled *So very white, white.*

Don't be sarcastic, she looks lovely.

And she did. In a simple robe of calico, barefoot, she came towards us.

'Welcome,' I whispered.

The ritual was gentle it seemed to slide right through us like snow melting through a sieve. When the women held hands, the circle was made, such was their friendship and the bonding that had strengthened it over the past 24 hours. My words were lifted into the breeze and fell around us, as the laughter of the stream came and went from my consciousness.

When the time came, she stepped from her circle of flowers and, undoing the buttons, let he robe fall with a dignity that belied her shyness, her inhibition overwhelmed, her chin raised in her pride and determination to be a woman amongst us. The eldest, a lady who had left her blood moons behind her, walked forward with the bowl, and Melanie listened to her words, every intonation. Dipping her hand into the bowl, she brought out a dollop of mud that was thick and smooth as cream, and with it began to mark her body. Were she the child of a Witch, specific signs would have been used, but for her the initiation was not into a faith but solely into a new realm of life and responsibility. As she daubed it over her belly and legs, her giggling was sanctioned by the women's approving comments and noises. She marked her arms and her breasts with thick lines of the clay mud and looked at me, biting her lip and smiling.

Go ahead, I nodded.

She spoke the words she had composed herself: 'As spirit, I honour the spirit of the Earth. As body I honour the body of the Earth. It is not dirt, it is sacred.'

Across the circle her mother clenched tight the hands of those on either side. Again I nodded at Melanie, who took from the grass by her robe a little jar, wrapped up in a red velvet pouch. Opening it, she dipped in her finger and again she marked her body, this time with almost invisible traces. At first she was uncertain, but then something changed and her mind was suddenly totally focused, dipping it into the blood water and touching it to her body, running her finger down between her breasts and under her belly button. Closing her eye, she drew circles on the cheeks. Every woman in the circle was utterly entranced.

His time she needed no prompt, but spoke her words with her eyes still closed. 'As spirit, I honour the spirit of my ancestors. As body, I honour their body through my bloodline and through my blood. This is my blood. It is not dirty, it is sacred.'

Only when her mother gasped, trying to hold back a sudden rush of tears, did she open her eyes. For a moment I held the energy, but the young woman in the circle did not give way to the child within her whose mother wept with the pain and love that every mother knows. Instead, she smiled, so scared and brave and proud, as Katy walked forward, also holding a bowl, which she gave to me.

'This water is moon-blessed.' I offered her the bowl. 'Be you blessed by our Lady Moon, for now you walk in her cycles. Drink of her blessings'.

Melanie held the bowl to her lips, her mud and blood-streaked face, and sipped. Then panic swept across her eyes.

'I've forgotten what to say,' she whispered.

'The waters of life - '

'Oh yeah...' She looked up instantly centred again, with that graceful innocence and pride. 'The waters of life flow through me and all around me. I will honour the tides as they rise and fall within me.'

'Then feel the sacred water', and I couldn't help but start to laugh, 'the rather cold sacred waters of our Mother Earth around you.'

In a whirl of movement the circle swept her up and over to the stream, where in a furore of squeals and splashes and screams of laughter, Melanie washed in the mountain water.

That was an hour ago. Finally wrapped up in a towel, shivering and shining with vitality, she was taken back to the house and disappeared to robe. Now, before me, her cheeks still rosy, her hair replaited with catkins and cherry blossoms, she lifts up the bunch of yellow daffodils and makes her call: 'O spirits of the winter, of the places where we used to go on holiday near Windermere, of the snowflakes and the stories by the fire, I thank you for all that you have given me and all that I am.'

Her robe is quite beautiful, hemmed in red silk and the ribbons around the flowers and in her hair dance in the cool breeze. When we've walked the circle together and she has cut the ribbons and shared the daffodils with everyone there, an older woman starts to sing, in a voice that is deep and syrupy, about love and womanhood. It could be a Billie Holiday song. Perhaps it is. In the stillness that follows, I say to Melanie, who is now sitting beside her mother, 'You've been meditating, travelling, in the way that I taught you, to see if you might be given a new name. Has one come to you?'

She nods, 'But I don't think I'm ready to use it. It seemed like more of a special name, like a sacred name.'

'That's OK.' Her mother hugs her.

'Would you like to share it with us anyway?'

'Fawn,' she whispers, looking up at me with what I realize are those big doe eyes.

'That's beautiful. Keep it inside you.'

She nods, glowing with pride, until someone says, 'Eggs!'

* * *

Eggs?

Over the few weeks that surround the eight festivals of the year, it's usual for Druid priesthood to be attending or arranging half a dozen ceremonies and rites of passage. So it is that, a few days after the menarche rite in the Wye Valley, I find myself sitting in another circle of women. There's very special energy generated within a circle of just women. I have no way of experiencing an all-male circle and so no way of commenting on it.

Neither have I experienced a women's circle where there is overt sexual energy, so I cannot talk about that, nor offset my thoughts because of that experience. Certainly I do have doubts as to whether working solely with one's own sex is sufficiently balanced, but admit that in these things it is impossible to generalize. My joy in working with women was expressed in one way through the menarche rite. Celebrating in the forest with a group of experienced priestesses is quite a different thing. There is a voluptuous crudeness about it, a rich and somehow sated feeling that hangs about us, as Pagans, as women, celebrating the earth as if without men we are free to interact belly to belly.

Each sabbat festival has its key symbols, such as the Yule log and dressed evergreen of the midwinter. The spring equinox, often named after the goddess Eostra, or *oestrus*, or indeed Easter, has a central theme that has reached over and become part of the secular English Christian culture: eggs.

Our circle is described with yellow flowers and fallen branches, yet for this festival it is just slightly stretched, oval. Around the fire, which glows brightly in the dusk, four women sit, robes hitched up to their knees, comfortably cross-legged, breathing in the warmth of the embers in the cold air. A shower of spring rain has just soaked us and one of us begins a song or a chant which is slowly picked up by the rest, each concentrating, looking down in the twilight at the work in hand. The chanting rises with joy and rhythm til the dryads are humming, and the little people who sit hidden around the edges of the grove start to move with it, ever so slightly. As the energy peaks our voices start to soften til there is silence again, a few moments of calm. Twigs and fingers dip into the pots of natural dye as we paint, in burgundy and blues, browns and black, the eggs we hold in our hands.

Sometimes between songs we chatter and laugh, speaking of our hopes for the season of growth, for the seeds we are planting, the symbols we are depicting. When Naomi, a long-term Witch in her early fifties tells us of the operation she has to go through, we stop for a moment and feel the energy we have raised within the grove, adding to it with our intent and her prayers for her healing. When Willow talks of the fears she holds for her wild son quitting college, we laugh and tease, and talk of the dead ends of our own adolescence, the lack of direction of the men who have flowed through our lives, and again we focus, and a song begins about growing and finding freedom, making mistakes.

'How was the rite you did in Wales?'

'When were you in Wales?'

'I did a First Bloods rite in the Wye Valley just last week.' I tell them of the two days and the extraordinary grace of the young girl's dedication.

'Will she stay with it? Learn the craft?'

'I don't know. I couldn't help but look at her sometimes and wonder what the hell she was going to tell her school friends about how she spent the weekend. I got the feeling that she had nobody to tell, nobody who was on her level.'

'Not even her mum?'

'Not really.'

'I apprenticed a girl,' Naomi says, shifting on the ground. 'Came to me when she was 23. Apparently she first met me when a friend of her mother's came for a pregnancy session, wanting to talk to the spirit of the foetus. She'd come over with her mum to pick up this woman and I'd given them all tea while they waited for the expecting lady to ground again. The girl was 14 and at that moment, she said, she knew she wanted to study the Craft. It took her nine years to come back. She's an excellent priestess.'

'Is that Trudy?' asks Willow, nodding. 'Beautiful, I've seen her bring through the flower maiden, Blodeuwedd. High Priest Tony Marlin. Had him almost licking the floor.'

We laugh a mixture of giggles and pride.

I wonder about Melanie, remembering her concentration, that magical focus, as she painted her body, acknowledging, accepting, diving into her wanting to learn, to shift, willing to see the world in a very different way, willing to be different. She had learnt about beauty and, without knowing what she did, she had transformed, embodied her goddess in beauty.

I sigh. 'We were sitting around in the circle, towards the end, the fire was lit and we were painting eggs, and we did the sharing part, when we give up our secrets to the young girl, the deep enigmas of womanhood.'

Naomi grins, guessing what I'm going to say.

'No! It was lovely, everyone was so strongly together, so trusting, real friendship like you so seldom see. But every time, every time, that advice bit just makes me giggle.'

'Shit, yeah, don't tell me.'

'Especially with non-Pagans, it can get so New Age and serious.'

'Sure but there are usually 90 per cent worthwhile tips.'

'Your earthbound handy hints!' laughs Willow.

'Oh crumbs, I know!' It's Skye who speaks in her soft Edinburgh accent. She's a priestess of Brighit in her mid-thirties. 'I was assisting at a rite and this old woman started talking about sex. I mean, of all the women I'd have expected to get into the subject, she was the last. She must've been about 88, no kidding. And she was going on to this woman about it was her responsibility – both to herself and to the goddess, mind – to make sure that her lovers knew where her clitoris was and exactly what to do with it. Too much!'

'Hey don't knock it. I could have saved myself a lot of frustration if someone had given me the courage to do that 30 years ago!'

We laugh and as the stories bubble up about men's failings and our own, and the crass and embarrassing, we holler our laughter and the grove buzzes with energy. Gradually, around us there settles a poised hum. The last satisfied touches are put to the eggs and we place them by the altar stone, amongst the daffodils and apple blossoms, as the drums whose hides have baked by the fire are taken up and another slow beat begins. Darkness is falling fast.

One by one we stand and stretch, and over the earth caller drum the rhythms start to weave and skip. Skye is the first to dance. She swirls and spins around the fire, and we sing with no words the expressions of our souls, *Maa-yaya-oo-ama-ayay*, gliding on the thermals and breakers of our urges, pushing at the tensions that hold life together, weaving and dancing, building and casting to the breeze, trancing and guiding, beating and whirling with the drums, round and round. *Hai-ai-oh-mamamm!* Women join us, spirits of the woods, ancestors clapping and stamping, laughing with joy. We are children, we are too old to mate, we are mothers of the forests, we are the wind and the soil, and the old crone dryads hold our energy in wizened bark hands.

I am dizzy dancing a step before my body, pausing to feel the shift click back in, calling through the drums, twirling and singing with the fire sprites and pixies and devas, as the energy we have generated over the hours of our ritual is brought into one current, *Oo-mama-ayay-oh!* One flow.

Through the air I think I hear the flute. I stop singing, leave my drum and float and stumble a little back from the circles of the dancers, calling through every cell of my being, *My Lady of the Forest! I hear your pipers, come to us... come to us...*

The drums are stopping. The air is thick, as if with storm clouds, yet intensely bright, though not with light. We drift together, our hands touch, our eyes close. It isn't long before I feel my wolves are there, the fox with his vixen, my cat by my feet, and the great stag bellows as a sweet song rises. It is Naomi, and her voice curls around us, trying to touch the beauty to reach that high, yet accepting with deep reverence that we cannot, not in human form. Through her music, I weave the *awen*. Slowly the harmonies of our four voices come together and the forest around us seems to resonate with the sounds as the dryads join us, the earth humming, warm, and our spirits climb as if enchanted by the star people. Then somehow we know we are as high as we can be. The silence hovers.

She steps that last step, through the bounds of our sacred circle. And energy, like sweet mother's milk, pours through the glade cool and radiant. As I open myself out, in perfect surrender, it floods through me, a waterfall of exquisite power.

* * *

There is no ever-loving goddess in my Craft, no concept of one who will always care for me, self-sacrificing entirely for my best interests. The gods who come to me and those of my tradition, emerging out of the natural world, are not working for our benefit. They have their own tasks and will listen and blend with us only if it is to their own advantage. Nature is not cruel, nor is it kind. Nature is not good. Nature simply is. It is born, grows, survives, adapts and releases, dying to the ever-flowing system of creation, sustain and decay. A goddess such as Blodeuwedd, created by the gods out of wild flowers, is well reputed to have little compassion for the human race and its petty cravings. Most Druids recognize that for us to offer healing to the goddess Earth is preposterous. She adapts, changes and exists according to her own desires, holding the power to eliminate whatsoever she should wish from her skin, to scratch any itch. It is our concept of Earth that we fear to lose, not hers.

The gods who come to us through the human psyche, those who express and reflect for us and to us the archetypes, the ideals of our souls, are potentially as cruel and as kind as humanity itself. Just as we might feel the need to revere a god of judgement, who will declare for us what is and what is not acceptable, so we might call up a deity of love. It is not, though, my belief that these gods exist to look after us. They have better things to do.

This is an attitude that is fundamental to the way in which we treat the gods. Our focus primarily comes from the basic law of balance. If we want something, we must give something. It won't happen just because a god loves us. In less clinical terms, we know we must create a relationship. It's not an ordinary relationship, for deity and humanity think in very different ways, but it is based on balance, on equal exchange.

In Druidcraft, when we have an idea of what we want, whether that is inner peace, purpose, a new house or lover, a healing or vision, the focus is on finding the inspiration that will allow it to manifest. The Druid looks for a breakthrough that will give her the clarity she needs in order to know that her path and purpose are true, and which will inevitably and synchronistically bring the energy needed for the process. It could be said that this search for inspiration is in fact the pivot of all Druidcraft.

Life brings its moments of breathtaking inspiration of course, even when we don't craft it, but the active focus on finding inspiration – and on the ways in which it can be accessed more often than the usual unreliable and erratic flashes – is an important part of the tradition. Inspiration, in Druidry, is understood to be more than simply the relief at a piece in a mental puzzle clicking into position. It is seen as the action of connecting (or of reconnecting) with the source of the spirit of life that flows through us, body and soul. That flow of the life force is called *awen*.

Translated from the Welsh, the word means 'flowing spirit'. It is emphatically not just the essential spark of life, but that force in motion. It might be compared with the Hindu *shakti* (as opposed to *prana*) and perhaps the Christian Holy Spirit. In Druidry it is often associated though the Bardic tales with the Celtic goddess Cerridwen, who brewed (brews) in her cauldron the elixir of perfect being, of divine inspiration: *awen*.

But where does it come from, where is that source pool, the spring of inspiration, of exquisite *awen*?

As with every aspect of faith, the Druid's search is a uniquely personal journey. For many the most effective way to begin is by focusing on the glimpses that they do catch, on meditating with the spray of the ocean waves or the patterns of the stars, or whatsoever it may be. The Bards of our ancestors used sensory deprivation techniques, remaining swaddled in a darkened room for a night and a day. Somehow the mind must be entered by opening a very different door. Within Druidcraft, it is understood that what makes that shift most effectively, allowing the *awen* to flow through, is the relationship forged with the gods.

Wherever the journey will take us, to whatever spring, in Druidcraft we begin with respect. That respect is part of the absolute personal responsibility that we hold for our every action, for everything that we manifest, knowing that all life is still in the process of creation and that our every thought and action affect its form. It is through respect that we formulate our intention to call upon that perfect source, and working on our intention, crystallizing our hopes, we dream our future realities.

So, through respect, we look to the gods. In perfect respect we call upon them, so finding a channel for the reverence which is our commitment to the interaction, to making or further building a relationship. It is in reverence that we cast and consecrate our circle, setting aside a place that is dedicated, that is sacred, so expressing our commitment and our intention.

Through perfect reverence, we discover a medium for our devotion. Devotion rather than worship, for that is a word that has been degraded, bringing with it connotations of a judgemental and dictatorial deity whose rule is law. Devotion in Druidcraft is the process of giving. We make our offerings, our songs to enchant the gods, our art to inspire, our food to nourish the spirits and the little creatures, our dance of joy and our physical ecstasy, our commitment of energy, our dedication of time and change, all of which are ways in which we honour creation, showing our thanks, our respect and our desire for a deeper relationship.

Sometimes we aren't quite generous enough and a little more is required. Every priest and Pagan has experience of when, after the libation to the gods has been given, the bottle tips over and emphatically the Earth drinks what she deems to be her share. A spirit of place will often take blood, a fire sprite the energy of pain, in response to insufficient devotions.

When our gifts are accepted, we know it.

And after that exquisite pause, there is communion. The gods respond. Having stretched to our potential, often into naked vulnerability, we are touched by them. We are given the perfect gift of *awen*.

It comes as a cool lake of peace. It comes as power, empowering, driving, winding us up so that nothing can block us. It comes as a suckling for the soul, bringing profound satisfaction, a total security. It comes as the crack of lightning that splits us like an oak, shattering our every paradigm.

How we feel that response, how we interpret it mentally or subconsciously is entirely dependent upon our experience and our relationship, and which god has been called upon and has joined us in presence. What is without any doubt is that the deeper we are able to allow that relationship to become, the easier it is to reach the state of communion again. The more we trust and accept the energy that flows, the higher our experience, the more potent the force and the more transforming it is. The closer we are to our gods, the more intimate is the interaction.

Most people have their only experience of intimacy through sex. That may be an interaction which is purely physical, or it may have emotional intimacy with it, through love or fear or pain, even anger or grief. Intimacy on a mental level, true openness and stimulation, can and does happen, although for most it is a sadly infrequent event. Intimacy on a purely spiritual level is very hard to achieve in itself and tends, I believe, to be wholly detached, transcending the other realms. Indeed, it is often confused with the experience of transcendence, rising above the mental and consequently leaving behind the energetic responses of the emotions. It feels free, carefree.

The intimacy of communion, of perfect devotion accepted and reciprocated by a deity, is an intimacy on all levels. For in Druidry, there is no belief in a transcendence of matter that does not first take us into matter. We transcend by way of spirit, but through the essence of matter, of the human body, of pebble and rain, of tree and fox and all creation, for the essence is spirit.

* * *

She is seated on the rocks by the water. I stop and stare. I've walked up by the stream, along the mud and new grass of the bank. Crossing over, stepping from stone to stone in its bubbling current, my feet getting wet and cool, bending down to wet my face with the same freshness waking my soul, I've come up through the oak and pine to where high in the hills, there is a glade of ash and wild cherry. It's where I often find her. The white blossom of the cherry is beginning to open, rosy buds fat and bursting, while the ash, still bare but for the seedpod keys, hum their awareness. The spring, the source, is hidden in the thick grass and steps out like a serpent, emerging to pour down over flints and mossy rocks into the pool.

She has her back to me, as if she were gazing out over the forest below, through the leafless trees, but I know she isn't looking at anything at all. A part of me believes that I can just reach out and touch her. But I couldn't, I wouldn't. Such a rash venting of my craving to feel her would send energy surging through me at a volt that would knock me senseless. Still on soft and silent paws I creep, through bluebells not yet flowering, along the trunk of a fallen birch, around and about and towards her, until I feel that the shift from bobcat back to woman won't bring with it the cacophonic crash of my confidence. I kneel behind her, sensing with me an older dryad of the ash people of the grove. I breathe once again, whispering my prayer of dedication, affirming my intention yet letting myself go, bringing from my pockets the bread, crumbling it, scattering it, with my prayers for the spirits of the land, the creatures of the forest, of the burrows and trees, all the while aware in my physical body of excruciating pain sliding and pushing up my spine, the pain that is heat and tingling and more. I bend over, out of the rays of the sun, into the shade just beside her, but I've bent too far and I'm falling, falling into the pool, into deep, deep water.

Some knowing kicks in and I glide through the fear, open my eyes. I am looking up at the surface, at the light glinting, at bubbles, vague shapes of the trees above. I let go of physical constraints more and more, relaxing my muscles to release the grip. Then I breathe, not air but an expansive strength. It fills me with the energy that was the pain and as I rise with it through the water I call out to her where she sits on the warm stones, still apparently unaware of me.

My Lady, I cry, *how do I revere thee! You are my love, passed mouth to mouth, breath to breath, and in that love I am your beauty. Touch me, O sweet Nemetona, and I will be your flowing dance!*

But in a moment that is first panic and then exquisite joy, I know that I am the water she takes into the cup of her hands, lifts to her lips and drinks down, cool and shimmering with darkness and with light.

I stand up and feel muscles stretching with extraordinary brightness. I bow gently to the sun that kisses my face with warmth and walk with a floating ease, fingers brushing against the dryads that reach out to me, feeling the subtle earth under my feet. With my every move the forest responds. My robe is made of the fibres of the breeze, soft and swirling around me. As I touch the bodies of the trees, I rise up and seem to swim and stretch and dance in their canopies. Breathing deeply, as if refuelled, prepared, I balance to land on a high oak branch. I am owl. I watch, invisible, the world shivering with its vitality. Then

I lift off and fly through the trees without a sound. Until I see him, standing alone, in a grove of beech and holly.

He is a stag, and he seems to be listening to all that breathes and yet all that exists seems to watch and wait for him. He weighs his dignity with the reach of his antlers. I can sense him in the air, filling my lungs, and I'm filled suddenly with a lust so great it tugs and draws me down. Slipping to the ground, once more in ethereal human form, aware of the silvery shimmering of my robe, I walk in silence to the holly that separates us and call to him, just audibly. My voice is like the music of the maiden dryads of the forest, laughing shyly, seeping through the tension that is pulling me, through the light that flickers through the leaf-budding trees, *My Lord, O Prince of the rich Wildwood.*

He looks towards me and I can hardly breathe. His eyes, so dark, pierce through me, reaching into my womb. *So at last you come to me,* he says softly, *you who are my energy and my inspiration.*

My Lord I bow, *my love. It is you who gives me my form and my purpose.*

Ah, you bring me perfect joy.

Then let nothing be between us.

He moves and as he does his body changes into that of a man, young and strong, his face still soft. I am aware too that I am only newly come to womanhood. I can smell him now, musky and hot, and I'm scared. But I know I will be his. He will be mine, just as the sun in the water and the rainbow in the sky cannot help their merging, their union. The holly responds to the touch of his breath, leaning back so a gateway is made.

Come, my Lady, he whispers. *There is nothing between us.*

But I smile, in my fear, my shyness overwhelming, knowing he is mine. And I close my eyes, sinking back, and, taking to my owl's wings, I am gone into the wind of the canopy. He watches, smiling.

It is not yet time.

V

SEX AND DRIVE

BELTANE: RELATIONSHIP IN THE RICHNESS OF THE SOUTH-EAST

Within the freedom of the sacred cycle, we watch the year passing. And as the wheel turns we walk with it, reminded of the cycles of life, each marker point giving us opportunities to understand more deeply the nature of our own existence. As we walk those paths, within the circle, within the inner planes, our steps take us all the way through life, again and again, from our conception in the darkness of the womb, through the sweet innocence of our childhood adventures and out into the world where we declare and pull at our defence. And it is within the sacred circle, consciously remaking that journey through our life, that we are given the opportunity to make those first committed attempts at regaining trust.

The mother goddess, who gave birth to us in the depths of winter, who nurtured us through infancy and guided us through childhood, has quietly moved back into the shadows, receding with the long nights and frosty mornings, letting go as the child of her womb finds its own five-toed feet, watching without a word at its determined attempts to reach out for independence, making its mistakes, reaching its significant goals.

The young adult is emerging, now barely even glancing homewards, fizzing with energy, utterly immortal and making the most almighty din revving up the 125cc. Music shakes the house, everything is rejected, clothes are wild and wrenchingly uncomfortable, food is low priority unless it's there on a plate.

In terms of the sacred circle journey, we have walked over the windy eastern hills and below us lie the meadows of Beltane in the south-east. The sun is shining with its late spring freshness and there are people gathering for the festival of May Day. Exhilarated with anticipation, the excitement of all it seems to offer, we set off at a run through the wind, only to trip on a stone and tumble half the way down. We crash land, stoned and laughing with shyness and enthusiasm, into graphic adolescence just when it's leaving home – or everyone wishes that it would.

Back at Eostra, across the schoolyard, a young couple notice each other. Their eyes meet, if fleetingly, but their bodies respond. They turn away and blush deeply. He turns up his Walkman, she turns to her friends, each painfully aware of the other's presence. It happens all our lives – a glance that lasts just a moment too long, bringing with it a bolt of energy that shakes the whole system.

· The first if mostly subconscious intimacy is with the mother and, if lucky, the father too. The strength, the intensity, the physicality of that first connection doesn't come again through the years of play or friendships. The memory of it disappears until that strange and gripping moment of overwhelming attraction which brings such a longing to release the energy it evokes, to feel once again the joy of perfect intimacy.

It's a difficult time, heading down the windy hillside towards Beltane when the beautiful white blossom, soft and subtly sweet, hides those impenetrably defensive spikes of the blackthorn. The little child's innocence has long gone, the quick release of masturbation been found, the crises and pains of life have already built those barricading decisions which are now hauled firmly into place. We've found out how to survive and to discover that our souls are now begging for intimacy totally opposes the protective independence we've come to believe life requires. So it is that, while not fully understanding our needs nor the laws of consequence, we stumble and hurl our way through the dark unknown of our adolescent relationships.

But when the blackthorn petals are falling like wet snow in

the spring rain, all along the hedgerows the May blossom starts to open, the hawthorn, with petals not quite so starkly white but tinged with pink. By the time the hawthorn flowers there is a little more knowing, a little less awful fumbling in the dark. We are getting ourselves back onto our feet after the rush and surprise of our clumsy tumble down the hillside, and the meadow is before us, now littered with daisies, buttercups and soft rich grass. There is music and dancing, and we are old enough now not to blush and turn away. Beltane is here.

Opposite Samhain in the wheel of the year, Beltane's moontide strides through earthy Taurus but reaches its fullness in the sensuality of Scorpio. As Samhain, there is a freedom from the constraints of normality or convention at this time. It is said that after the Beltane feastings couples would disappear off into the woods and fields, filled with the energy of the rising summer, the sweetness of the mead, bringing the magic of their lust to the growing crops and forest fruits. Some say Beltane was a time for weddings, but I rather think that the formal commitment of a wedding wasn't a concern unless a child was conceived. It was by the Lammas fairs, three months on, that any pregnancies might be surely known, and at Lammas that bonds of commitment were declared before the community. Indeed, marriages tied in the lust of Beltane can be risky business. Notions are fuelled by the warmth of the Beltane fires into wild ideas, all conceptual and rich devouring passion. Even now, with the sap rising strong in the forest, and the birds and the bees out there chirruping and buzzing, Beltane is a time of rich sexuality.

Though often traditions of earth spirituality are referred to as fertility religions, our modern understanding of science and nature means that neither the young couples of the community nor the Pagan priesthood are any longer required to go out and make love in the fields at Beltane in order to ensure a good harvest. Yet many Druids will still take their prayers into the crops and meadows, calling to the gods so that the harvest will be rich and bring with it abundance to all the community. They may even celebrate those rites out in the fields in the belief that their energy will flood through the corn. For so many people in our over-civilized culture, the separation between the food that we eat and the corn that is sown and growing green in the fields around us brings with it a misunderstanding about the nature of nourishment and fertility. A strong part of modern Druidry is the addressing of this disconnection with nature and the issue of fertility is still central to the tradition.

In our calm and pleasant land it may not simply be the crops that we are concerned with, nor animal husbandry nor the conceiving of children. It's the fertility of our personal creativity that's often foremost in our minds, including all that we are responsible for, all that we manifest, both consciously and subconsciously, be that health, ability, music, global visions, whatever. In modern Druidry it is the struggles and crises of our daily experience, the tensions and paradoxes that provoke us to change and grow, that are taken up and drummed into the virgin clay, into the furrows of the fields and the seeds that are shooting, the crops that are greening, that their own power might be used to propel instead of block us.

As we study Druidcraft, raising our awareness of the cycles of the Earth, the natural tensions of life become poignantly evident in both the external and internal environment, and it is these points of natural conflict that are seen to be the most potent places of creation. They are areas of tension that are eternal within time and space, and so hold within them an infinite source of energy. They are not points of stress, which is untenable, but are powers of fundamental creativity. They are dualities, which are both contrast and paradox, which play within and around us, prancing and bouncing through our conscious minds: male and female, earth and sky, sun and moon, sea and shore, day and night, life and death, light and dark and so on. One might perhaps add the balances of stability and freedom, intellect and emotion. The play between the two, pulling up and down, together and apart, is a natural part of childhood, like tiger cubs rolling and biting and pouncing on the tip of their mother's tail. As children we are testing the forces of nature, the tensions and stresses, playing with the powers of hunting and mating. As adults so often those natural conflicts become points of crisis, traumatic.

Man to woman, woman to man, soul to soul, we push and pull, assertive and passive, dominant and yielding, giving and receiving, holding on and letting go. Subconsciously in our daily being, in our relationships and decision-making, we are working with the tensions that hold the world as it is. More consciously in our Druidcraft rites, particularly those of Beltane, we are acknowledging the presence of those forces, celebrating and sympathetically releasing the stored energy of all nature, the aeons of tension that formed and continue to form the universe. By releasing ourselves into the tension, working with our ability to trust, the energy becomes a part of our empowerment. Getting into the saddle, we ride the tension, faster and faster, adding to it the fuel of our own motivation, building it up, yowling with the joy and awed exhilaration. We are integral in the explosion, the ecstatic union. It is our energy, our thought and emotion, that helps to tear apart current reality and, as the raw essence settles, it is our inspired visions that help to guide the formation of a new manifest state, bringing a new reality into being.

In much of modern Druidry, there is little overt sexuality. The very male-oriented Druid renaissance that got underway in the eighteenth century developed out of a Nonconformist Christianity and a growing antiquarianism, and had no desire to understand Druidry as an earth spirituality, drawing more upon a romanticized archetype of the ancient philosopher than an Iron Age priest. In the last 30 years, the influence of Orders which have developed a Druidry for distance learning programmes using much humanistic psychotherapy and academic research, has given the tradition the reputation of being a gentle art, filled with poetry and philosophy.

The work of Orders which celebrate publicly has also affected the general perception of what the tradition holds within it, for where ceremonies are held in the public eye, rituals that evoke powerful surges of energy are not appropriate or effective, and any rite where there may be families and children present would not be responsible if it were to include or allude to any sexuality or shattering tension beyond the level of what might be found in myth and fairytale.

In the Druidry of the prudent mailing course, the public ceremony and open gathering, the point of natural tension that is held within the rite is that of the interplay between earth and sky. It is the biggest, the widest and that which affects us with every breath and twitch of our living bodies. Within it lie the under-standings of the seasons and the cycle of the day and of the moon, of gravity and laughter, of our stomping human influence and our less that speck-sized insignificance in the vastness of the universe.

Though the sun and the earth are often gendered, it is as elders, parents, with any sexuality abstract and symbolic. The sun reborn, beginning to rise higher in the sky, touches the earth with his warmth, drawing out of the womb soil that's been hiber-nating, germinating. Every creature looks up, the animals stretching with their energy rising, the plants reaching out and into his light. Yet when he is moving through his greatest strength, he is overly dominant and once more the plants recede, creation hardly daring to move, creatures searching for the cool of the earth. The earth has taken over, every creature looking down, until the sun sinks into the ocean. There he stays til he is born again...

The energy of the Druid rite focused on this source is not drawn down into the circle through priesthood, although there may be a priest and/or priestess who speak the words of the invocations. Indeed, in most Druid circles or groves, there is no main priest or priestess to focus the rite, bringing a sense of equality around the circle that might not be felt otherwise. The flow of energy, the exquisite *awen* that pours down, fills the whole Grove, spreading out from the centre, through each person, through every soul that stands within that spiritual kinship as a balance between the powers of earth and sky.

The tree, regarded as sacred in Druidry, is seen as a perfect example of that centredness within every dimension, reaching roots down into the soil and branches out into the sunshine, standing firm within the sacred space of its own being, its circle made between the spread of its canopy and that of its roots. So the Druid grove is created not only by the circle of the trees but also by each person standing as a tree, centred and balanced, honouring the above and the below, honouring the sacred space of each spirit in the circle, branches just touching in the movement of the breeze, allowing and feeling the currents of life energy that flow through their bodies and souls.

Deeper into Druidcraft, behind the open gatherings, more poignant sources of natural tension are invoked. Earlier I spoke a little of the conflict that exists between life and death, between the animal need to survive and the human craving for release. It is the hardest to work with simply because it requires such a deep understanding of the powers at work even before one can begin. Many work from the edge, as if perched on the cauldron, with only a few flying down into the apparent void of its depths. Only a few choose or accept being chosen to work with the dark goddesses and grey gods of death and the underworlds. It most often takes a deeply disturbing, usually near fatal experience to shift the psyche sufficiently to be able to access these realms. And the tension brings with it the stench of its own substance, of decay and darkness, and the emptiness beyond, which cause most people to turn away with a chill of revulsion or fear. Certainly it is not an energy that is ever evoked in an open Druid gathering or Grove, nor are these deities evoked in such rites.

The point of natural tension that is the dance of male and female is more easily and commonly used, bringing us back towards the idea of fertility religion. It's the crisis of sexual polarity, the buzz of attraction, but again it is very seldom evident in open Druidry. If it is seen at all it is at Beltane. At the early summer festival the Lord of the Greenwood, the young and fertile god of the vibrant new growth, beats the drums with his companions, pushing and pulling with their rhythms the laughing maidens who swirl and tease them with the dance of their ribbons about the May pole – til the Greenwood God takes the hand of the May Queen and together they dance, showering their blessings throughout the grove. In an open ceremony, this would be performed with a playful innocence, with music and laughter. In a private Druidcraft rite celebrated by a loving couple, such a dance consciously done could generate an altogether deeper and more potent energy, as through the spinning movement the two slip into semi-trance, weaving and sliding into the heart of that tension, where the magical energy of creation shivers with waiting.

The male/female relationship can be extraordinarily poignant, far more so than can usually be accessed by humankind through the conflict of gravity. Its essential tension can so easily be evoked in most, triggering energy and instinctive response through what are basic animal needs. The union between souls, unlike the pull between life and death or earth and sky, most often the only one of those critical tensions through which we've experienced explosive energy, and memories, expectations, anticipations guide us on as we dance.

To work magically, spiritually, with the power of sexuality is not easy. It requires a considerable consciousness and control of emotional energy and of underlying motivations, and a profound honesty if it isn't to be damaging to either party – and eventually destructive. Where there is such a relationship and understanding, working with it in a sacred manner can be both extremely beautiful and deeply healing. The critical element is, of course, trust.

Out in the darkness, beyond the known, lie the myriad worlds of every other soul. With people of our own sex there is usually a sufficient measure of understanding; we can at least empathize a little, even if we can't agree. But the mind of the other sex is mythically obtuse and impenetrably so, evoking the eternal conflict on the rocky dark shores between threat and desire.

I spent a good long time wandering through that part of the sacred circle that is the venue of the Beltane fair, stubbornly determined to understand men. After wasted years I eventually realized not only that I'd never get there, but that I wasn't supposed to. I sank to the grass with giggles of relief.

I recall being male in previous lives and working with those memories, journeying from feelings evoked within them, I was once drawn into the auric form of one of my principle gods, his energy filling me as we merged into one. It taught me a great deal. Primarily it taught me never to do it again – my whole balancing system was utterly thrown, leaving me physically dizzy and sick for a horribly long time. It didn't help me to understand the male psyche from a woman's mind set, but it did provoke me to consider that if I was to find a clearer state of joy, my wisest course would be to learn how to relate to it/him. By 'relate' I mean just that – work on the relationship and the potential it might hold, not despite but because of the natural tensions. It took me into learning of the most powerful and appropriate ways in which we can come together as male and female, drawing out the polarities, weaving their natures and surrendering to the union in the exchange of energy.

As a priestess, I revere a number of male deities as well as the female. Most of my gods hold within them to various extents elements of the feminine, in the same way that most men do. Needless to say, the same can be said of women and the goddesses they love and honour. There is gentleness and music within my Lord of the Moon which is so tender it is quite exquisitely effeminate. Even with my Lord of the Hunt, who drives me through the barriers of death and fear, there is some tenderness that I can relate to. Though he may take me through the darkness of the forest at shaking speed, in my terror I am not afraid of *him*, for in some strange way and through my catalepsy, I know he is simply my guide into other realms, and that nothing can truly hurt me but own fear.

My principle male deity, however, is *all* male. He scares me. Without any female aspect, he is entirely beyond what I can understand. He is the lover of my Lady Nemetona and he has been invoked for me by many names, as has she. He is the Lord of the Wildwood, Rigonemetis, the Green Man. For me, he is the mythical wild Robin Hood. In the movies and TV shows, Robin is portrayed by what is considered to be the most attractive to modern women: Errol Flynn, Kevin Costner, Michael Praed, all men with a beautiful balance of feminine energy. Not my Lord. His balance comes solely through his relationship with his lover and in this way the tension that is held between them is more acute.

It is because of this that I am not often able to reach him in my human state. He can simply be too terrifyingly overwhelming. I can bathe in his strength, in his light and his love. I can dance in his fire and watch myself change. I can float and glide in the music of his pipes. I can listen and be guided, I can learn so very much. However, it is only as priestess to my Lady that I can feel his touch, only when I let go and allow my soul to be filled with her light. Surrendered to her, walking in her grace and through the relationship she holds with him, I learn of perfect trust. And through perfect trust I am filled with *awen*.

* * *

It is a grove of field maple, a circle of trees with canopies spreading wide and just come into leaf, standing on the edge of a band of old woodland. The meadow is left for grazing, with rolls and slopes too steep for growing corn. It's our place. It belongs to a friend of a friend, an old farmer, who chuckles at what he thinks we might be getting up to. Though we seldom find the time to get here, we know for sure that nobody else does. Occasionally the old chap laughs out loud as he tells how he keeps his grand-children out of it, telling them of the crazy Witches and faery folk who come to play there. I grin with the warmth of it and thank him. Each time we return, the fire pit is always just as we left it, though the nettles that tether the grove to the woodland are high or dying down according to the time of year, and the maples are at different stages of their leafing.

From where I am sitting beneath the hawthorn, the maples are silhouetted against the dark blue horizon. Behind me the sun is melting gold as through those beautiful trees the moon is rising. I shift my bum on the soft earth and am tweaked by a thorn.

'Ow!'

Do you dream?

No! That hurt! I'm watching – just being here.

A thrush in the hedgerow chortles his song of dusk. *This is it, this is all there is, oh yes, so here are my sweet songs, my songs of thanks, and I wish you all adieu, oh yes, this is it.*

I laugh. *Thank you, brother mistle thrush, that was just beautiful. It is time for me to get moving too.*

Are you as prepared as you should be? It's the soft croaky voice of the dryad behind me.

My Lady of the May, you well know that beneath your branches I have journeyed to find my intention for this night. What is it that you doubt in me?

My sisters tell me that he is there.

Her words make me breathe in deeply, almost sharply. Getting to my feet, my legs all shaky from being motionless too long, I stretch and look down to the far end of the meadow.

I can see the fires flickering.

My sisters tell me that he is there, she tells me again.

Thank you.

I know she means more than I am picking up and inwardly call for guidance as I dig into my bag for offerings, scattering hazelnuts and raisins for the little creatures there. I bow to the hawthorn and ask, *One last things – might I take a sprig of blossom for my hair?*

You'll need it.

As I near the trees I search with my eyes but can see him nowhere. The thick new grass is cool and damp around my toes and I tiptoe, avoiding the young leaves of thistle, ducking under the low branches, into the grove. There is nobody there. The fire is strong and flames lick into the deep colours of the earth and grass. For a while I stand and watch the flames, drawn in by the heat yet, still wrapped in the insights of my meditation, less aware of its warmth than of an inner coldness within myself. A breeze moves through the trees and I know it's time to begin.

At the edge, I put down my bag, laying my clothes over an old fallen trunk, wondering what will happen, dreaming of times past. Skyclad but for a silver ring and the hawthorn blossom, I comb my fingers through my hair and take the fallen strands to give as witness into the fire. They crackle and spit as I call to Tyroshai, opening my heart with thanks for this sacred place, asking for his inspiration and blessings on the rite. The cool breeze and the heat playing on my skin, I lift my sacred dagger into the flickering light and cast the circle within the trees, according to our way. And although I cannot see him, I cast him, into its bounds with my intent. I consecrate with incense rich in sandalwood and rose, the charcoal in the hollow of a smooth chunk of flint, and waft the pungent smoke over my body with a swan's breast feather. Then, with water from our sacred spring, steeped in last year's flowers of damiana and elder, I consecrate again. I make the signs on my body with the cool water before setting down the chalice on the altar log. Without words I dance my calls to the high spirits and animals of the four directions, as above me, through the new leaves of the canopies, the sky is blurred and moonlit black.

For a while I do nothing but drift around the circle, whispering to the sky gods, feeling the weight of my hair moving on my back, waiting for the moon to rise above the trees, humming to the earth damp beneath my feet. Playing with natural highs and dips of the grove energy, the thickness and emptiness of the air, I sing to the fire sprites and the dryads and devas, listening to the rhythms of their songs and letting my body dance. I sway to the music that seems to fill me like rolls of thunder, yet when I stop and gaze into the edges of the grove it is barely perceptible, so high I can hardly hear more than the faintest tinkling chimes.

I am not building energy in my dance; I am drawing myself in, spiralling and gathering the dissipated focuses of my daily life into one place, letting the chaff fall. But with each step I am more aware of just how scattered I am. There has been so much to do, as there always is at this time of year, with weddings and babies and festival rites. Those who have slept through the winter are suddenly impatient, everyone wanting everything manifested right now. It takes a while before I feel present enough to sit down on one of the flat stones around the fire. I gaze for a long time into its bright heart. My body looks golden in the light, resolved, smooth. I wonder at the serenity. Yet it takes me in and the motion that had led me around the circle leads me into myself, gliding, spiralling, into a centre point.

Calm. Certain. Nathair, from a distant grove within, looks towards me. Her voice and her lilting ballad soothe me as for a while I am lost in an ancient melody,

An owl calls and for a second I am not sure from which world, but the response, a husky *whooo*, seems to come from so close by that I look up. It's him watching me, sitting in the crook of the oak roots on the edge of the wood. How did he get there? I want to laugh with surprise. But I'm aware of myself in the full light of the fire, while he sits in the shadows. I can feel his eyes. They touch my golden skin and my love of the grove, they touch me as I have danced for him, aware of where he was, and they peel off the layers of my insecurity, as my heart thumps in my stomach and I crave to hear any whisper of guidance. For when he has taken off that last layer of self-negation, those eyes touch the ice of my deepest protection where the scars of millennia are but slowly healing. Achingly naked, I plunge into an inner world and run and run til I've pushed for enough energy to take off into the wind, and I keep flying on and on til I am sure that I have reached that thermal where I can glide, gently descending, turning, spiralling down to the pool on the mountain glade. My feet touch the ground by the dark water where the circle of the moon floats in the silhouettes of the trees, bobbing in the swell. I drink through the moonlight, feeling the fire rising, and through the silence I hear his steps coming slowly across the grove towards me. In that state of trance, swaying with dizziness yet unable to move, he takes my hands, whispering, 'My priestess, my Lady.' My consciousness drifts between the glade and the grove as he sings the love song that is his invocation, enchanting me to surrender into perfect trust, enchanting Nemetona to fill my soul.

When I open my eyes with the fire beside me, I am centre of my world and he is centre of his and we are but an inch apart. And when I lose the grove, and the moon on the water shimmers through my floating body, I speak the words of my goddess, and the priest who kneels before me stands, no longer a man but god of the wildwood, and his face is dryad and hawk and wolf and his arms are velvet moss on oak. When he lays me down and gives me the kiss with those sweet words, I am a forest bulb stretching out its tenderest shoot, aching for the warmth, I am the corn that sways sated with the sunlight, I am the ocean reaching into every curve of the cliffs, and in his face I see every man he has ever been to me and beneath his fingers my skin tears. I am cat, I am blood and claws, I am mud and we glare and he snarls, his wolf eyes unblinking, and I am doe as he howls and I am the blood in his veins and the blood on his lips.

As he walks away and I know he has my soul in his hands, I watch the light of the fire playing over his skin, his beautiful body so perfect. Then I'm on my feet and I pounce and we fight tooth and claw, falling like tiger cubs laughing and growling, and I gaze at the rich wine that he pours into the pewter chalice and I walk away, across the grove.

When he comes to me and we kneel by the fire, reciting the words we have said so many times, as the steel blade of my sacred knife slips into the wine, his breath is a waterfall that keeps plunging through me. We drink and the wine spills from my mouth, the starfire exploding in me. We give to the gods, pouring our libation, and sinking back with love and laughter.

We are children and we run and scream, and take to the skies, great falcons chasing, driving. Claws locked, we drop through the air, crashing into the earth, and he is every man who has raped and violently abused. And he laughs and marks my face with mud and he is every man who has deeply loved and not been understood. And I am painfully tender and I am utterly to blame. As I lie in the leafmould, his face glows with golden light. He is my Lord. And in my love for him I give all that I am.

Stretched out on his cape beside the fire, utterly sated, sipping wine from the chalice, his fingers run along my back. I am dripping in sweat. 'I melted,' I laugh.

'I'll be your fire any day.'

'As you are, Silverwolf.'

* * *

Freedom.

Consciously delineating the bounds of our mind by describing the sacred circle, we began our Druidcraft journey up in the north, in the quarter of the element earth, by delving into the soil beneath our feet and confirming where we are, in time and in space. Then, lifting our eyes to look around, we stretched our wings, taking off with the strength which that basic security has given us, to fly and discover the outer reaches of the mind, gliding into the east. We started to glimpse our own potential, our dreams filled with visions of what we could do, who we could be.

That is, if only...

We aren't alone in the world, nor are we surrounded by other creatures who have no agenda of their own. Each of us wants to move in a specific direction in a certain way. Someone, some group, some institution, something that is created or motivated by other people and their ideas will get in the way, no question. We're blocked. All our great ideas are demoted to impossible dreams. Those glorious visions of fulfilment are flying fat pigs. We can't afford to invest energy in dreams, so *forget it!*

Except that in truth what stops us from achieving our potential is not anything outside ourselves. The 'if only' that throws our fears back out into the world, to where they loiter threateningly at arm's length, becoming something we can blame, is not tenable within the sacred circle, where concepts of reality are not fixed, where our visions and our manifest world are perceived to be equally illusory. As we journey along its paths, walking through our inner worlds, watching for clues within its scenery, the colours and creations of our natural associations, we come across the monsters of our self-negation, those little sods who are all set to make sure we don't find our own power. Tattooed across their chests is 'Don't look at me, scum' and they laugh and scowl, snarling, *Face facts, dreamer!* Their job is to convince us that, if we were to find and grab hold on our power, life would be worse than ever. We are destined to fail, it is written – in big childish letters – as those primary protective decisions that are stored down in the bottom drawers of our subconscious mind. Trying would be futile and deeply embarrassing. *Keep the dream, kid, keep it precious.* Nice and intangible.

As we walk within our scared circle, our awareness shifts and increases. The inner planes reflect what is happening in our subconscious world, and the creeps that live down there in the dark and sticky corners where they can adjust our motivations without being questioned continue to block and entangle our path, unaware that in the circle we can see them as clear as day. Finding them, confronting them, some are vaporized by the force of the limelight that is simply the adult mentality, but some fight, using the weapons of their twisted but flawless logic. As they are caught, disarmed and hurled into the cauldron of transformation, under threat they start to holler and kick shins, yelling, *Hey come on, kid, whata ya doing? Can't you figure that it's you who's the victim here?*

According to our circle, at Beltane south is still ahead of us: south, the heat of midsummer, the place of fire, the point of vitality and burning power. But if we are to reach it without being scorched or blowing out its spark with all our hot air protestations, we must deal with this crisis of blame. The ex-spouse is often number one on the list. The boss is a favourite. The government, of course, takes in the whole dominant authority archetype. Most people, after digging into the heap of debris that blocks the path, find that it's their parents who are the culprits. The mother is often the final contender, a marvellous *coup de grace* for the determined victim being that the one who, if anyone, should have loved us unconditionally, from womb to breast, is the one who's destroyed our potential to be all we want to be.

As our tendency and ability to blame increase, our ability to relate honestly slides into the mud. We hold on to our masks, sensing the world as a threatening place, denying ourselves the opportunity for true relationship, let alone intimacy. Our barriers are reinforced and painted red with loud warnings.

But we are not alone in the world. Til now, on our journey through earth and air, our focus has centred on ourselves. In the south-east, through the transition between air and fire, we start to look at how we relate, at our attitudes to those around us. We stop and consider those key relationships which have provoked, sealed or healed our fundamental belief systems, both the protective and creative.

In the same way that a tree exists within the sacred circle made by the spread of its canopy and its roots, the energetic field that is our aura is our own personal space. In Druidcraft we are encouraged to be sensitive to that personal space, our own and others, being aware of how that energy responds through our various relationships. At the mere thought of somebody our aura can flinch violently though we may be giving the impression of calm ambivalence, while others we are happy to have brushing against us and a few can slip into our space, our energies blending peacefully. Without such sensitivity, time and time again we manage to deny our true feelings, ignoring our best interests with our self-negation.

So in the process of understanding relationships, we acknowledge the needs that stem from our basic paradigms. In my classes I talk about the crate of bottles that each of us hauls about with us, each bottle labelled with what it is that will fill it to our satisfaction. Our search for relationships is the search to find someone whom we believe can fill a few of those bottles, while in return we can fill some of theirs. Sometimes it works beautifully.

Sometimes it goes very wrong. What he expects us to fill we never had any intention of filling, only we didn't find that out until we getting ours nicely done and what do we do now? Sometimes some of our bottles are ones that should be smashed, ones that keep us safe in the status quo of our self-negation, such as one labelled 'I'm horribly overweight' that's nicely filled by him as he gapes at those twiggy 17-year-olds parading along the beach, or the one found in so many crates labelled 'I am always used' or 'I can't get what I need' or 'I'm not good enough' or 'I am unlovable'. Sometimes we simply get to a point where we've run out of what we can give and our own are still half empty, evoking the quarrels and the resentments that are so common within relationships where honesty is not absolute.

In Craft we talk of the two ideals of perfect love and perfect trust. The concept of perfect love is based not on unconditional giving but on perfect balance. Where the energy or resource exchanged is not balanced, the side that is giving most eventually gives out. It is as true with emotional energy as it is with physical resources. At times it works that we give in one direction and receive from a different source, but the intentions must be clear and where there is conscious expectation, there must be trust that the expectations will be fulfilled. Out of perfect trust, love naturally follows.

Where there is love, only the positive bottles are filled and in perfect balance within the relationship, even those precious ones we keep coyly tucked at the back, while the big ones with their URGENT stickers and labels stating negative protective beliefs are gently pushed to one side. Yet where there is love the only need is to fill the bottles which heal, like those with the label 'I am who I want to be'. What love actually brings is beyond the needs and so takes us in a rising spiral into deeper relationship. Love is the interaction which begins with such blatant evidence of soul honesty it inspires in response an awed and profound trust, a trust that breaks down those limiting defences, itself inspiring intimacy on every and ever deeper levels. It is a relationship that empowers, vitalizing and activating us on every level of our being, breaking through us with visions of our potential creativity. We start filling our own bottles and hell, is that fun! It is soul joy shared.

In Druidcraft our adventures through the meadows of Beltane are ones which teach us about relationship. We learn of trust so vivid it inspires freedom. We learn the tender art of surrendering in love and in trust. Yet as Druids our aim is not only that we should learn this art with our friends and lovers, our colleagues and family, but with all creation and the gods beyond. For in developing our ability to trust, to let go into our freedom, we are able better to listen and interact with the deep unknown, believing better our intuition as to what we can survive, and so able to step further into its dark brilliance and the tides of its energy.

Through sliding in, with perfect trust, to the heat of what otherwise might be a point of hopeless conflict, of painful tension, we come close to the essence of life, where we can feel the flowing energy of our existence. Here is the cauldron of *awen,* of divine inspiration.

We come to understand that inspiration is not only about the fullest breath that lifts us into the wide skies of freedom and potential, but is also the ability to see that all around us is inspirited.

* * *

His face is so clear in my mind that when I close my eyes he is standing before me. I shake my head and stand up, brushing dry leaves and twigs from my jacket and walking on. The late morning sun is warm and shines through the pale, almost translucent leaves of the beech trees. It's a glorious wood, a National Trust reserve, nearly all beech and few over 30 years old. There are no discernible paths at this time of year and no undergrowth. For someone more used to the ancient forests of oak and ash, thick with holly and honeysuckle, hazel and thorn, a place like this seems strangely open. But it's bright and vibrant.

There's a wonderful sense of mischief, as if hiding all around me the wood pixies are waiting to pounce. I laugh and stretch and run for a while, feeling them running with me, and reaching out to touch the trees as I pass, giving thanks for the beauty of the rising summer.

At one of the few big old trees I stop and pay my respects, entering into his aura slowly, checking acceptance with every step, calling as I circle, attuning, singing an old chant under my breath.

You've not been here for a while, hums a beautiful velvet voice.

I came in the cold moons while you were sleeping.

What is your uncertainty, priestess?

I lay down my bag, taking out of it my mouth organ. I tried to take up the tin flute once, thinking it an integral part of my British Pagan culture. The forest spirits were not encouraging. In fact they were rather offensive after awhile, but then again I guess I did make a dreadful noise. My father's jazz was just too strong. So it is that for a while I play, leaning up against the smooth trunk of the old tree, meandering through harmonies, rolling the cool metal over my lip. Dryads and plant devas crook their heads, stretch and watch, listening, then chatting, and dry leave dance in little eddies of the breeze out in front of me. From my pocket I scatter nuts and herbs and I drink from my water bottle, giving some with a prayer back into the earth. I lay my head back against the tree.

Who is this soul? he asks softly, after a peaceful silence.

His name is Tony. Antonio. I sigh. *He has asked me to apprentice him.*

And why do you hesitate to give your refusal?

I don't know.

He is smiling, young nervous, so eager to learn, to know. Trained in iridology, studying homoeopathy. All in his head. This reluctance is much more than just my usual resistance to taking on a male apprentice.

He makes me nervous. There's something about him I don't under-stand.

What is his world?

Urban. London.

But what does he see?

I hesitate, but he pushes me. *Go on.*

Centring, I follow the inner paths to see the world from his shoes. Instantly I am thrown, flinching from the noise and speed. I clutch at the pain in my head. *I can't get there, it's too much for me.* I reach back into the dryad, who seems to flinch too. I let go of the image and we slip back into each other's quiet energy. I rub my eyes and sigh. *I'm too sensitive, I'm sorry, I can't cope with the city like that, in such a rush.*

He laughs. *Neither would I.* There's a moment of quiet before he murmurs, *What would he see if he were here?*

I go another way in, calling to his soul and connecting through our joint need to know how to address his request. Acknowledging our separateness, I enter into his aura and open my eyes. I don't know how long I stayed there, probably no more than 15 seconds. It felt like 10 minutes of terrified catalepsy.

It was dead. The forest was dead. Not leafless and decaying, but empty, lifeless. Though the colour was still there, it was pallid, anaemic as if the blood sap were no more than a mixture of chemicals. It was motionless, the branches swaying mechanically. The air was replaced with hollow space. The sky was a million miles of emptiness away. The worst part was the silence. Every noise was a jangling of leaf on leaf. There was no spirit.

When I come back to my presence I am gasping in horror and revulsion. The energy of the dryad is gently wrapped around me, while the little people close by watch, giving, waiting. From a few trees off a little voice calls out, *Music!* and I bite my lip and nod and pick up the mouth organ beside me. The music that I play is rich and doleful, but through it I release the pain in my soul sufficiently so that after some time I am able to ask through my sliding melodies, *My Lord of the Beech, how can anyone get to a point where they see the world like that? What could cause that to happen? How can they survive like that?*

He sighs a deep sigh that shivers through his branches, shakes his old head. *I have no knowing about these things. But here is a wizard older than I who can guide you. Listen to his words, priestess, but lie here in my arms still, for I sense there is much to know.*

It is Seabhac who is strolling up through the woods towards me. I smile in deep relief.

So you're looking at this Antonio fiasco, he mutters with a sceptical smile.

Shit. Is it bad?

He walks up and a wash of affection softens his face. He touches my forehead. *Close your eyes, my little cat. Let's journey.*

Antonio is there again, standing stock still right in front of me, staring. For the first time I look at him long enough to see into the lad's expression. It is empty, dead, lifeless. From some distant place the word 'loveless' comes to my ears. I blink long and look again, and his face is the face I know, with all his young enthusiasm. That emptiness is but a flicker in his eyes and I realize that it's that flicker that has scared me. Focusing on it turns his enthusiasm into desperation. I remember the first words he ever said to me, so polite and excited, 'Excuse me. You don't know me, at least not any more. But while you were giving your talk I had this vision that you used to teach me.'

Ice rolls down my spine and for a moment I can't move.

Breathe, whispers Seabhac.

I open my eyes and as I do a memory floods through me. I am old, an old man, tired and aching, sitting around a fire talking to a couple of youngsters who are listening with big eyes. One of them is Tony. I am aware of his name, though I can't translate it through the shift in time, but it brings to me an image of a skylark, rising up on its fluttering wings and exuberant song, high into the blue. I am the teacher of these young people and I recall that we've spent a great many moons talking and working with herbs and energy, spirits and prayers. I have taught them the songs and the power of the drum. But the picture brings to me a feeling of overwhelming tiredness. I am ready to die. I am losing interest in all other things.

So I did teach him.

Seabhac nods and makes some gesture that shifts the energy and I am thrown into another scene. I am walking towards the mountain in whose guidance we lived. The eyes of my daughter are on my back, and a few other souls too. I hear her whisper though the wind her love and her goodbye. She knows little of this dreadful weight in my heart. Slowly, as I walk the mountain into the cold, I think of Skylark - so full of energy, so full of compassion, yet so full of conviction that when his sister was dishonoured, raped, his anger was master. And I had taught him, I had taught him of energy and invisibility, of finding his power and using his emotion, I had taught him of healing plants and of poisons, but I had not taught him enough. He still wanted to change the world.

So when his sister, in her childish grief, scorned and cursed him for killing the man she believed she loved, a part of him died. He didn't blame me, but he was too ashamed to come back to me, to sit at my fire or look into my face. No, he never blamed me. But as walk up the mountain to the gods who will receive me, looking over my life like leaves blown up in the autumn wind, I blame myself.

Beneath the great beech my open eyes begin to see again the wood about. I stretch out my legs and breathe deeply, unravelling my fingers, so tightly clenched round my mouth organ.

Was it my fault?

It was not your intention.

I need to release it. I pick at an old beech nut. *What did I miss out? What was it I taught badly?*

It wasn't what you missed out. You forgot to watch for what he didn't hear. He understood that the web existed, for it was a natural part of the culture and your teachings. But he forgot what his part was.

Hmmm, whispers the old beech.

Seabhac takes out his old pipe and, after tapping it a few times on a root with a smile, fills it quietly from a pouch. We all watch a squirrel land and scamper along a branch.

* * *

Druidry is an animistic faith. Spirit is seen to be the vital force, the life energy, the essential (in its literal meaning) and eternal core of our being. It is with the spirit that we activate our own conception. It is the spirit of the deva that activates the germination of the seed. Soul, on the other hand, is the main body created from the spirit. The soul exists transincarnationally, holding the memories of our entire existence. It has its characteristics born out of its experience, but it has no specific personality or appearance. It is from the soul's library that we are able to create who we are in each lifetime. We lose parts of our soul living in different times at the same time, getting too attached to things and places, getting hurt or traumatized, and so on.

In animistic belief, then, everything has spirit, a life force, and everything has soul. Everything lives: tigers, rabbits, shrews, ants, catfish, tadpoles, daisies, acacias, oak trees, plankton, starfish, rocks, sand grains and Uncle Bob. Each creature, in whatever form it exists as an expression of creation, has memory and a sense of purpose, direction, time and space. Yet the differences are so extreme that it is hard to give as much acknowledgement of spirit to a pebble as to a whale, to a blade of grass as to a majestic sequoia, to a golden retriever running through the wood as to a cow on its way to be butchered.

There isn't an equal level of individual consciousness in all creatures. An old beech is quite different from a single grass plant, or indeed from a plantation of young beech trees, where there is more of a collective consciousness. It is hard to talk to a mouse; I find I'm constantly getting confused, as if the little fellow is always conferring with 100 others. It's impossible to talk to an ant, for the consciousness of the creature comes through the ants' community. None the less, the spirit and the soul are still present and vital.

An animistic vision comes hand in hand with the ground rules of respect, patience and tolerance, where any concept that the Earth, her body and her inhabitants are resource for one species is entirely anathema. Perhaps the most extraordinary and the most beautiful effect of the vision is the knowledge that, where everything is animate, animated and vital, rich in sound and colour, everything communicates.

I don't mean necessarily in the way that I do. Through my hypersensitivity, I hear and see and smell beyond the norm. Perhaps some might say that my imagination is a little too busy. Yet even those animists who have no psychic or sensory sensitivity still understand that everything communicates. After all, we are made up of energy – spirit is pure energy of the highest vibration that we can conceive of, while soul is energy patterned by experience – and our energy systems, not bound by the physical form, connect, creature to creature, in a perfect web of being.

Along the threads of the web hums the news of our consciousness. There is never any sense of being alone in an empty world. Neither is there ever any chance to forget that we are responsible for every action and every thought, for each wave of energy that passes through our bodies and minds also travels out, vibrating across the threads. We exist in an integrated world of co-operation and collaboration: a beautiful orchestra, a perfect web. Only the human race, now and then, creates the most almighty fuss. Forgetting we are part of it, in a paranoid delusion of threat, we believe we are entangled and struggle like a crazed thing in the fine silver threads til we have half throttled ourselves to death.

Some people have a sense that they are connected, but, terrified, they hide. Some are scared of the effect of others, but most are hiding from themselves and from their own potential, scared that any measure of empowerment or stimulus will activate a torrent of energy out of their control. The fear of anger is epidemic. We are scared that any opportunity for self-expression will lead us to be dangerous.

* * *

I am aware of every movement of my body - my foot down on the clutch, my hand over the gear lever, my hair on my shoulders as I look into the rear view mirror. Rolling into my drive, I can feel every pebble crunch under my wheels. I cringe at the noise of the garage door closing. My husband looks up, my son runs towards me, but neither says a word as I look at the stairs for a moment, unsure how I will make it up them. My back is aching with the weight of all I have seen, the woman's face purple, red and grey, one eye swollen blind, bandaging the wound across her arm, putting broken crockery into the bin, watching her as I make some calls, her child wide-eyed and breathing shallowly. Why does she stay with him? *Why do you stay with him? Why do you always come back?* You crazy woman, one day he will kill you.

Her voice of a four-year-old: 'He's not a bad man. It's just he gets drunk and -'

And, I know, you have said it with all of your body, be it now battered and bleeding, you really 'love' him.

I close my eyes, my head sinks as my shoulders move forward and I drop to all fours. The weight is suddenly bearable and I am up the stairs on silent paws in just a few seconds, slipping into my sacred room. On the rug I push out my front legs and tense the muscles in my paws, extending the claws, picking at the carpet threads to intensify the stretch. Then the back legs, pushed so the stretch lifts into my spine, weaves and pulls through my vertebrae, with my neck at its limit. Every muscle worked out, I slowly, muscle by muscle, lie down in a wonderful pile of limbs, gradually curling myself round into a comfortable shape. The door shifts behind me and my little cub patters in. He walks around and, sniffing up to me, checks it's OK before slipping into the curve cuddling up to my tummy, resting his head on an outsized paw and falling asleep, moments before I do.

I float out into dark space. I drift.

Then it opens and *fwooosch*, I am out in an extraordinary leap that spans the whole gorge, huge paws pounding over the earth, the blood pulsing through the muscles up in my head. Just one image fills my mind, my body powered by the scent, driven on by the one thing that will feed the craving, that intensity of desire that fuels every cell of my being. So quickly I am upon them and now the smell is all I breathe and I spring at the vision which has drawn me, claws tense and teeth ringing. When I bite into the hide and warm flesh spills into my mouth already wet with anticipation, I am excited beyond knowing. Then that exquisite moment comes, filling me with a sense of who I am, spirit released and flowing through me. I lick at the stream of blood now trickling down the hide. Then, as if given permission by the force around me, I tear into the meat, ripping and tugging and shaking my head to break off chunks, slicing with claws and teeth to get to the dark softness of inner guts. Now and then I stop with a paw on the neck of the young steer and the satisfaction ripples through me.

The sound of water draws my attention. It's my son quietly chuckling.

'What?' I ask, cuddling up to his lovely warm body.

'You were going *nyup nyup nyup* in your sleep. Were you chasing rabbits?'

'Mmmm,' I purr. 'That kind of thing'

'D'you feel better now? Daddy thought you'd probably had a

bad time at work.'

'Mmmm, better now.' I'm slurring and shift my body a little. "Cept I'm still a bit tigerish. Mmmmm. Time to be human.'

* * *

There are many situations where we are forced to suppress our emotion because it is simply not acceptable or appropriate to release it, as it is, at the moment. My rage at the man who could beat up his wife in front of his child again and again was so powerful that I was unable to access any of it to help her until I had processed a good part of it. It's a situation that is not uncommon. If I had to fight physically to protect her, that force of rage would have been ample fuel. In a crazy world, however, she needed an example of calm and centred control. My rage had been suppressed, but its energy was still burning inside me and it needed to get out. I could have run, danced and beat the drums around the fire in the forest, but that day my body released the energy by shape-shifting into a tiger. This time all the energy was played out in an inner world but often that is not the case - and not always appropriately.

The phenomenon of werewolves is a kind of shape-shifting. We have modern accounts of people who, because of some abnormality which removes their control, believe that they change into wolves. There are reports of men committing crimes in order that some policeman will lock them up for the night to ensure they don't harm anybody, anticipating the release of an extraordinary rage held deep inside which is impossible to express in human form. The mind is certainly powerful enough for us, trained to shift, to get to a point where we are convinced that we have changed. It must be the same with those for whom shifting is not an active choice.

I have often wondered what the difference is between what I do and such hallucinating insanity. My definition is simply that ultimately I have personal control, even if that includes the times when I release, surrendering into the unknown. In my experience, madness is about losing that control.

It's a fine line. Surrender is not complete if we have any kind of safety-net or pull-out clause, and any experience is constrained without the commitment of full surrender. That doesn't mean an experience is negated or not worthwhile otherwise, but its freedom is limited. Yet remaining alert through a wider consciousness of worlds on many levels, while not requiring any to be so real it becomes rigid, and remaining aware of our responsibilities in each of those planes, it is possible to find the balance between release and control necessary for appropriate and powerful shape-shifting.

As in so much of Druidry, the reach for soul freedom is the most distinct motivation. The idea of walking for hours to the edge of a canyon and not knowing what it is like to take off and play in thermals for me takes an awful lot out of the deep pleasure of living.

VI

DOING WHAT

MIDSUMMER: UNDERSTANDING POWER IN THE HEAT OF THE SOUTH

As the last leaves fell from the trees in the icy wind, I backed up my muted tawny owl wings and silently clasped my talons over the drying branch to land, then slipped down in my sleepiness, down to the ground and into the rich earth, relaxing, expanding, til I was thick with fur, a big Kodiak bear of the north. As the snow came I gave birth deep in my hollow, and as the first sun touched my cub and I stretched up into its light, breathed its freshness, I took to the air again on the lightest wings and with a sweet melody, as a blackbird, then raising higher, til with the hawk's keen vision I crossed over the plains way out in the east. Coming down to land on the sun-blessed stone, my four paws stretched out claws and I was off in pursuit of a scent, a mate, wild cat hungry, stalking through the forest ... But now, when at last I reach the south, stopping to flex my body in the midsummer heat, to watch with pride the reflection of my strength in the noontide sun, who am I?

In Druidcraft, the south is the place of vitality, where the pulsing of life can be felt in fingers, claws and hooves, where the energy can be tasted in the air, the muscles shiver with anticipation and with the stretch. The south is the place of doing, as opposed to (and opposite) the north, the place of being. While the north is where we feel the mud of the earth, the flesh of our body, the south is where we experience its physicality. It is the quarter of fire, perpetually in motion and looking for more.

On the first journey we make around the circle it is not until we've fully covered a half that we have the opportunity to work with the reflections and balances. When we move into the south and are faced with the unpredictable force of fire, glimpsing or even grasping a greater understanding of our own power, there is suddenly a deep comfort in sensing the path that runs from there back up to the north. Reaching out into the high blue sky, up to the glorious shining sun, we become poignantly aware of the state of our roots and all that is keeping us grounded and stable. If our foundations are shaky, our stretch will be disastrous. Our actions, ungrounded, will have no secure basis and the energy will be burnt up without use or purpose.

We call this the place of the wild, the untamed, the unpredictable. It is often seen as the height of masculine or male energy, of assertiveness, thrust, push and growth, the linear and overt: the opposite of the dark embrace of the north. It is the place of power. Yet we can only understand what is meant by that when we realize that the edge of the circle only ever expresses a part of world, of our psyche and potential. It is in the centre where we are creative, in the gap between experience and expectation, in the moment that is now, and in Druidcraft it is understood that our ability to create is entirely dependent on the clarity and balance that exist within the circle as a whole. When we talk about the south as the place of power, we mean not the holistic empowerment of the spirit, but the power which exists behind the force of our action. It is the spark of our courage, fuelled by the oxygen of our thoughts and the old wood of our past experience, all of which make the fire that is our drive.

The whole concept of power, though, is dangerous ground. It pulls without feelings at the roots, testing, testing our resolve and our ability to deal with the consequences of our action, licking the air with its hunger, eating into the woodpile, spitting, roaring, crackling – or it reveals our weakness, barely managing a flame. To grasp our power is frightening. It is our ability to act, which means it's also our ability to make mistakes and to fail. All too often the south is avoided. On the Druidcraft journey it's where a student will get skippy, hoping to jive her way through, giving the scenery scant attention, desperate to dive into the cool waters of the west that are such perfect relief after the hot sands and scorching of the south's bright light.

But such avoidance doesn't teach us. To learn, to grow, we must stop, find our courage. So in the Craft we turn to look at the beliefs we hold about power. We look at the energy, the unpredictability, the force of the fist, the effect of clear vision when the world is well lit. We look at fears that shudder deep down when, no longer blocked or blaming others, we know we're being offered the energy of action. We acknowledge the thoughts which we've not allowed the energy they need to express themselves, fearing just what we might do if we did. We come to understand what we believe to be strength, courage, power, both within our adult minds and also in the depths of our subconscious, where our attitudes are those of the child and the wounded.

If we were to ponder on what would be our male archetype, we might chuckle and snort over ideas of what is man, what is perfect, what is probable. He might be all sweat and pectorals, all Cernunnos and Sly Stallone, or he might be beautiful, androgynous, wiry with grace, Mercury gliding, David Bowie. The female archetype makes us stare and wonder, from the sweet skinny Hepburn to curvaceous Monroe, from ethereal Titania to the warm thighs of Demeter. If we allow an image to leap into our consciousness it might be a very different one from what our thinking would produce. Is our vision that of someone who embodies our view of male or female qualities, or is it how the perfect male or female would or could be embodied? It's an interesting exercise in sourcing our attitudes and perspectives.

When we come to search out our archetype of *power*, quite another vision most usually arises, the form of which reveals a great deal too. There are the two sides of power: the dominant, controlling assertion of personal energy motivated by threat; and the enabling, centred and directed expression inspired by freedom. Where beliefs about power are based on the dominant; it's hard to imagine the freedom. Most of us have known both, but our lives are most often directed by the subconscious need to control the unsafe, unstable environment felt within us and perceived around us.

In my teaching the Craft, people have shared with me a wonderful diversity of power archetypes. To begin with the negative images arise: authority crises come leaping in, kickboxing or glaring, the whole issue of power bound up in the dominant, the essentially abusive. The primary beliefs that have inspired these archetypes are then carefully acknowledged and gently disintegrated through the process of healing. Once the idea slips through that it is possible to be oneself, to express oneself in a way where blocks and limitations simply fall away, where there is no one to blame and we are free to do what we wish without fear of hurt or hurting, then the positive archetype steps forward, through the trees and out into the sunshine of the south. It's a wonderful moment both to experience and to witness as light breaks through after living so long beneath cloud.

Sometimes a person's principal animal ally will take this place as residence, or the strongest deity figure, or spirits of people from past lifetimes will come forward, people whose strength and courage has seemed to us unbreakable. In others' circles I have come across wolf packs, the great stag, Pan, Boudicca of the Iceni, the mythical King Arthur, an African princess, a boddhisatva. Each one expresses the circle's creator, their hopes, their fears, what it is they truly wish to do and what it is they need to find the courage to put into action, out there in the light of day.

I am a priestess. I work with the many layers of creation as I perceive it, with the gods and guides with whom I have a relationship, with those of the spirit world who would share and teach me. Essentially, my spirituality is entirely individual and exists outside any specific tradition or doctrine. It is the same with most people. Mystical spirituality exists beneath the level of community and the framework of any religion.

Yet I am known to be a Druid. It is a label that I'm happy to give myself and be given, though it only describes the language, the robes, the colours and tools which I use when I work with others or in public. Wearing that label gives me the responsibility of holding an edge of the big white sheet which is the public reputation of Druidry, bringing with it the threat of politics and conformity, which is in itself a disincentive. If I am a priestess of my gods and my grove, working my *nemeton* in private and in public, why do I use the word 'Druid' at all? What does it give me?

Druidry holds within it an exceptional archetype, one which offers me just that inspiration of courage I need in order to express myself outwardly, to put my inspiration into action. The rolls of its letters produce a beautifully clear image that is commonly held within our culture. The Druid is a peaceful sage, in harmony with nature, serene and directed, in touch with but unruffled by the great mysteries of life. Knowing and wise, he (most often 'he', though our ancestral Druids were men and women) has no need to shout; his words are well heard by those who would listen. He is someone who retains a distance yet stands in the centre, giving advice with no need to fight. Obviously powerful (and empowered), the Druid has no need for public wizardry, being perfectly in tune with the cycles and flows of energy that create and sustain and destroy our creation. He heals with his understanding of the essence of life, teaches through the example of his own living. All these are attributes which my gods and guides challenge me to hold as my own whenever I slip through the gateways and into the world of shared reality.

The word 'Druid', then, is a reminder of that challenge, but why I chose that one image and not another which might hold the same challenge is a part of the mystery which is our mind and our memory. As a child, had I ever been asked what my archetype of power was, I would have pointed to my cartoon book. But it wasn't to any super hero, not to Spider-man or Captain America. My finger would have pointed to the old Gaulish figure of Uderzo's *Getafix*. At six years old, and with editions that were often in Spanish, Goscinny's puns and ironies drifted high over my head, yet I gazed at the caricature of the white robed Druid, intrigued by the prickly feelings of familiarity that it evoked in me. It seemed to me to be an image that came from the land beneath my feet and I would softly touch the page, the long beard, the red cape and golden sickle, internally watching as he wandered through the forest in search of his herbs and mistletoe, feeling quite sure that I had come across the utterly invincible. All of Rome could not perturb let alone conquer this soul. I was hooked.

Growing into adulthood and searching for the potent essence of life, I spun through a decade chasing and diving into spirituality of the earth. What I found had no book that could be held with any certainty that all the answers could be found within the pages, just teachers who would guide and poke and disappear. It was like fine black sand – the more I grasped at its substance, the more it slipped through my fingers. It was like a fantasy lover, whose scent was somehow always around me, intensifying my longing, but who disappeared into the crowd whenever I glimpsed his face. In the privacy and isolation that was both my sacred space and my life, I studied and discovered its laws and magic, coming to understand how to slip through with the sand, to disappear into the scent, quietly finding my sense of self and beyond. But it held me within its rich darkness and with no language that was appropriate for me to share publicly.

When the vibrant energy of my soul's healing was so strong that I could no longer ignore the longing to express it openly, I sought once again the Druid archetype that Uderzo had painted in my mind. Slowly I came across groups who would share with me the sources of their inspiration and teach me the spiritual language that was easily acceptable in the world around. To my joy I found that my own old teachers regarded this step into Druidry as an almost inevitable move through another aspect of their own religion of the moonlight and the trees and humming stones, and instead of abandoning me they simply adapted to the new ideal, the image of the Druid which had drawn me out and into the warm beauty of daylight.

Still the dark cave that had been my temple did not leave me and when I looked at the archetype of the Druid, at Getafix, at the mythical Merlin, at the priest of 2-3,000 years ago, wondering how that image would express itself through me, the mud didn't all wash off. The peaceful sage was for me not the clean if eccentric intellectual of the patriarchal Christian, the antiquarian romantic, the Theosophical and Victorian Druid revival of the last 200 to 300 years which continues to inspire many in the tradition today. My sage had rough feet from long walking the earth. She brought counsel and balance, calm and vitality, and her words were clear, her rituals a poetry of movement and certainty. She wore soft hide and fur and carried in the pouch tied around her waist sacred stones and fetishes, gifts from those spirits with whom she'd worked. She wore feathers in her hair and her eyes sparkled with moonlight and knowing. She knew that her standing and her power lay not in status or doctrine but in her visions and her presence.

It is a rich image, an archetype that continues to exist as it did through Neolithic Britain, the Bronze Age and the era of the Celts. It is of a priest still practising, listening, through the invasions of the Romans, the Saxons, Angles, Jutes, Vikings and Normans and on through time and through the moments that pass as you read these words. In body she may now wear woven wool, robes of sanctified silk or animal skins; she may wear designer clothes, have a law degree or e-mail. As an archetype she exists as part of the spirit of the land, as a voice of its experience and the sanctity of its nature. That understanding is one which is shared across the spectrum of modern Druidry: Druids are a people who are drawn with a profound love of the spirit of the land on which we live. It is not an ordinary love, but a love so intense it *demands* expression, through total respect, through reverence and devotion, craving connectedness and exquisite communication.

If we are to believe Caesar, whose information came from the Gaulish Druid king Divitiacus, Druidry originated in Britain. In *The Conquest of Gaul* around 58 BCE, he wrote, 'It is believed that [the Druids'] rule of life was discovered in Britain and transferred thence to Gaul: and today those who would study the subject more accurately journey, as a rule, to Britain to learn it.' (H.J Edwards, *The Gallic War*, Leob library, 1917, as quoted in T.D. Kendrick, *The Druids*, Methuen & Co., London, 1927, p.78.)

We will never know how much his writings were true and how much the flourish of his status and ambitions, but my understanding of Druidry attunes with this idea. Its essence comes from the land of Britain, its teachings and attitudes were inspired by this land and are imbued with its nature and qualities. Yet, through its spirituality of the land, Druidry is not relevant to just one landscape, but is a philosophy and practice which is relevant anywhere. And an aspect of its nature comes from its history.

By 58 BCE, Britain had already been populated by a constant flow of peoples. There were no large-scale invasions which brought massive and abrupt changes to the culture, though this was the general belief for some time amongst historians. It seems more likely that small incursions of perhaps 30 people or so would come across the waters or move deeper into the country and, when enough land had been gained by battle or agreement for life to be tenable, families would be sent for to establish communities. Before long there would be intermarriage with local tribes and the cultures began to merge.

These early invaders were all Pagan peoples. *The Oxford English Dictionary* still defines Paganism as 'any faith that is not one of the three established monotheistic Middle Eastern varieties',

But the truer definition is more embracing: it is a religion of loyalty, i.e. it is where the devotees revere the spirits of the landscape around them, the water courses and wells on which they depend, the soil of the fields and forests around them, the sprites and elementals, sometimes to deification. It is a basic attitude in Pagan mentality that the spirit of the land is the most potent force.

When a community moved, the people would take with them the practice of honouring the gods of their homeland, for these were by then gods of their ancestors and were as much a part of their people as of their land. But there was also the knowing that if they were to interact successfully with a new place, to survive, to hunt or cultivate food, to predict and work with the climate, the local gods would need to be acknowledged. Without honouring these spirits, it wouldn't be known whether the land had accepted them and the community would shake without this sense of security or belonging. Stories of these processes are wrapped up in the ancient myths of all cultures – tales of these peoples and those, warring and retreating, dying and wedding and fighting again, learning how to appease the spirit of the land, how to work with its deepest powers.

If Druidry originated in one land, as a merging and developing of human experience, its wisdom and relevance cannot be contained within that land. The same principle applies to any culture associated with it. It was the Roman Diodorus Siculus, writing half a century after Caesar, who said, in his *Histories V*, that Druids were the priest philosophers of the Gauls. Nowadays it's often proclaimed that Druids were the Celtic priesthood, but such an idea is riddled with problems, the first being that any definition of 'Celtic' is under constant debate. The Greek Herodotus (fifth century BCE) gave us the term *Keltoi*, describing a people who lived around the area of the Danube. Over the next 500 years their culture, which was strengthened by their skills with iron and the use of horses in warfare, spread out from central and eastern Europe to Turkey, to Portugal and southern Spain, down to northern Italy and Greece, up to Scotland and Ireland. When Caesar was writing, the tribes he called the *Celtae* were tribes who lived in central and southern France.

When mid nineteenth-century archaeologists made finds in the Danube region, they took Herodotus' idea of the Keltoi, and with the concept of the noble savage, a romantic Celtic identity was born. Reprints of Classical literature were becoming available, inspiring Druid revivalists. Through poets and mystics such as A.E. and W.B. Yeats' inspiring ideas about the magic and spiritual past of a Celtic people, together with translations of medieval literature by such people as Lady Charlotte Guest (who produced her *Mabinogion* in 1849) and Lady Gregory (with her edition of *The Book of Invasions* in the 1870s), the Celtic Twilight thrived.

So 'Celtic' is a concept. In some ways it is part of the romantic dream.

The second problem with declaring Druidry to be Celtic is the implication that the practice of Druidry, its sources of inspiration, its deities and myths, must come from a Celtic root. Such a constraint does not allow for the deeper philosophy of Druidry, which is concerned with the flow of divine inspiration. As each of us has a different experience of living and the land, each perceiving in different ways, working through different beliefs and learning different lessons, it is inevitable that our inspiration must flow from different sources.

Within Druidcraft then there are those whose altars and offerings are made to the gods brought to Britain by the Romans. There are those who revere the Saxon gods and their white dragon mysteries, and those who work with the Norse gods, Odin's Runes and Stav, brought here by the Vikings. There are some whose inspiration comes through the medieval millennium, given its language by Arthurian myths, coloured with dark forests and courtly chivalry, proud with the self-regard of the Norman invasions. And though by nature Druidcraft is Pagan, there are those who walk its paths and call themselves Christian or Christic, holding Jesus to be the Christ but with a pivotal awareness of the Earth as a perfect expression of God. Some bring into their Druidic practice the gods of their ancestors who were not of these lands and never have been here, yet through reverence for the ancestors these gods must still be honoured.

There is no unbroken line of Druidry. The evidence of the Iron Age priesthood is scant. Though Roman emperors issued edicts against Druidry, it was their political power (and their power over trade), not their beliefs, which was the threat, and with many Celtic tribes aligning with the Romans there is no evidence of these edicts being enforced. Beyond Roman influence in Ireland, hereditary Druids were still advisers to the kings of Cashel as late as the tenth century.

With many of the surviving Irish and Welsh myths written down by the ninth century, information on Druidry within these has some validation, despite most being committed to paper by Christian monks (who embellished and censored according to their own faith). Yet there is little here too. Over the last 500 years even more has been lost through Christian fear and intolerance.

Yet what is lost is history, not Druidry. Druidry by its very nature is a faith which adapts, changes, like nature itself. It can't be held within an era, just as it can't be caught by land or culture. It is an oral tradition. I was told many years ago that the Druids believed anything written was dead, an idea pinned to lines of script was no longer free to grow and change, and as with anything caged it lost its spirit, its life, its energy and validity. The magic of the Bard certainly rests on the value of the living tale in prose or ballad, and Bards were and are judged by their powers of memory. The Celtic alphabet, the Ogham, thought to have originated around the second century CE and handed down to us through translation of medieval texts, was 20-25 letters, each associated with a tree and a galaxy of facts for which it was mnemonic. Though it could have been used, as it is now, for divination and talking in private, priest to priest, through hand signing and letters, it was seldom committed to ink or stone. Although the ancient Druids were said to speak and write Greek, this was not a part of their faith but a tool for the mundane workings of politics and business.

Stepping out into the public domain as a Druid, the questions I'm asked most often begin with, 'D'you really believe that you are practising the same religion as they did thousands of years ago?'

The answer is, 'No, we don't practice the same rites, we don't use the same prayers, we don't wear the same robes as the Druids of pre-Christian Britain or Ireland, those of 500 BCE or 900 CE. We don't hold the same positions in society.' It's not common for a monarch now knowingly to seek advice from a Druid (though it has been known). Life then was very different. There were no high security gaols for psycho killers, mental health programmes or anaesthesia. Violence was common, as were battling and raiding. Blood sacrifice was a part of the Druid's Craft.

But perhaps all that has changed is the context in which we work. Our role is still to create space for healing, for celebration and change. The ancestors guide us, the trees hold us, the songs of the land waft through our minds. In this way the Druids are the same as they ever were.

* * *

It's early June. The sun plays on my skin as if waking up every pore and I lift my face to its light, absorbing the glorious warmth. People are starting to arrive, mostly in small groups, the occasional person alone, and the chatter is like the sparkling of the sunlight in the grass. There's laughter, everyone jesting with some comment on the weather, wondering if it will hold after the cold of the week before, gazing around, debating what the global climate shifts will bring. I watch my son playing with his kite in the breeze.

The hill where we have gathered rises up out of the plains, a wide stretch dark with deciduous woodland lying just below us, and beyond fields of wheat and barley, sprinkled with red poppies, a few fields of oil-seed rape, its yellow just starting to fade into green. Villages are soaking up the sunshine, settled in the converging of lines and hedgerows. Over to the north the great chimneys of the power plant are belching their smoke and steam into the clear blue skies.

'Ghastly, isn't it?' Susie puts her hand on my shoulder.

'Yeup. It's why we're here.'

'Someone's asking for you. Over there, the fellow in the brown wax jacket.'

I take off my shoes and, feeling the grass between my toes, stroll over to the copse.

'Hi. Mr Dunstan, is it? I'm Emma'

We shake hands and look back over the people who have gathered and up at the skies, at the jackdaws and the chaffinches, chatting as we laugh and smile. He's the warden on duty for the trust that owns the land and I can see that he is slightly relieved. It's the first time we've asked to hold a large ceremony on the trust's land and there was some concern that we might be a bunch of weirdos and anarchists.

'It all looks fine, doesn't it?' he ponders.

'I did try and tell you that we were normal folk,' I laugh. From here it looks rather like the meeting of a ramblers' association.

'Well, you know we haven't had much contact with Druids. I

had no idea.'

'Just tell us when your next tree planting day is and you'll get to meet some more. A lot of us would be glad to say thanks with a day's work.'

He's still watching the people as they arrive and settle, putting picnic contributions onto the rugs, sitting on the grass. A handful of little kids, chasing each other with shrieks and giggles, suddenly stops to watch a pair of butterflies.

'So what is it you believe in?'

We talk for a while about tradition, about his job, about not just looking at or looking after the trees and birds and wild flowers, but feeling a part of it too, about our mutual love for the land beneath our feet. At some point he starts to feel the link between us and he nods his head in a warm understanding. It's his life, his breath and purpose, and I can see that he doesn't understand the need to celebrate it in a group of people. We shake hands as he wishes us a beautiful day and he makes his way down the track into the shade of the woodland. I walk back towards the people. Somebody's calling me.

'Bobcat! It's the local radio people – '

I turn and for a moment watch the warden as he disappears.

There are some 40 people in the sacred circle, Druids and Bards, Wiccans, Pagans, Christians and Buddhists, environmentalists and more, children holding on to hands and skirts, bright-eyed and waiting, as a priestess walks the circle, casting with her voice, a song that is waves of sound, prayers that ripple around us.

As the sacred space is created, the spirits and quarters called and honoured, I look out over the fields to another hill close by. An ancient burial mound lies at its top, guarded by old dryads and held within their energy.

Hail, ancestors, I whisper within myself. *Blessings of this day.*

The response is an exquisite hush which flows through me, so rich that I can relax and feel myself held by it. The radio reporter had wanted to record parts of the ritual but we had recited bits and pieces to her, given her enough of the poetry well mixed in with our intention for her to wander off shortly before the rite began. She watched from by the gate with a few reporters for a while, but looking round towards her now I see that she is gone. The last of the photographers is getting his pictures. As ever they seem a mite disappointed that we are not dressed in white with long beards, carrying flaming torches.

'So what's the point of this do, then?' one of the reporters had asked.

'It's a time for us to focus on the Earth, to reaffirm through ceremony one of the basic tenets of the faith, our connection with the Earth, with the spirit of the Earth.'

'You've found a spot here which is very beautiful, but you've got the power station out there in full view of the proceedings. Are you protesting against the modern age, like a "back to nature" thing?'

'No, this isn't a protest. It's about reminding ourselves of our purpose and our place in the world so that we can live more honestly, be truer to our convictions. If others express an interest, we would hope that our actions are triggers to awaken an understanding of how as a culture, as a race, we are so cut off from the world that we can drain her resources with so little thought for the consequences. We aren't dreaming of any idealized past. We may work within an ancient tradition, but we are more concerned with the present and the future. We would all support a reasonable end to investments in fossil and nuclear fuels, in favour of using and researching wind, wave or solar energy. But to us that seems to be more about sensibly looking towards the future than holding on to the past. Getting stuck in current economic traps based on the past and denying past mistakes are still creating these problems.'

'So is your ceremony about healing the Earth?'

'In our philosophy, an intention such as to heal the Earth

would be seen as awfully self-important. Can you stay? Listen to the ceremony and hear for yourself.'

He isn't by the gate and for a moment I am disappointed, wondering if I gave him enough. We don't solicit publicity, but there are ways in which the media find out about what we are doing. We don't hide. One newspaper had run an article in its local weekly stating that we would be here, a fact which was picked up by others. As ever, our fear is that they will write assumptions and not facts, perpetuating misunderstandings about the faith instead of bringing us further into the light.

The Druid prayer brings my focus back into the circle. An old friend, a solitary priest, declares the intent of the rite and I feel the blessings of the circle, that deep sense of kinship.

A Druid walks forward, a Grove Mother from the south coast, holding in her hands a large wooden bowl filled with earth. In fact it is rich crumbly compost from her garden and watching her the memory of its sweet smell fills me as she begins to speak in her warm voice:

'The Earth is strong. She does not need us. She follows her own cycles, steady and sure, through Ice Age, through times of warmth, through winter and summer. Yet she holds us. Let us become aware of the Earth beneath our feet, the soil and humus, the leafmould on the forest floor, the richness that nourishes us, the many layers of rock, the gems and ore, the mountains and valleys that give us our stability. Let us become aware of this globe that is our home.'

A stillness holds us and I close my eyes, allowing myself to descend through the energy centres in my feet, down through the grass and into the soil, roots wrapped around my stones, the fluidity deep down of the shifting rock, the fire of the centre, and from the centre I am suddenly aware of the whole sphere and am struck by its beauty, fascinated like a child gazing into a marble, as if I am re-experiencing the evolutionary shift triggered by those first photographs taken from the moon of the blue-green planet held poised in space. There's an extraordinary sense of love which is almost nostalgia, for within it there seems to be no ache of need, just awe.

'Let us reach out with our hearts and minds across our Mother Earth.'

My words come next and I breathe in the energy that shimmers in my bare feet. I call, as loudly as I can muster:

'May the rocks and the very earth be honoured with love.'

So may it be.

A priest walks forwards into the centre, carrying with him a paraffin candle, which he pushes into the hole prepared behind the wooden bowl. The flame dances yellow as if licking up the breeze. He closes his eyes for a moment. His energy is everywhere like the flame, nervous in such a big group, but he is a fine priest and in an instant he is focused. His words extend like rays of light, projected as if into the core of each one of us:

'Above us the sun shines. He does not need us. He follows his own path. Yet he blesses us with beautiful warmth and light. Let us become aware of our great Star Father, for he is the power that draws the seedling up and out of the dark earth, urging the leaves from their buds and the tender blossoms to open. He is the power that leads us into action. Let us feel the creatures of the wild. Let us feel the wilderness that stirs deep within us. Let us become aware of this power that is fire.'

An energy runs through us, each soul drawn into the bright light of the flame, some mesmerized and some energized, but all around me the strength rising, a confident glow.

'Let us reach out with our hearts and minds across our Mother Earth.'

And in a stronger voice I add,

'May the sacred fire and fuel of energy be respected.'

So may it be.

A Bard steps forward and into the centre, a shining blue tabard flowing around him over his long white robe. By the bowl and candle, he sticks the quill of a huge swan's feather into the soil. Turning, he addresses us all in his melodious voice:

'All around us is the air. It does not need us. It dances as the breeze and races as the wind, yet it is our very breath. Let us now become aware of the air as it touches us, inspiring us, giving us the opportunity of life within time and space. Let us feel the expanse of the skies above, the birds and insects in their freedom of flight. And let us become aware of all the people of Earth, of all the many different cultures and faces of mankind. Let us become aware of the power that is thought.'

By my side my son, who thinks this Bard is just brilliant, breathes in a tremendous breath. I join him and he looks up at me, proud, and we giggle between ourselves. As I look up I see the people who have gathered around the edge of the circle, folks out walking dogs, flying their kites, even kids that have been chasing each other through the woodland below, watching with a stillness. Behind them, over the hill, the smoke of the power station silently forms into clouds.

'Let us reach out with our hearts and minds across our Mother Earth.'

As I say my words, I can't take my eyes from those vast chimneys:

'May the air and four winds be fresh and clear.'

So may it be

A priestess comes forward carrying a beautiful conch shell which she places on the ground the other side of the bowl. She wears a deep green robe that shimmers like velvet, and walks with a lovely grace. She is a healer and a seer, an Ovate. Her voice drifts around and through us like music as she slowly speaks:

'Circling our sacred isles lie the oceans and the seas. They do not need us. They flow with the tides, rising and falling, waves upon the shores. Yet these are the waters of life, waters through which we birth, waters that bless us with cleansing rain and sacred springs. Let us become aware of the creatures of the seas and streams, the finned and flippered ones who swim in freedom. Let us remember those who are still pursued by humankind. Let us become aware of the waters that flow through us, of the power that is love and desire.'

I gaze at the grass. It's as if only these words, directing our thoughts into the deep oceans, could make us feel truly the pain of our separation. I squeeze my son's hand and wonder at my well of emotion as a tear breaks over my eyelashes. The Ovate says softly,

'Let us reach out with our hearts and minds across our Mother Earth.'

Our eyes meet.

'May the oceans and streams be vibrant and pure.'

So may it be.

So may it be, she murmurs.

As the *Awen* chant is called and its tones cascade around me, I am drawn from my intention, that great and noble purpose in my head which led me to organize the day, into the *experience* of why I had felt such a need to. How easy it is for us to assume that we are always working sufficiently consciously. How bloody pretentious.

I listen to the words, as peace is called through the four directions, and I feel the human world in all its tension and confusion. I hear the call that mankind may live together with all the creatures of the world, with the forests and the plants, the stones and the stars, the spirits unseen, in peace and in harmony, with respect and honour, and I know that it means me.

It isn't until the Eisteddfod is well underway, with tales being told, songs sung and shared, the picnic spread and people eating and laughing, that I take a moment to feel deeply the strength that is the knowledge of the web, the knowledge that every thought and every slightest action do affect the whole. Then I see the reporter whom I'd asked to stay. He's reaching forward, accepting with a smile a hunk of bread and cheese, his eyes far away and thoughtful. I turn again to the gate to see if the others have gone.

A couple of policemen are just coming through. I get to my feet and make my way towards them, but they are with me before I can go too far.

'Hello...'

'Yes, madam. We're looking for an Emma Restall Orr?'

'Yeah, uh, that's me...'

'Ah, great.' The older one held out his hand. 'Sergeant Peters. We spoke on the phone. Everything alright then, love? Looks like it's been a big success.'

* * *

There are two points in the year when the media get especially itchy for contact with the Pagan community. At Samhain calls ripple out across the telephone wires to any known Pagans, preferably Witches, who might make some comment. And it's a good festival for it: not only have the Pagan roots been hard to weed out – as often they are, being deep in our heritage and thickly instinctive, chewy and salty to our bodily tastes – but it's a time of childhood memories, Hallowe'en and trick o' treating, a time to shake a stick at the monsters beneath the bed, blow the raspberries into the darkness, challenge it, tame it.

The other is the summer solstice, when the days are long, the wheat starting to ripen and editors send out their crews in search of the Druids. The obvious place to look has for a long time been Stonehenge, although its Druid connection has been much debated, for if the Druids are defined as having been the Celtic priesthood and the Celts are said not to have reached these shores til a thousand years after Stonehenge was finished, when religious focus was on water, not circular monuments, then it can't be a Druid temple. The current standing stones are most probably on or near the site of a previous wooden structure, ageing still further. If on the other hand Druids were the native priests of this land, given the name later by the Celts, it may be their temple, but there is no evidence of this. Furthermore, while its connection with the summer solstice is impressive, there are said to be some 112 solar, lunar and stellar alignments over and above that one sunrise at the temple.

The link with Druids has, however, been distinct for the last few centuries, with Druid rites taking place there throughout the last hundred years, and the classic image impressed into the public due through old photos in the press, reproduced postcards and caricatured cartoons has long been that line of white robes, lanterns lit in the dawn, moving towards the great stones. In fact, the Druid Order portrayed in those old photos, an Order that grew out of the eighteenth-century revival, celebrated the solstice there at midsummer's noon in 1977 for the first time in a decade, having no desire for the publicity their presence had evoked.

Indeed, the vast majority of Druid ceremonies are not held in public. For many there is no reason to express their spirituality in any circumstance that is not private space – be that their own garden, grove a deep in a forest, a circle in a meadow or out on the moors. To have an audience would be incongruous, almost anathema.

What does motivate Druid groups to celebrate in public differs according to the place and the priesthood arranging the event. The Gorsedd of Bards of the Islands of Britain, an affiliated group to the British Druid Order, organizes ceremonies with the intention of bringing Druidry into the open, making it more accessible. These gorseddau have been termed as 'folk Druidry', with ceremonies that are family events, free for anyone to join in – weddings and relationship commitments, the blessing of children and their welcome into the heart of the community, the honouring of those who have died. There is the opportunity to initiate as a Bard of the Gorsedd, to give a witnessed dedication to the spirit of that sacred place and to one's own growth and creativity. The cycle of the year is celebrated with myth and drama, devotions are made to the gods – and with people present of so many faiths, celebrating within the spirit of Druidry, a great many gods are honoured there! – and the mead (or ale or juice) and the bread are shared as the circle is filled with the eisteddfod, the talented and the beginners offering their songs and poems, stories and music.

The Gorsedd began in Avebury in 1993 and has since travelled to other sacred and ancient sites in Britain and America. In a place such as Avebury a ritual is inevitably public, and the gorseddau enjoy the interest of the tourists, who often get involved. The joy of the ceremony is magnetic, inspiring others to express their spirituality more openly, creatively, with a pride in their ancestry and native heritage.

Where Druid ceremonies are held in public and a significant number are expected, a relationship with the landowners or site caretakers is developed so that any fears or queries can be allayed, permission gained where necessary and conditions understood. It makes no sense for a gathering of Druids come to celebrate their faith to end up in confrontation over a small misunderstanding and the overwhelming majority will honour the private ownership or specific guardianship of a site.

As in society at large, there are sadly also the antagonistic elements. In Paganism, these tend to express an extreme sense of ostracization and the subsequent anarchistic rejection of wider social values and structures. Public ceremony preformed by these folds is often linked with the desire to gain attention for a political cause and, though the situation is now improving, in recent years much of this has been focused at Stonehenge.

In the late 1980s, with numbers of over 40,000 arriving for the free festival and the associated problems with drugs and violence getting out of hand, threatening both the site and the local community, an exclusion zone was set up barring access to

Stonehenge over the solstice period. Perhaps inevitably, members of the fringe Druid Orders and Pagan warbands each year protest the decision, attracting others from outside the tradition who simple want to fight an authority that denies them their 'rights', creating havoc with security and police in their demand for free access. Whatever one believes about the validity of their demand, the confrontation – with its attraction for the media – is an issue that's awkward for the majority of Druids. The detrimental effect this handful of people has had on the public reputation of Druidry has spread right across the board.

Celtic tales are filled with battle and disputes, but they make it clear that the role of the Druid was not to fight. In fact, all who had trained in the tradition had particular status which protected them in times of war. The role of the Bard was to spread the tales of courage and strength – of his own tribe or the invaders – that were the history of land. When times were more peaceful, his stories were essential sources of teaching. The magical skills of divination and healing were always needed and gave the Ovates their protection. The Druid, advisor to the king or tribal chief and the community, having studied the deepest laws and knowing the language of the gods and spirits, was able to walk between warring tribes without risk of harm – and his role was to do so.

It's a role which is still central within Druidry today. Weaving together reverence for the spirits of place and the spirits of the ancestors, the understanding of history and the essence of the present, the physical body and the importance of spirit, the living and those not incarnate, the day and night, darkness and light, the Druid creates the pathways that stretch between. There are many areas and issues, such as interfaith, environmentalism and the law, where Druids actively work in conflict resolution, building bridges of communication. Where there is untenable stress, miscommunication or breakdown of relationship, Druids tread gently, using the natural tension to bring the crisis into a state of creativity and growth.

When a young Bard, a friend of mine, was living up a tree along the proposed route of the Newbury bypass, struggling to understand the situation he was in, playing his mandolin and telling stories to soothe the battle fever all about him, he asked if I might organize a ritual that would bring Druid energy to the frenetic tension of the place. While the extraordinary courage and dedication of the young folk who are willing to risk their own lives for the sake of the forests and the meadows, the wildlife, the SSSIs (Sites supposed to be protected because of their Specials Scientific Interest), never ceases to amaze me, most Druids would not work at the cutting edge of confrontation. What we did was a good example of Druidry in practice.

The day before the ceremony I was given live air time on local radio and asked by the interviewer, 'So is this a Druid protest against the building of the road?' I had to answer that the purpose of the event was not to protest, although that wasn't to say that there'd be anybody at the rite who *would* support its construction. He was confused. Then he grinned, 'So do you object to what the protesters are doing?' Again the answer was no – I had great respect for the tree people and felt their courage outweighed my own. I wouldn't condone any violence, from either side, to people or the environment – but then neither would any of the protestors I'd met.

'Then what are you doing?'

We were bringing our energy, our honouring of the trees and meadows, the beauty that was about to be erased, in the hope that we would strengthen that place with our awe. And in the hope that attitudes would change, with our presence we were highlighting the mentality that could run a hard grey line of noise and pollution where before there had been peace, pointing at the separation from the natural world out of which such a decision must have come. Druidry is concerned with the art of waking up.

Despite a press release, two TV crews and media

photographs, on top of the local radio broadcast, there were no police, no security guards, no conflict when, one Sunday morning, a little over a hundred people came from all across the country. Encircling an old oak in the middle of a meadow, in robes of many colours, with music and passion, with calm and with honour, we chanted the *Awen*. An oak sapling was blessed, to be planted with many others, replacing those which had been felled when the time was right. We filled the air with poetry, laughter and tears. Then we disappeared back to our groves, where the work would be affirmed, leaving the old dryad humming and shining with pride and dignity, his branches adorned with blessings of ribbons and strips of cloth.

As it happened the road plans were changed. The bypass was built, but that old oak was saved to become the centre of a round-about.

* * *

Bobcat. Time to go back.

Grrrrrrr.

Your work here is finished for now. Come on. Time to go back.

The smell of elder flowers hangs like a mist around me. I know that if I return and open my eyes it will leave me. But Seabhac's voice is too strong and my mind too used to trusting him and through his words I have slipped out of my inner grove and back to the place of my physical body. I take a moment to awaken my senses with my eyes still closed, challenging myself to remember where I am.

Breathe, Bobcat.

A cool breeze touches my arms and face. It must be dawn, almost 4a.m. The songs of the first birds are breaking the silence. I smell the air and the aura of the priest who sits in meditation beside me. His Druid name is Alder Bear. He has thick brown hair and soft eyes of longing, claws that can't retract. I can smell his bear fur, damp with the dew, and taste in the air drifting scents of where he has been roaming through other worlds.

As I do so an energy rises in me with a new strength that forces me to stretch out with my spirit, across the land and through the air, like a glorious yawn that shakes off the sleep of many hundreds of years. But I don't yet want to ground into my body. The smell of the elder blossom, the taste of a kiss, a sacred kiss, lingers inside me. And as my yawn subsides, I sink into the earth, wrapping myself around the rocks just beneath the rough grass, and start to feel where I am and why.

Around midnight we had arrived, walking slowly, deep in thought, with memories of the last few days drifting through our minds. Both of us were expected to have travelled on to various events, rituals and ceremonies, but we needed time to process all that had been going on, with a clarity that a night shared with two dozen others would not afford. I guess it was a normal summer solstice – my energy was high but there was so much happening around me I had started to spin.

We had walked through the warmth of the evening, listening to the foxes and the tawny owls, heading south over the Downs towards the great ridge of Wansdyke, that vast earthwork and barricade built between the Celts and the Saxon invaders. And through our thoughts and our silence we'd strolled along the top, quite some way above the fields, which glowed blue in the moonlight, watching for the shooting stars in the cloudless sky. The crackling, spitting fires of the midsummer energy were still flickering within us, lighting images I didn't particularly want to see again, the high spirits and wild assertions, so much aggression. Every so often I'd pause, close my eyes and centre. Now and then Alder Bear took my hand and our eyes met in gentle acknowledgement. A long day was almost over. I'd sigh and remind myself of the wonderful pictures of the day, the extraordinary drumming around the Avebury stones with the women, the earth shivering with life, and the crowd, some 300, sitting on the grass, picnicking, some standing, laughing and cheering the Bard as he finished his song with a great strumming of his guitar. It was just one marriage crashing with dreadful suspicions that could no longer be hidden. It was just half a dozen people angry and drunk.

It is the solstice, the highest point of light, the longest day. Spinning, I feel both utterly exhilarated with it and yet desperate to breathe, to bathe my aching feet.

In the softening dark we stopped, high above the ancient burial mound that stands like a platform over the Saxon countryside. It's a powerful place, one the Christians could not dismiss, long ago renaming it Adam's Grave. To us it is Woden's Barrow. Seeing it in the moonlight I can feel the imminence of the turning tide of the year, and sitting down to watch the night, I lay my head on Alder's shoulder.

But for a moment, somehow, the familiar warmth that had flowed between us jarred. I turned to him confused and in the half light his face had changed, physically changed, as if the thoughts in his head as he gazed down the barrow had transmuted his whole form and in that instant he was a stranger, yet a distant part of me strangely knew him. I pulled away with a sharp pain in my heart. But the face remained, shifting back and forth with the Alder Bear I knew, like two slides merging and interchanging on a screen. I stared, sensing something within me starting to slip, foundations breaking up, knowing I had no choice but to move with it, ignore the fear, like a raft on a lava flow.

When I do suddenly catch my breath, I am breathing a different air. The land is again ripped apart with fighting, warbands travelling so that we are hungry and scared to move from place to place. We have lost so much. All that I have and all that I am is held within a small stone, oval and white, like a tear that glistens in the moon's light. It is a stone of the sacred spring, given to me by my guide and teacher, who is of the old blood, as am I. Her face, her dark eyes and black hair, shimmers before me, reflected in the dark water of the pool fed by the hidden spring, for she is gone now, passed into spirit, and I am alone. The grief and fear of the whole village seem to hang around my shoulders. I am but their priestess and who knows who is now king? Few have journeyed and returned from the walls of our village in the past few moons.

It's hard to breathe.

As I gasped Alder Bear looked into my eyes. For a moment the vision was lost. I'd half smiled and he lifted his hand to touch my face with tenderness. But I found myself wanting to pull away and I'd moved, got to my feet, walked a little way by the thorn trees and elder. Slowly it began again, creeping back into me, the earth sliding, shifting...

I am wondering who these gods are who can give such advice to battle, to storm through another land, another kingdom, taking the lives and the dignity of all who step into their path. Who are these gods whose only pleasure is blood and crazed vengeance?

There's a panic, my heart is racing, strained with holding such a weight. This is a track that I cannot continue. If it has always been so, then I want no more. As I hold my head and pull at my hair, I cry out to my gods, *Is life not sacred beyond the games of men?*

The power of the emotion that hit me threw me, for a moment, back to the present and, with fingers still pulling tightly at my scalp, trying to ease the pressure, I saw my feet on the grass. Lost, sliding through 1,500 years, I looked up, needing to find Alder Bear, needing to know what he was triggering in me. But he was no longer where I remembered leaving him. I held to the regression, panicking, confused and stilling the urge to look around me, pushing myself into the fear that was pouring like molten rock through the hole in time, bringing with it the blinkers and filters of a different reality.

I am out here alone on the ridge, for I have been drawn here by spirit. This I know but little more. My mind, aching with fear, grasps at all that I have been taught, pulling from each breath and uncertain step the strength and pride I once had. *For your people, for the old gods,* I hear in the wind, and I am aware of the little people, the ancient dwellers of our lands, watching me as I stumble on the bank. My shawl is snagged on the branch of a rose in soft pink flower and I struggle to get free, fingers shaking, bleeding, as their voices rise around me. *This was our land. This was our land, priestess. They came and tore it from us, that we must now dwell in a place that is within and beyond. So others come now to tear it from you. Will you too be chased into the mists? Will you?*

'I cannot, I cannot!' I scream beneath my breath and the wind. *How can I,* with the grief that twists my guts each time I walk through the village, with every starving child that is brought to my hearth?

Then do what is asked of you by the ancient ones. Do what is asked of you, priestess of the land.

The wind is sharp and my legs are stinging with the thorns that I walk through as I try to be silent. I breathe slowly, trying to listen, to become calm, and then make my way with determined steps, slipping, scrambling down into the ditch and up the chalk rubble to the top of the ridge. But what I see makes me shriek. I gasp, trying to hold myself in and together, but too late. A man, huge and wrapped about with thick fur, is standing 20 paces from me facing out towards the sacred mound of the ancient king, his arms held high, a huge dagger in one hand. At my shriek he swirls around and looks directly towards me. My heart is thumping into my lungs. I daren't move, though I know that I am marked plain by the horizon and the moonlit sky behind. But he does not come towards me, just stares into me. I stare back. He brings the hand without the blade up to his face and holds his head as if he were seeing beyond a veil.

Is this why I have come? I whimper into myself and out into the chill wind.

Be gentle, priestess. *Do you not see he is in pain?*
I see he is Iloegwr *and I see his blade is sharp.*
Remember who you are, priestess.

Slowly I find the courage, the strength from the ancestors, to make those steps towards him, shaking almost too much to walk, not knowing what I might say nor whether I might be walking into my dying.

'I ... I suddenly knew you'. Alder Bear was frowning, rubbing roughly at his forehead.

'What happened?' The question was so vast, as if it spanned all time.

'I was looking out over the long barrow and I got struck by this...' He shook his head. I knew that at some time he would tell me. All he could say now was, 'I ... I had a vision ... of Woden.' He half laughed. 'Bit bloody disconcerting for a Celtic Druid like me.'

'You work now as a priest to Celtic gods,' I whispered.

'I saw you on the top of the ridge.'

'I think I screamed.'

'You did. But I couldn't go near you.'

His eyes asked me if I was OK. Shaking, I nodded, but our eyes drifted into each other's and in those moments, as we clasped hands in the moon's light, I saw the rest, as though I were dying and wondering at my life from outside its hold. As Celtic priestess I had surrendered into the trust of my gods and been led to this Saxon warrior. In his childhood he had been taught some of the ways of the spirit guides and the magic of the forest, but he was pushed into fighting, pressured by his father. Half out of his mind with pain and confusion, unable to continue to find reason to kill, up there on the ridge, he was crying to his gods. Yet his gods were not there. His gods were resident within the hills and forests of his own distant land, and so it was that he had cried out to the gods of this land through the love of his own land to guide him through this pain. And I had walked forward

SPIRITS OF THE SACRED GROVE

as if out of the dark sky.

My land was taken by the Saxons. But through our pain we had been bound together, this Saxon and I, and through the moontides that followed I had taught him of my land with a language of gestures and signs, and I had shared with him its beauty and spirit. And slowly to that language had come laughter and affection.

Hand in hand in the darkness, Alder Bear and I walked down over the fields to the long barrow without talking, sensing the change in the energy between us.

I whispered to Seabhac, *Do you know of these things?*

I was with you in body during that lifetime.

Who?

My name was Edern. I was advisor to your uncle, in whose house you spent your childhood. It was I who sent you to Tangwen, daughter of Gweir, to be trained in healing and the mysteries of the gods.

Walking up to the great long barrow I began my prayer of greetings to the ancestors, and reaching the top, I looked down over the valley before us. Somehow it felt as if it were the first time I'd seen it for a very long time and I was filled with the joy of feeling it humming beneath my feet again. It was as if seeing the valley again was a gift to me from Alder Bear and I turned to him, swollen with my love of the place and my deep gratitude, with the awe of trust between us. A ritual of thanks and communion emerged around and through us, with few words but with an intensity that directed our actions, pulling me out of my frame into trance. Flying high up along the ridge, I hovered on eagle's wings, gliding over the barrow, then screeched and dived, coming down like a golden dagger of lightning that fused us together and into the earth. We kissed, as if with it some ancient bond of peoples were sealed. And in the darkness of that short night I danced until our circle was done.

Sitting together in the damp grass, looking out into the night, my eye caught a flicker of movement. The elegant form of

Seabhac walked towards me out of the mists. He sat down beside us, gazing over the dark fields.

Much has happened, little cat, His voice was soft, like a cool breeze on a hot night. *You should go now, loosen your form, free your body for these things settle well. Such power needs a body which is deeply flexible. Allow your joy to shine through. Run, Bobcat, find your freedom.*

I closed my eyes, smiled for a moment in thanks. My heart was so open, to breathe I had to sigh, and as I slipped back, out of my form and into the cat, a shiver of pleasure ran through me. When I looked round to him now my instinct was to push against his hand with my cheek, to lick with a rough tongue, to half bite with affection. And then I was away, searing with brilliant energy, into the dark undergrowth.

I open my eyes into the quiet. By the light it seems that the sun has broken over the far horizon but it is yet blocked to our view by a high ridge, the valley before us still thick with mist and shadow. It won't be long before the soft rays are flooding over us. There's not a cloud in the sky. I am loathe to shift entirely back into my body, for I sense the pain in my spine from sitting motionless for so long through the damp of the night and on hard ground. I know I'd have to get up and stretch to release it if it were to hit into my consciousness.

A sprig of elder blossom lies in my lap. I don't recall picking it, but its smell is still sweet, encouraging me to breathe deeply, and I start to hum my devotions to the beautiful world, to the sun that rises on this sacred morning, this day after the longest day. An old love song to the star gods slips into my mind, but I am singing within me, making no noise, moving only my eyes.

Alder Bear, the sun is rising. Seabhac, don't let Alder Bear miss it. He is coming.

As I watch, an extraordinary exhilaration starts to trickle into my soul. It warms me, fills my legs with light, tingles til I am all around my body and I have to shift, not from pain but to move the energy that's now flooding through me. The first fingers of the sun creep over the ridge, and then the first curve of the sun, and I can't keep with the quiet dignity but throw my head back and stretch and laugh and shriek.

Look ahead of you.

I turn to Alder Bear and his smile paints beauty all across his face, and he chuckles with me and at me and pulls me into his arms.

'Merry sabbat, crazy priestess.'

Look ahead of you.

What, Seabhac? What?

'Look!'

Beneath us in a field of barley, now golden with sunlight, is an enormous and spiralling crop circle.

VII

SAYING YES

LUGHNASDH: COMMITMENT IN THE WEALTH OF THE SOUTH-WEST

No, I'm not going to declare that I or other Druids know what is causing the crop circle phenomenon. Certainly some circles have been made by human hands, but others would have required tools that only wild boffins could conceive of. Furthermore, the effects of the circles, both on the visitor and on the corn itself (such as altered DNA), are wonderfully inexplicable.

Up to my waist in the midst of a field of swaying golden barley, the edges all scattered with scarlet poppies, bathed in that beautifully English sunshine, the breeze humming, the green and yellow hills like the waves of an ocean, the undulating currents of the earth's bright energy, every breath is pure *awen*. It fills me with such joy and inspiration that I am either left in a daze and liable to drift up and up into the thermals like a feather of down, or I am unbearably animated, swirling and singing, rising and diving with the exuberance of the skylarks. When in the middle of such a field there is a crop circle, I am more than liable to be even worse.

I have heard indirectly from those who have seen circles being made. During the day or night, within 15 minutes, sometimes 90 to 130 circles, with linking passageways creating the spiralling shapes and symbols, emerge out of the corn, each individual stem bent but never broken. These eye-witnesses speak of an energy hovering, shimmering, or small shining discs that spin at extraordinary speed. Most are down-to-earth people, embarrassed by the experience of what they have seen, people who would never consider speaking publicly about it.

In the pattern made in the barley field just over the Wansdyke in 1996, within the flattened whorls of the circles, by chance we came across a few little pockets of wheat still standing bolt upright. Despite our searching for it, we could find no wheat that had been bent. The conclusion we lay folk came to was that whatever had created it had linked into the barley's energy, transmitting to its collective 'consciousness' the pattern of the circles that was the symbol, effectively getting the barley within that area to respond by bending down. It therefore did not affect the wheat. I guess not many of us took it seriously, but we laughed and wondered.

I have no wish to know how the circles are made. It is a glorious mystery and we acknowledge too few of those in our modern lives. For me, the experience of being there, of feeling that heightened energy, is enough. As with many other issues I have touched upon in this book, I am happy to know that such things are part of our potential reality, our living and growing mythology, our extraordinary world in which anything is possible.

While being quite sure that a good many of the circles are not human-made (or could only emerge from the mind of a fantastic genius), but at the same time are far too complex now to be 'natural' phenomena such as wind or earth energy, I am also sure that they are not made through any sense of territory or an asserting of power. Perhaps that's why being inside one feels so exhilarating. If power is about the ability to express oneself from one's deeper sense of being, through the intellect yet centred in confidence and certainty, accessing the energy to relate and do so consciously, then these circles are a wonderful expression of power, power that is not unbalanced or distorted by any sense of threat which requires an assertive action, a statement of strength. The energy in these circles is so freely shared that it fades, dissipated within three days or so, to blend beautifully with the environment that surrounds it.

My personal favourite theory is that the circles are made by space brats – kids from a significantly higher state of being who have fun zooming into the atmosphere of planets populated by us dim-witted lower lifeforms, lifting symbols from the brighter areas of our collective conscious and painting them across our fields. They aren't trying to teach us or send any cryptic message. They have 'evolved' sufficiently not to get their kicks out of provoking fear, and of course it wouldn't be so much of a laugh for them if they weren't then to hang around and watch us pondering and scratching our heads, coming up with wild and silly theories – rather like this one.

Power with any negativity or sense of threat is no more than a defensive assertion of the emotion present. In most cases it is anger, for fear and grief are often seen as weakness and lacking in power (though through these states there is often an undercurrent of manipulation). Anger is commonly expressed and perceived as power and, even where the emotion is not obvious, it can be a potent force and easily deceiving of those searching for strength. In many people the anger is so deep down, the danger rationally denied, that the motivating emotion is only revealed by the person's goals, which are bent on seizing territory or evoking fear, both of which will allow the soul more control and a greater sense of freedom from the threat it perceives. The targets are often simply projections of the original threat.

Power without negative drive is a perfect flow of energy, streaming out of the soul and guided by its natural direction: sweet expression. There is no pushing it, no shoving and making a big effort, no ungainly grasping and fumbling to contain it or clinging on so damn tight that it starts to get twisted. It just flows – like the little child whose eye alights on a brilliant butterfly and who, letting go of your hand, runs down the lawn in a burst of energy, so absolutely directed, perfectly guided by its purpose and freedom.

It was on our journey through the south of the circle, in the heat and light of bright midsummer and its festival of the zenith, that we celebrated our greatest strength and vitality, and we worked on our understanding of power and how we could access it in its purer state to use it positively. But now what will we do with it? As we make our way forward, walking with firm steps, tall and strong, our journey leads us on towards another cross-quarter festival: Lughnasadh, the place between high summer and the red skies of autumn.

We have completed half the circle. On a journey of regeneration from conception deep in the womb of the mother to the height of our physical potential, from a deep inner being to our greatest outer doing, we have travelled from birth through our childhood and adolescence, with all their crises of learning and growth, and through the striving to find acknowledgement and validity, aspiring to take our place as adults in our society. But now midsummer is over and, the solstice behind us, we no longer need to work at growing up and making a statement of our existence.

We might believe we have got so far that now we are beyond the need to grow, or beyond the ability to absorb new information, and can only stagnate til the chill winds of the reaper come to take us away. Or we can find a way gently to nurture and work with the cycle of growth, of learning, of changing, of understanding afresh. The latter is hard to do. The direction is changing, the days will grow shorter and the weather will in a while begin to feel cooler. The wheat that was rich and green in the fields is starting to dry, to die. We need a different way of working, a new attitude.

So it is that the second half of the cycle is a period of learning to be the child again. In our struggling and striving to grow, to take action and *do*, we have forgotten how to simply *be*. With awe and wonder, the child interacts with the world. With trust and without any negative expectations, it discovers its current reality and emits its pure responses back out into its world, a world so filled with mystery and possibility, a wide and unlimited world.

Though the children we were, growing up in the real world, reaching forward into the flames to find out that they burn, have from the beginning of the journey been making their decisions about life and love and safety, creating barricades, the child-self, the magical child within us, is still free. As children we didn't have the consciousness to change our minds, to reconsider mistaken beliefs as the walls grew higher. Through the Druidcraft process of the second half of the circle, we step gently into the heart of that wounded self-limiting child, and discover within the bounds of the sacred grove the crises of our self-negation.

Far ahead, through the waterfalls and rivers of the west, lies the still lake of Samhain, the festival of endings, the rite of death. As we make our way through, letting go of all that for so long has held us back from our true nature, relaxing into our honesty, that childish awe returns, and those last steps into the gateway of passing are taken in peace.

As with every long journey the starting out is hard, but it is eased as we acknowledge the turning tide and adjust to its flow. As we stride forward, it is eased still further, though strangely so til we stop, now and then, to listen more closely... There is music and laughter drifting through the trees in the heat and stillness of the early afternoon, and then across our path sometimes there passes a wild free soul, with dancing eyes, who shares with us some weird old tale, or throws us a riddle like a shining fresh apple, or skips with a rhyme that makes us spin. At times the music is so enchantingly sad our path starts to blur in the mist of our tears. At times it gives us a rhythm so fast we can barely walk for dancing...

The Druid tradition is taught in many ways. Most begin by covering the basic tools of attitude and ritual: establishing a safe and sacred space in which to work. Many go on to focus on the elemental building blocks of earth (north), air (east), fire (south), and water (west) – often in that order around the circle sunwise, though others choose to focus on other correspondences, such as earth (physical), water (emotional), air (mental) and then fire (spirit). Some begin with the east, uncovering the philosophy, and ending with the practical, up in the north. It is either after the basics have been grasped or consecutively with them that the student is usually taken into the teachings and practice of the Bardic tradition.

The archetype of the Bard is for many of us close to that of the wandering minstrel or court musician. Finding a modern image, many see the lad who sits by the hearthstone, playing lonely ballads on an old guitar. As with the Druid, the common image of the Bard is often male, but the working Bards of the modern Druid community come in all shapes and sizes, from the fellow in his sixties who carries his harp in a chamois case, calling her Isabella and touching her strings with utter devotion, to the young girl with a long auburn fringe whose Celtic poetry leaves the gathering clutching their stomach with laughter. There are as many women as men, each finding their inspiration from their own unique vision, from an era that is special to them, each working their vocation: to tell the old tales in prose or verse, creating the new form quietly watching the strange twists of life and love, to travel on and study the truths beneath the words, to play the songs of the hills, the streams and the dryads for those who would listen but cannot yet hear. These special and beautifully gifted folk are still rather few, for the way of the Bard is as magical a path as that of the Druid. It could be said to be the path that begins just past the zenith, in the dawn's groggy light after the wild midsummer festival the night before, in the wasteland of bodies that was the field of battle and is now, for the Bard, the source of another tale. As a mystery tradition, it is a path of learning how to listen, listen deeply. It is a path of learning how to create silence and how to fill it – while still listening.

There are certainly many great poets and songsters who have managed to make a name for themselves by writing through their grief and rage. But in magical Bardcraft this is not the way, for no truly great Bard will invade his art with his own emotion. His aim is the portrayal of another event. He hopes to take his audience into the precise moment of its happening, to set them baying with the hounds then get them bleeding with the stag. The master of the tale is a master of emotion. He has found a way through to joy and to ecstatic clarity, and it is with these that he envelopes his tale, allowing it to be rich with its own emotion.

Though it may never be our central role, the teachings of Bardcraft are a critical part of Druid training. In many Druid Orders or teaching groups, the creativity of the poem, the tale and the song are strongly encouraged as a form of expression and spiritual release, even if what is produced is never sufficiently coherent to share. But the simple essence of the Bardic craft is much more widely accessible and, according to those who taught me, it is during the journey from the fires of the south towards the ocean in the west that the first lessons of the Bard appear on our path.

So far we have captured our inspiration. Now, like a deep breath, that inspiration must be exhaled. Bardcraft is about learning how to do just that without the fears that have held us back – the fear of negative feedback, of judgement or failure.

Emerging from our limiting inhibitions is seldom a scene of sparkling success. Our first journeys with the Bardic guide can be like climbing a rock face just to get to the top of those defensive barricades. When at last there is sufficient courage to let out a splurge of energy, to create a little something here quietly in the corner, the reaction can be dreadful, as the wonky clay pot is hurled *splat!* against the wall or that rage of a fist slams into those crumbling cup cakes, or we trip on the twist in the end of the rhyme and the audience stare expectantly just when it should be laughing and all we want to do is hide. There has, after all, been a *reason* why we haven't tried before. For starters, it hurts like hell when it all goes wrong...

Slowly we learn, understanding which of our assumptions and attitudes are actually invalid and self-defeating, where our motivations are misguided and how our creative energy can best be used. We learn to be our own free selves. With our enthusiasm and courage still firmly held in our grasp, we make our way with sure resolve along the dusty track into the afternoon, into that strange mixture of the purposeful and the soporific.

There is an honesty rising with the reality of the coming harvest. The wheat and the barley are ripe and drying bleached and golden, shimmering like water. The festival is just ahead when the first sheaves will be cut and thanks will be given to the gods of the land. People will gather from all around, bringing barrows of fruits and vegetables, crafts and livestock to trade and compare. There will be races as the best of the horses are shown off and the strongest young men compete against each other. Disputes will be taken before the Druids and lords to be resolved, oaths will be sworn, laws declared, witnessed by all who have gathered by the Gorsedd mound. It will be Lughnasadh, the festival of the Celtic god of light, and the gifts of the sun will be displayed with pride and celebration.

In modern Druidcraft we call it the festival of first fruits. The harvest has only just begun. There is still perhaps a whole moon's cycle of hard work before the crop is safely stored and dry in the barns. In the trees and the hedgerows, the petals have long since fallen and the fruits have been swelling: the first taste is an explosion of sweetness and sharp juices that those under tender secretory glands.

On our alters lie the first stems of corn, a loaf blessed and offered to the gods in thanks, and bowls of fruit – strawberries, raspberries, blackcurrants and plums. We gaze with awe upon the first rewards of our cycle's work, knowing that what we see is

just the beginning.
    This is no time to relax, no, not quite yet.

* * *

Over a hundred are gathered around the great fire in the centre of the circle, and the sun bakes down on the yellow grass and cracked mud. The rhythms of the drums are rolling and diving, and the mandolin plays as the Bard sings, each word thrown down like chunks of dirt out into the crowd:

'There were three men came out of the west
Their fortunes for to try
And these three men made a solemn vow
John Barleycorn must die...'

And the joker prances between the people, his mask strangely disarming, and the kids stare at him in wonder and giggle in their nervousness, tickled by the anticipation of not knowing his next move. He disappears and emerges somewhere all new, and he drums an invisible drum and half sings silently, and out of key, as the Bard continues, holding our gaze so intently:

'They ploughed, they sowed, they harrowed him in
Throwed clods upon his head
And these three men made a solemn vow
John Barleycorn was dead...

Then they let him lie for a long time
Til the rain from heaven did fall
Then Sir John sprung up his head
And so amazed them all...'

The king strides out around the circle, his crown made of stems gathered of wild fescue, brome and meadow barley, with wheat from a nearby field, corn marigolds and feverfew, his face aglow with pride. As he passes me our eyes briefly meet and a flicker of a nervous giggle twitches over his lips, but on he walks to the widest rhythm of the drums as if he were leading them, head up and shoulders broad, his robes flowing all about him.

'They let him stand til midsummer
Til he looked both pale and wan
And Sir John growed a long, long beard
And so became a man...'

And the circle cheers and a conch is blown as the king gives a marvellous flourish. But the Bard, with his talent to hold his listeners in his hands, suddenly creates a hush within the music and colours, a pause just a moment longer than is expected. And, as the mandolin strikes the jaunty pace, out of the circle sneaks a figure, all in black, eyes hidden by his hat, with a long curving blade, stepping into the king's pace just behind him. The song begins again with a slowing lilt:

'They hired men with scythes so sharp
To cut him off at the knee...'

The blade flies up and comes slicing down over the king, who crumbles to the ground. Only the blade is of card, and the children screech with joy, for they have spent long hours painting and glueing together the weapon. The joker screeches amongst them and curls up into a ball of mock fright as more come forward upon the king.

'They rolled and tied him by the waist
And served him most barbarously...'

Now the bloodthirsty crowd are a-hooting and clapping, as the drums stamp their rhythm, and I am filled with a mixture of uncertainty, fear, lust for the thrill and a deep warm glow of the magic that is being here replayed, a wild sensing of the divine spirit that is coursing through the circle like the pulsing response of the earth to our feet that move with the beat of the music.

'They hired men with sharp pitchforks
Who pricked him to the heart
And the Loader he served him worst than that
For he bound him to the cart.

They wheeled him round and round the field
Til they came unto a barn
And there they made a solemn mow
Of poor John Barleycorn.
They hired me with crabtree stick
To cut him skin from bone...'

And the youngest kids in their poster-painted robes step forward with sheaves and beat them down upon the ground. One of them drops his handful of wheat, entirely entranced by the music that fills him, and he moves his little body to dance a crazy dance, unaware of the effect of his freedom on the crowd, til the Bard finds himself enchanted and for a moment throws up the song and comes to dance with the little child. The sight of it melts the great wedge within me, and I hold and kiss the hand of my own beautiful son, as my body sways.

Then the singer weaves his way through the children to a woman. He bows to her. She is his lover and takes up the song again:

'And the Miller he served him worst than that
For he ground him between two stones.

Here's little Sir John in a nut brown bowl
And brandy in a glass
And little Sir John in the nut brown bowl
Proved the stronger man at last.

For the huntsman he can't hunt the fox
Nor so loudly blow his horn
And the tinker he can't mend kettle or pots
Without a little barleycorn!'

Everyone is singing, and the dancing begins with the jingling of
the Morris bells, the whole gathering a-skipping and weaving
around the circle, some going one way, some the other, in a
whole-hearted mess of chaos and music, of laughter and swirling
ribbons.

Someone is crying and I stop on my way. *OK?*

'It's alright,' she sniffs. 'It's just good to be here!'

My arm is grabbed and I am pulled into a dance, circling and
reeling around the fire, laughing with my abductor, who is a
beautiful Bard in a billowing shirt and trousers of violet. But then
I spy my young son, the gentle thinker, serious old soul, snarling
with aversion at the whirlwind around him. I go to him and
laugh and he snarls at me. We move out a little and hug,
watching the action.

*Yes, I know, my love, it is all very, very childish. It is how we express
our freedom, how we celebrate the beauty of our lives, of this fertile land,
the wonder of the first sheaves of the harvest that is our soul's wealth.*

'Hmph,' he says, with an old man's disapproval. *Too crazy for
me.*

I am about to console him that the serious part of the rite will
continue soon when a Druid priest walks into the dance and the
Bard's wand brings the music to a stop. The people move gently
back to form the circle as it was cast. The centre is a wide and
open space, filled with the energy and waiting. More wood is

thrown onto the fire and as the priest speaks I slip into the earth, opening myself into the beauty of the thanksgiving.

'... of your womb was our king born, and through your nourishment did he grow, strong and tall, fat with the blessings of your abundance, shining gold with the light of your sun lover. Now he has given his life for us. Blessed goddess...'

It is time for me to play my part and as he speaks of our essence and our sustenance, ground between the flattened stones, blessed and mixed with air and water, set before the fire three times, and of the deep magic transformation, I come to the centre with the loaf of the sacred feast. It is a foot wide and designed in intricate details with sheaves of corn and the high summer king set against the base of the flaming sun.

Another Druid comes towards me. He is a priest of Lugh. His green eyes sparkling, he holds in his hands a fine polished grey mead horn. 'Blessed be, my Lady,' he says quietly and I bow my head. *As blessed is.*

I hold out the bread, calling out the thanksgiving, as the energy of the earth pounds through me, the sun washes into me and the loaf in my hands seems to come alive, tingling with a thick and warm vibrancy. I make the first break in the name of our sacred Mother, offering some back to her body through the spirits of nature by crumbling it upon the ground, then offering some to the ancestors through the flames of the fire. Breaking off another piece, I call within to my Lord of the Sun, and whispering the blessing, I offer it to the priest. Through that exquisite tension, he takes it into his mouth. Then he raises the mead horn and makes the thanksgiving for the first fruits, gives the first draught as a libation to the Earth and then offers the blessed mead to me. I sip and its strength and energy kick into my solar plexus. I close my eyes and it flows through me.

As I open them again, the circle around us returns to my consciousness. We bow to each other, then greet the couple who come to help us. I break the loaf in two, giving the other priestess half, and in pairs we move off to share the sacred feast around the circle, breaking off a piece for each person and with a kiss whispering, 'Blessings of the sacred bread, blessing of abundance.'

Around the fire, another Bard begins to play.

* * *

The bond between a tribal Pagan king and his land was always critical and there are many tales of the wedding – both symbolic and initiatory – that creates and affirms that connection. As the people knew, if the spirit of the land was not happy, if the king had been disloyal to the vows of the marriage, the natural world would give every sign of doubting their right to remain. The health and wealth both of the land and their king were therefore of paramount importance, for the two were woven together through a magical union.

Out of this fusion emerge the ideas about sacrifice that exist within much of modern Paganism, with all the imagery that shapes and paints them. The connection between the tribal king and the king of light, the Sun Child born at midwinter who grows up to be the saviour, the great hero of love and justice, is one which is played out many times, and one which eases the meeting place with Christianity. In Paganism there is also the blend between the sun king and the green god, who dies each year, to be reborn with the seasons. This blending is seen in the tale of John Barleycorn. At the solstice the sun king was at the height of his glory, but things have now changed; the year is beginning to wane, and it is clear that his beauty and strength have been spent, poured into the corn which now glows with that golden light. As the corn is cut, the weakening king is slain, his life blood spilling over the fields as they are harvested, his essence returned to the land.

The element of sacrifice is important. Whether in times past a young man was really killed or not in place of the tribal king is not relevant here. More important is the fact that it is neither a natural death, which happens later in the year across the plant and animal realms with the spellwork of the winter gods, nor is it murder. It is about the relationship between humankind and the land, about what is taken and what is given in return, ensuring the continuity of the perfect balance.

The symbolic sprinkling of the fields with blood at the very start of the harvest and at times throughout the process ensures that the harvest will be good til the very last is cut. We don't want to lose it! The seeds we kept dry and safe through the winter, sorted through once again before sowing in the spring, nurtured into seedlings and then into plants, protected them from pests, watered through dry spells and showered with our delight, have started to bear fruit. And knowing that in order to receive fully, sufficient must be given in return, the Druid makes offerings to the spirits, to the gods of the land who have guided and inspired the work, bringing the crop to its fruition. These offerings are potent symbols of our life force – we let go of something to keep the balance, pledging our harvest with the sacred intention that it may be used for the next step of our lives.

Of course, sometimes things do go wrong. By Lughnasadh it is quite clear what kind of harvest it will be. We can't deny what might be too dreadfully obvious. Did we choose the right seeds? Did we sow on fertile land? Did we neglect the seedlings in the late frosts or when some other project diverted our energy? Do we actually want what we have grown? Will it nourish us, body and soul? Are we proud to show off and is there sufficient to share as we would wish? And, if it is what we need, have we grown enough so that some can be put aside for next year's sowing seed?

If we have done our work well, found a sure foundation, and in clarity and freedom thought through our ideas, claimed our sacred gift of responsibility and with it the strength of our empowerment, the next step is not a decision that needs to be made. Like the child who sets off across the grass after the butterfly, there is only one way to go.

It could be said that the whole journey, from our place of conception to this moment of decision, has been no more than a preparation, finding a path on the map and packing the saddle bags. We are moving towards the west, the place of flowing movement, of water, of life.

But at Lughnasadh, when we first come to it, we are not at the gentle spring which seeps out from the dark earth. Where fire and water come together there is all too often the power of the summer storms, the crack of lightning and the deep rumbling that reverberates through the soul before the rain comes down. Lughnasadh is the river that cascades down the mountain with a momentum that can shake you to the very core with anticipation. It isn't like Beltane – you can't afford to pussyfoot or play around. If you aren't careful you can lose the moment and at Lughnasadh that could mean losing the whole harvest. It could also mean losing your footing and that could be fatal. The slightest hesitation could send you smashing against the rocks of some harsh reality, or plough you down into the depths of some unforeseen black emotion. But though in our caution we may be trembling over the stopwatch and fiddling with our zips and gloves, these are merely tools that stop our shaking hands from flailing through the ungraspable. We must take that step, knowing that we have the power, that the active energy which we need is ready to be released the instant our course is set. Holding firm to our responsibility with the confidence of our knowing, we face the white water, the force and flow of the current. It's that horrifying concept we all come to one day: commitment.

When we are poised on the brink and looking down into the churning froth, ducking and hedging in the conflict between intellect and emotion, our reasoning and our fears, our justifications and our intuition, the power that we have is put to the test.

Looking out over the prospects of committing to a direction can be somewhat scary, but the time spent just looking while those demons fight in your guts is time that is wasted, and with that wasted time the energy starts to dissipate.

Once we have understood the freedom of air and have found the centred potential and strength of fire, we have this sense that we are in control – or at least sufficiently so. Earth and air are fuel for our fire, but water is different. It can drench, drown. It can put out the fire.

Water, not only in Druidcraft but in conventional psychology, is symbolic of emotion. Emotion I would define very simply as 'energy patterned by thought', more specifically by the belief systems that we store in the subconscious. It is our fear of the unknown reaches of our emotion that kicks in and holds us back on the edge of our commitment, our fear of the unstoppable force of its current. Yet a part of us knows that the force of that white water crashing through the gorge is the force of our own emotion. Water itself is a calm neutral energy, but our response to the world, our thoughts and beliefs, has changed it, coloured it and set it in motion.

Most of the beliefs we hold are those that allow us to live fairly effectively. They give us the motivation to eat and sleep, to find a partner, care for our children, to nurture, to integrate. In comparison the protective decision and the invalid assumptions that limit us unnecessarily are very few, yet because these lie in the subconscious and are seldom brought to the surface in any way which prods us to awaken to their presence, we carry on for decades quite unaware of their influence – which can be considerable, for as part of our belief network they are subconsciously referred to in every decision that we make.

Every action we take is fuelled by energy that is patterned by the beliefs that we think are most appropriate to the situation. If something happens which triggers a certain energy, an emotion, that is based on a belief which is seriously non-progressive, our whole body is affected. If we simply can't understand our own reaction, either having no concept of the underlying motivations or no scope to see that the belief is invalid or self-destructive, the emotion – which is the both the momentum and the direction of the energy – leads to a feeling of being way out of control.

In most cases, the hesitation which plays for time and allows energy to dissipate doesn't end in cataclysmic disaster. As energy leaks, the pressure eases and the situation can feel less uncontrollable, even if the basic poor beliefs are not addressed. If enough energy is lost, the original motivation breaks up too and the challenge disappears. So we go on, year after year, getting nowhere.

Until perhaps there comes a time when we are not only sick of our stagnation, but are sick of being sick of it, and sick of that too. When that state is sufficiently acute we are willing to go through the hell of being dunked and slammed against the waterfall, just to break through to a new reality, determined, as we gasp for air in the deluge, to get a vision of the core problem and the subconscious motivations that are holding us back. We are not going to create another disaster, we are not going to stop ourselves from succeeding through a fear that we might just fail. But how do we find the courage to take that dreaded step and actually *commit*?

We need to affirm that we have *sufficient* control. No more. Standing on the edge, determine to do it this time, feeling the inspiration and the reservoir of energy filled and ready to burst out and wash lifegiving water over our dry plans, we call to our gods and guides for help that we might successfully contain and distribute the flow of the energy. In Druidcraft, we cast the sacred circle, creating the *nemeton*, the sanctuary for our process of change, within which we can affirm our safety and our centre. The bounds of the circle hold in the energy – both that which we have found for our purpose and that which has been triggered in response.

Then, with clear intent, opening to the guidance and

protection of those around, we step forward into the circle, into the task, the act of making the commitment, opening up the flood gates for the energy to pour through and into our creativity. It can be the most painful step we take. We are sacrificing what we believe to be our safety, challenging protective decisions that have held us stable and secure, albeit at the cost of our lack of fulfilment. So a part of us dies and is reborn as the Bard.

Not surprisingly, then, Lughnasadh is the traditional time for Druid weddings. Though all through the year wedding rites are celebrated, it is a Lughnasadh that the sacred vows between king and land are made and broken, and often in Druid ceremonies at this time the sacred wedding is replayed according to myth or imagination.

At the open Druid festivals, couples are wed or 'handfasted', giving their dedication and proclaiming their love for each other, witnessed by a priest, their friends, their grove and, at large gatherings, the whole crowd of those assembled. Many of these 'weddings', though often beautiful and profound, are fairly quick, a simple public statement of two people being joined in the eyes of their community and before the gods, but only 'for as long as love shall last'. It is traditional that, should a marriage be ending, the couple return to the place of their vows and there, with respect to the spirits of the place and the ancestors who witnessed their binding, retract their commitment, turn and walk away.

The full Druid wedding is quite different from the festival handfasting – and different from the wedding ceremony that most of our culture knows through the Christian Church. To being with, the couple are asked to write their own vows. After all, if we really are going to take the risk, to jump into the current and through our pain, we may as well do so fully conscious.

* * *

It was on one of those beautiful late winter days, a light frosting of snow just covering the fields, the sky so high and strangely blue, that I first met the couple at their house in the Cotswolds. They had heard of me through some long and complex grapevine and we had spoken briefly on the telephone to arrange a time to meet.

It's always a vaguely awkward moment. In some ways it would be easier if I had a business card with a profile and photo I could send out in advance. It's hard for people not to build up a picture in their imagination. By the expression of Jack's face when he opened the door, my actual appearance just didn't correlate with his expectation.

'Emma...?' he asked, seriously doubting himself.

I had to laugh. 'Yes. You must be Jack. Good to meet you.'

'It's OK. I know it's difficult – what *does* a Druid look like?'

His expression quite distinctly said, *Well, not dressed in a long coat with suede boots and a wide-brimmed hat.* 'Come, come in,' he stammered, smiling through his bewilderment and ushering me in. 'Darling! Emma's here.'

Sarah concealed her surprise a little better and we greeted each other with big smiles, but sitting down around the oak table in their cluttered farmhouse kitchen she giggled over the coffee. 'We thought you'd be much older, didn't we darling? Oh, not that it's a problem, it's just that we've been trying to work out what you'd look like from your voice and we'd rather made up this image of, well, a rather eccentric old priestess, I suppose. You're...'

'Well, you look very normal – '

'Jack!'

'Hey, it's OK. But you can be assured – it's all camouflage. Inside this outfit, I'm mad as a hatter.'

And we'd laughed away any tension and the English embarrassment.

Since that first meeting, we have met a couple more times,

securing the date, walking through the fields that stretch along the valley as we pondered upon this and that, discussing flowers and musicians, photographers and robes. We have talked through the ceremony and ways of incorporating the vision of their dreams, ways of making the relevant changes. I have sat beneath the three oaks that make a grove at the end of their garden, talked to the dryads and the spirit of place about the wedding to be held beneath their canopies.

A week ago I came down and spoke to them separately about the vows they would make, walking with Jack along the river, chatting with Sarah at the table, aproned and in the midst of making raspberry jam.

Not only are the vows in a Druid wedding created by the couple, but the time scale or conditions through which they must be kept is also defined. There is no basic 'til death do us part' we must somehow 'love and obey'. This avoids the possibility of the priest sensing that the prospects of the couple keeping their vows are less than good and compromising his honesty and integrity through completing the ceremony. Working with a lot of people, taking them through these processes, it's easy to get a feel for what is true, for where the honesty is profound, where relationships are nurtured through mutual support and nourishment, where the love transcends need.

For some couples, there is a feeling that one wedding ceremony should be sufficient. However, if the vows that we make are reachable, and the relationship grows, changes and deepens with the growth of the individuals, it is often the case that the couple come to a point where new vows need to be made, a new commitment made through vows that take into consideration and honour the changes, vows that help us to stretch just a little further.

So it is that I stand at the fireside now, a warm wind blowing through the leaves of the branches of the oaks above us. The sky is darkening blue, but there is not yet the scent of rain. I call to the storm spirits to hold off a little longer, breathe deeply and watch as the priestess working the rite with me makes the call for peace.

Around us the circle is marked out physically by great logs of an old ash tree recently felled down by the river and half-barrel tubs overflowing with tagetes, golden cosmos and dark red pelargoniums. Two dozen little lantern are resting on the logs, their candles burning gently, spreading their pale yellow light across the wood and leaves, picking up the colours of the huge sunflowers that are tied into sheaves of newly cut wheat. With the dry August grass, the quality of the light and the flickering of the fire, the effect is beautiful. Beneath the oak behind me my Bard plays, his fingers flowing over the strings of his harp, painting the humid air with music. All around the circle of logs the guests are now standing – over 100, maybe 150 folks, friends, old and new, family of all ages, in fancy hats with flowers and veils, in jackets held together with uncertain hands, looking around, wondering, waiting. One or two have previously been to a Druid ceremony, but none to a Druid wedding. There is the dignified hush of a congregation more used to the stone and echoes of a church.

My assistant, Rowena, bows to me and the harp is quiet as I take my staff, leaving the circle to walk around outside the guests, casting with the jingling of the hawk bells, not to bind or separate from current reality but to gather in the focus. As Rowena blesses and consecrates, taking the censor with its plumes of pungent smoke round the circle, I can see the bride making her way towards us. Jack stands at the edge of the circle, fidgeting and breathing deeply. A little niece of his walks forward in a long dress of ochre linen with a belt of golden ribbon and a garland of tagetes, and I give her the chalice, blessed for consecration. The rose petals have been soaking in the water since dawn and nervous but proud she walks the circle, dipping her fingers in and sprinkling the rose water over the guests and the grass, occasionally flicking out petals to the smiles and chuckles of her audience. Rowena and I call to the spirits of the quarters in the soft waves of the harp music that shimmer and flow around us. Then, in a hush, I invite the couple into the circle.

Sarah is dressed like Maid Marion in long skirts of unbleached linen bound with laces at her chest and cords of gold around her waist. She stands barefoot in the grass. The crown woven into her hair is of honeysuckle, meadowsweet, oak and thyme. Her big green eyes look into my face like a child's. Jack's expression is one of such concentration, I can almost see the pounding of his heart. He is dressed in a long shirt and loose trousers in the same soft cream linen, tucked into moccasin boots. His hair is wild in the breeze and in his nerves, his 33 years have been halved. The couple stand at either side of the fire as I call to my Lady within, then lift my face to talk to the gathering:

'We stand together on this holy Earth and in the face of our star sun to witness this sacred rite of marriage between Jack Joseph Carter and Sarah Melanie Mason. In the name of all creation, I here call upon our goddess of love, of beauty, of the sweet songs of the earth and the mysteries of being.'

The energy slides into me, filling every cell of my body, swelling my heart. For a moment I wonder if it can be felt through the crowd, if anyone out there is sensitive to the Lady's blessing. But it's not a thought that strengthens my confidence and I turn again to call out through the mists:

'In the name of all knowing, I here call upon our god of light, of the rising of the sun, of the wildness of nature, of perfect truth and the power of doing. Hail to thee, in whatever form you so wish to come. Hail and welcome.'

After a pause, sensing the silence, the thinking around me shifting to waiting, I add:

'Let us take a moment to attune to the divine presence that we may bring our consciousness to this special moment.'

In the quiet whispering of the trees and the crackling of the fire, I watch a man walk through the crowd and across the circle to stand at Jack's shoulder. I am slowly aware that he is not in a body. *Who - ?* I start to ask, when he says, *I am his father.* I bow to him in greeting and watch with pleasure as, when he puts his hands upon his son's shoulders, Jack seems to gain confidence. I continue:

'A man and a woman are drawn together instinctively and in profound and natural search for a place of relationship, the deep wish to share in each new landscape, each new discovery along the pathways of life, drawn together by the memories, seldom conscious, rich in their souls, the deep feelings of familiarity, the cords and bonds of previous lives, the memories of having loved, joined, perhaps many times before.

'Now you come to this sacred circle and prepare to take the step of pledging your first marriage vows, of committing yourselves. In the intimacy of your bond your partner symbolizes for you your connection and attitude to all humanity, to all creation and to our holy Mother Earth. Where you dishonour, so will you anticipate and experience dishonour. Where you love and respect, so will you find and receive love and respect. Know that when you love each other truly, you will have grown to love all life. For in a perfect love do we touch our Creator...'

As I talk about partnership and the forces of life, the couple gaze at each other, turn to me, then back to each other. Tears are falling down Sarah's cheeks, leaving little grey streaks of mascara. When I ask if they have come to the rite of their own free will, she smiles through her tears and nods as she bites her lip, and he whispers, 'Yes,' as if it were the only decision he had ever truly made of his own soul.

'Mother of all life, ocean of creation, draw us deep into the waves of your embrace. Bless this couple with health, with strength, wealth, the warmth of growth and the light of pure joy.

Come together.'

I beckon them forward in front of the fire.

'Hold hands and behold each other in the light of the goddess. And, as if for the very first time, open up your hearts to each other. Know that this is a time of trust. Feel the freedom of that trust within which you can surrender.'

Such an open expression of intimacy is seldom seen, and within the bounds of the rite and their precious moment the couple drift as if on a raft in the midst of a calm and endless sea. Sensing the need for them to have this space and the guests starting to fidget, my Bard begins to play, so quietly and tenderly that at first I assume it's the songs of the dryads.

When Rowena walks forward, they look up.

'Come,' she says. 'Let us walk the circles of creation.'

They move slowly around the circle, stopping in the quarters to acknowledge the cycles of time, the tides of the seasons and the mystical powers of the elementals, to feel the blessings of the spirits that dwell within each realm, affirming their commitment through the possibilities of life, its twists and turns of certainty and potential. When they have walked the circle three times, they return to the altar, laid with its cloth of deep red and the tools for the consecration. Beside them is a pearly clam shell filled with water and shining in the water are golden rings.

'All things in nature are circular. Night becomes day, day leads to nights, which again gives way to day. The moon waxes and wanes and waxes again. There is spring, summer, autumn and winter, then spring returns again. These are the flowing rhythms of the cycle of existence. Yet in the centre of the circle is the stillness of the source, eternal and brilliant. To this rite you have brought your symbols of these great mysteries of life.'

I hold the clam shell into the sunlight which now and then breaks through the thickening clouds and call out a blessing. Then I take the bigger ring and hand it to Sarah. Jack lifts up his hand and she pushes it onto his finger, half giggling with the effort. Holding his hand with both of hers, she looks down and breathes in deeply. Then she looks up into his dace and offers him her vows:

'Accept in freedom this circle of gold as a token of my commitment. With it I pledge my honesty and my own freedom. I will not give you the responsibility of my own mistakes and my own needs.'

She closes her eyes and her voice is so quiet that only he can hear. Then, with her face to the heavens, determined and smiling with tear-stained cheeks, she says aloud:

'...and I pledge to love you and never to ask you to change for me. In the name of the goddess, these things I vow.'

I think I hear a murmur from the crowd, like a hum of resonance but it may be in my mind or the acknowledging energy of the oak dryads. Sarah turns towards her mother, who is weeping into a handkerchief.

I take the smaller ring and give it to Jack. As he slips it onto her finger, his father nods his head with a deep and encouraging approval. Jack says:

'Accept in freedom this circle of gold as a token of my commitment. With it I pledge to you all that I am, all that I hope I am. Through all my tempestuous artistic temperament, I vow always to honour you, to respect you, to be your best friend, to be loyal. I vow to give you the freedom to be yourself and to change and grow. Even if I can't always be on time, I vow to be reliable, to be there when you need me, when you want me. I vow... oh shit, I've forgotten the rest.'

He bites his lip and seeing the tears welling up in his eyes I look down.

'I just love you so much. In the name of my god, these things I vow.'

That does it for me; my voice is all croaky as I try to push the lump down that's now firmly stuck in my throat.

'Let these rings that you have exchanged be an outward sign

and a sacred reminder of your commitment.'

I turn to the altar to pick up the chunk of rose quartz and lift it to call for the blessings of the gods. A deep rumble of thunder rolls through the air. *Not yet, my Lords!* As I open my eyes I see my priestess suppress a compassionate smile seeing me surreptitiously wipe the tears from my own cheeks before turning back to the couple and the guests,

'This stone has been chosen by you as sacred. Blessed by the gods...'

A flash of lightning clears the sky and a few of the guests look up into the storm clouds that are gathering.

'...blessed by the gods and by the spirits of this rite, infused with the energy of this precious moment, stable and strong, in perfect beauty and unchanging, it is a symbol of the stone of your hearth, the foundation of your home, the light of your love. Upon this stone and witnessed by all who have gathered here today, do you, Jack and Sarah, swear to maintain your vows?'

Each with a hand upon the quartz, they swear in the stumbling of the thunder:

'I offer myself as your wife.'

'I accept with great joy. And I offer myself as your husband.'

'And I accept with great joy.'

'Then seal your promise with a kiss.'

A crack of lightning streaks across the sky and a burst of thunder follows. But the couple are lost in a glorious kiss. Slowly the church inhibitions are put aside and there's a cheer which evolves into more noises of approval and even applause.

I call out:

'O ancient gods, souls of our ancestors, spirits of all existences who join us in truth, accept this union between Jack and Sarah.'

The first raindrops are beginning to fall as again thunder rolls.

'By the power vested in me as priestess of the old Craft and on behalf of all, I recognize you now as husband and wife. From this time forth you walk together along life's path. May your way be blessed. May your strength and purpose sustain you and bring you great spiritual growth together. May wisdom bring you enlightenment and patient clarity, and may perfect love shine always through your lives.'

Jack and Sarah's smiles are radiant and they embrace again in a kiss. But the rain is now coming down and I give up.

'Um, perhaps we could leave them?' I suggest to the gathering of people who don't quite know what would be appropriate. 'It's necessary for us to close the circle in a sacred manner, but while the storm passes, let us move off into the marquee by the house.'

Standing looking out from the marquee, with the rain spitting in the fire and the lightning cracking across the sky, Rowena puts her arms around my waist.

'I saw you crying there.'

'Weren't they so beautiful?'

'Look at them. Totally oblivious.'

'May the gods ensure that all their storms are summer storms and pass right by.'

'We'll have to close the circle some time.'

'Let's see how the storm goes.'

An elderly lady offers me her hand. 'Excuse me, I'm Sarah's aunty. I just wanted to say that it was beautiful, really beautiful.' She shakes her head in that paradoxical way which her generation allows. 'I'm Christian, you know, and I didn't know what to expect, but I thought I'd let the young ones have their decisions. I'm jolly glad too. Very special. Very moving. Thank you, dear. And you too,' she adds to Rowena. 'Lovely.'

'I'm really pleased you enjoyed it. Thank you.'

As she walks away I overhear a young woman, expensively dressed to kill, no doubt a contemporary from the couple's London days, making her comment to a friend: ' Isn't this the most ridiculous wedding you've ever been to? Why couldn't they be sensible and do it in a church like everyone else? Bloody weather, *wrecked* my shoes.'

That's his old girlfriend, Jack's father explains, walking towards me through the rain. *Nice ceremony. 'Bout time he said yes.*

VIII

TIDES AND CHANGE

THE AUTUMN EQUINOX: LETTING GO IN THE TWLIGHT OF THE WEST

Why is it so hard to make that commitment? Essentially because we don't know – or don't use – any checking procedures to work out whether what we are plunging into is the right river at the right time. We are so used to thinking of the world as an overwhelming and highly complex barrage of apparent chaos within which is some order that we have wholly failed to grasp, that we assume a level of erratic competence must be acceptable. It seems to be the only option. Even when we have reached the state of being sick of being sick of our lack of achievement, it is hard to rise up and declare our new direction with absolute confidence.

Passing on from Lughnasadh, the festival of the first fruits, we journey through the moontide, the weeks of harvest. The summer draws on like a long afternoon. We work hard and the chatter in the fields starts to fall quiet, muscles start to ache and the sun casts longer shadows. As the end draws into sight, the last bales are bound and thrown into the cart, we give ourselves time to stop and breathe deeply, to feel the satisfaction of what has been achieved, to start to relax.

Sure, there are still essential tasks to get done before nightfall, but let the sun slide a little lower first, let the wasps settle in the eves. Later the sun will set, a deep golden red, beyond the far fields and into the western ocean. Now there is a lull, a moment of perfect stillness that is too precious to miss, a moment that feels almost as if time did not exist. We slow down, awestruck in the luxurious abundance, the rich verdancy of our land that allows us the pleasure of knowing it will be OK: we've done it. For a while, in softening sunshine, we snooze, bellies full of freshly baked bread and lips still sweat with mead. A year's work has reached its peak. The sap in the trees is now barely rising. The herbs and grasses are shedding their seeds into the lazy breeze.

But if our harvest is poor, as we trudge through the stillness, the future will hold no certainty at all.

In the late September sunshine, our gaze is drawn up to the first splashes of bronze in the forest canopy. There's no turning back. What we are storing now is not only our winter supplies but also the seed grain for the next year's corn. There's no point now in dreaming of what could be. All that's left is the bare reality and the might have beens.

We have leapt from the high river bank, plunging into the white water, committing ourselves to the moment and all that it holds, and there is nothing to do now but surrender to the current. Caught in the flow, if uncertainty kicks in and instead of lying back and letting the water take us we struggle for confirmation or, worse, a way to get the hell out, some kind of damage is inevitable.

Beyond the commitment, then, is the need to accept what we have done.

Our existence is so gloriously rich with paradox. *Is* the universe infinitely expanding or will it implode? We crave our independence and we long to be held. In order to find peace, we need to feel secure. While paradoxes push, pull and inspire us, it is this critical dilemma between security and satisfaction that seems to me to underlie a great deal of human behaviour.

Within that need for security is a deeper paradox. In order to feel secure we need to find a place of safety – now. Yet unless the threat is addressed it will stay there, either as an actuality or a looming dark potential. In other words, much of what we believe will bring us safety takes us into a hidden place where there's little opportunity to remove the threat that lingers outside. At the same time, to erase the threat means working too far out in the open, away from that safe space, which can be overwhelmingly stressful.

Unless we have lost hope, as well as security we also need to feel fulfilled, to have a sense of personal satisfaction. Without this, we stagnate. The paradox within this issue is that of wanting to progress, to experience growth through tangible results, but at the same time to want a life of ease and freedom. It's summed up in the problem of not wanting to do, yet wanting to have done.

In the natural world this paradox is addressed with ease. There's an instinctive understanding as to when to haul in and when to wander out and discover new territory. But in our human psyche, our self-consciousness, which gives us an awareness of our circumstance and the anticipation, leads us to chase our tails round and round, mentally tying ourselves up in knots. Leaping at our tails, we bite down – and wonder at the excruciating pain.

We know that holding back, holding on, is not the way we're going to succeed. So we try to let go, to follow our inspiration, but those screaming trembling monsters seem impossible to avoid. Affirmations rife in our culture and our language simply affirm our incompetence and our inability to achieve: life is hard, we must buckle down, no use chasing dreams, you can't fight the system...

Some folks simply give up. In our education system, it's not difficult to find kids who have already given up, believing with absolute certainty and resignation that life holds no great opportunities and that fulfilment can only come from acute bursts of stimulation. Some folks live without seeing opportunities for fulfilment, despite them sliding slowly by with shining handles to grab on to. They believe too strongly that such a rash move would lead to personal apocalypse, a public performance of failure which would paste their basic weakness on billboards countywide.

Some folks just keep trying and, with a fine mix of great courage and blindness, hurl themselves into their dreams again and again, hitting the rocks every time as some underlying bastard of a belief skids their ability to succeed. This is perhaps the very hardest way to live. I've seen people struggle for so long in the search to discover what is stopping them from making it and every time they get close denial hits in and the mind goes blank. I have seen denial so strong that for years a person will pour energy into what he believe he wants to do, with clear and strong intent, and never find success or any sense of satisfaction, because hidden deep down there's an alternative agenda that is sucking energy away. For most people this hidden motivation is security, though the form it takes can be inside out and twisted.

Finding out our basic motivations is a long process of awakening self-awareness. We watch and take note of our actions and responses, of emotion triggered and expressed, of any circumstance that evokes energy. We start to listen to the messages our physical body is giving us – pockets of tension, knots that tighten, shakes and twitches, internal and external. We learn to break through the barriers of our pride and know the ways in which we – so skilfully – fool ourselves.

There are two levels of belief stored down in our subconscious, variably accessible though affecting our every action and reaction. The first level is our assumptions, those beliefs that we consider to be the simple facts of life. The Earth is round. Your eyes are blue. Politicians lie. Life is painful. My body is unattractive... If somebody refutes one of these beliefs, the reaction is going to be either confusion or dismissal. After all, how could anyone think differently? *This is basic fact.* Sure, it might change but probably not before the pigs have spread their pretty pink wings. Any situation where two people, two groups or two aspects of the same soul, each hold an assumption that is fact to one side and incomprehensible to the other, communication breaks down completely and irrevocably.

The second layer of belief is that of attitudes. These are the ideas we hold on to as true. They may not, we can admit, be true for everyone in the whole world, but they are true for us, as individuals. If an attitude is questioned, the response will be an emotional outburst of defence. These are the understanding we have taken on about the world which allow us to live the way that we do. If someone injects doubt into one of these attitudes, it shakes us. We have our stability and understandings invested in this world view and these are things worth fighting for.

Religious beliefs based on blind faith are attitudes. In debates between evangelical Christians and Pagans, the Pagans are often quite bewildered by the emotional upsurge of the Christians. Most Pagans would agree that their spirituality requires no blind faith: Paganism is an experiential religion, where very little if anything needs to be believed. Concepts are understood to be merely concepts, opinions and ideas of potentials, ever changing and growing, until some spirit of place or some deity leaps out and thumps you, sending those concepts into the factual level of assumptions. Thankfully, most Pagans also understand that these facts are different for everyone and dogma seldom arises.

Attitudes are the branches that grow out of the trunk of each assumption. A girl might hold as fact that men are attracted to women with big breasts and flat stomachs and fact number two is that she is shaped like a comice pear. On that basis, her crippling attitude is that she will never find a man who wants her. It's no good how much her gorgeous friend tells her she's wrong, *doesn't she understand that it's just going to be that way, because it's too embarrassing to be ugly and not worth the risk of having it said to your face by some bloke you're aching for?* Furthermore, if some guy says she's beautiful, he's lying. And if he lies on that score (which is painfully important), how could she ever trust him at all? That's a very real if rather simple or facetious example. The results, the symptoms, could be anything from a girl with very low self-esteem and a catalogue of failed relationships through to anorexia or drug addiction.

The key problem in any situation is the most fundamental assumption that can be found beneath the attitudes, attitudes which are throwing up effects like wheels spinning in wet mud. Working with that assumption, bringing it fully into the light of consciousness, picking away at the calcification of its rigidity and stagnation, and getting the knife into all the cracks where denial is lurking, we start to open up into new areas of freedom. It might well hurt.

Sometime it takes someone else to point out that an assumption isn't actually a fact of life according to agreed reality. It takes an objective observer to see where the 'facts' are chains and metal doors to our freedom and fulfilment. It's my view that *all* assumptions are potentially dissolvable and this is a cornerstone of my Druidry. (Find the paradigm beneath that one...)

The process tends to work so that just when we find a really fundamental belief and break it open, beneath it we find another. All these are attitudes, for at some point we will come across the blocking assumption which seems to sum up our whole lifetime, explaining every mistake and self-negation in its dreadful repeating pattern. It's not only a fact based upon some occurrence and adorned with attitudes which are our protective decisions, but often it is also compounded by its own paradox, pulling us in two ways. Perhaps these are the very reasons why we have chosen to incarnate: this pattern must be broken.

Only when we start to understand which motivations we hold deep inside us can we begin to live effectively, consciously creating our reality, evading the erratic and destructive landslides. Life need not be a minefield. Perhaps we don't want to be checking every step against our motivations and intentions, our formulated or intuited goals, but when we are working directly and consciously with our basic paradox our self-awareness allows us to know very distinctly when we've taken a wrong step. The panic kicks in when we've leapt off the wrong bank and, careering down the river at exhilarating speed, our whole being responds in a way which grabs our attention. We know that we're heading down the wrong river. At such times a terrifying decision needs to be made which can often create havoc, as a whole barn of corn, the wrong corn, goes up in smoke. We lean and capsize or hit the rocks at speed, spiralling out into a period of emptiness.

It's equally clear when we have made a right choice. And without the tension of our indecision, it is easier to lie back, to relax and let the energy rise, to open up and start to experience the process of living with every cell and every nerve in all its rich and sensuous vitality. Racing down on the current, we needn't be passive. If we open our eyes, we discover that the river is a maze of tributaries through which we can steer. The current will take us on even if we do nothing at all, yet just the slightest shift of our weight will adjust the course and take us off another way.

These decisions, the slight adjustments and the balancing, are all a part of this next point in our journey around the circle. We are now out in the west and the festival we have come to is that of the autumn equinox. These opportunities are the distinct qualities of the festival. It is a time of understanding and attuning to, moving with, perfect equilibrium.

Many who are particularly sensitive to the cycles and tides of the year will say that the two weeks surrounding the equinox are a time of tension, when the need to accept and have faith is critical, for any blindness caused by impatience or frustration can lead to disaster. The sun is slipping from Virgo into Libra. All the options that face us have to be assessed, weighed and balanced really accurately and efficiently, because if we are to stay with the tide there's not much leeway for making mistakes.

Unlike the spring equinox, between Pisces and Aries, when the surge of energy rising out of the earth to meet the warming sun is so strong that the actual point of balance often passes us right by, the autumn equinox seems to draw us directly towards it. Yet as we come nearer, assessing the situation, taking in all the information and reaching for our decisions, we rise and fall with the tides, shifting this way and that, in our search for balance. It is only at the moment of perfect equilibrium that there is, for an instant, the inspiration of stillness.

* * *

On the brow of a hill, four old beech trees stand and watch the world as it quietens around them, while out on the distant horizon the mists of evening merge with the sea. There is not a breath of wind. From the hedgerows that edge the fields beneath the hill comes the song of a wren, drifting out into the silence of the softening light. I move a little close to the grove of trees, the only noise the *shush* of the robes around me, and close my eyes so that I might sense more clearly.

I listen to the murmur and soft footfalls of the circle being cast by our hostess and her priest. Candles are lit and the spirits of place invoked with a song so tender it seems to float on the air, lingering. A sparkling of herbs is put onto the charcoal, then the musky smell of the incense drifts around me. I breathe in the balmy evening and open my eyes to the grove, touching my thigh, which is aching. I have been working too hard, spend too much time on the edge. The Druid before me enters the circle, greeted by the couple, and I watch as he walks to the altar to honour the guardians, his cloak of black velvet moving around him like a liquid shadow.

'Blessed be,' whispers the priest.

Welcome, sister of the Craft, the priestess bows and ushers me in. The grass is soft beneath my feet, the circle delineated with flowers of deep orange, red and russet, thick candles with fat flames flickering in the open air as I walk to the altar and acknowledge the spirits, bidding my greeting with a curtsy.

Five of us, blending traditions, have come to honour the place and the season of the year. I am pleased I came. It's good not to be leading the rite as I have the others of this festival – I can open myself better to its energy and flow, letting myself be taken. It was an honour to be invited.

I walk to my place at the edge of the circle to stand beneath the canopy of one of the beeches. As I turn to the centre, another stab of pain rips through my back. I shift my feet, trying not to let it show, and it floods like a bleeding through the muscles around my spine, searing the nerves. With all I am I focus, not allowing any tension to add to the pain, but for a couple of minutes it's excruciating. Waves of blackness pour over me, filled with stars. At last this breaks and with a surge the heat rises up, filling my cranium, and I can open, let it out, grounding and stilling myself once again, feeling my body cool, waiting for the next one.

I open my eyes and slowly my blurred vision clears as I watch the priestess, in a long robe of olive green, weaving her energy through the circle, consecrating and invoking the forces that create her world. Her priest holds the sword and she looks to him with a love that is more than that between man and woman. He kneels at her feet in perfect reverence and adoration as he calls through his love chant to his goddess, and she radiates that love, radiates the power and the absolute knowing, lifting him to his feet and sharing the kiss. As she speaks the words of her Lady her energy spills out through the circle. Closing my eyes again, I move through my body, relaxing every tension that would hold me closed, allowing every cell to absorb the high energy, the air charged by the presence, feeling myself glow.

The rite is beautiful. When the time arrives, one by one, we walk to the centre and lay our offerings, our gifts of the harvest, around the altar. It is a flat rock, laid with a silken cloth of deep sea blue and set with the tools of their ritual practice. Crimson plums, purple black damsons, acorns, orange and red rowan-berries, apples, blackberries and corn dollies, a round loaf of bread flecked with sunflower and poppy seeds – each offering given by a priest on his or her knees, whispering words of deep thanksgiving. As I empty my basket of rosehips and elderberries, tears slide down my cheeks, tears of pain and of thanks. Another cycle of the wheel is closing, another year coming to its end, and yet again how very different I am after such a journey. How much love I have felt and been able to give, love that has shown that I've never truly known the power of love before. And how much I have learnt and found there is yet to learn, freeing my soul to express its desire. How much beauty I have shared, such rich laughter and ecstasy. How can I possibly offer thanks for so much?

With my heart so open, the energy that's flowing between my soul and the altar rock, rooted into the earth, bonds us together. I whisper my dedication for another year of learning and devotion to my gods, feeling all too clearly what I still have not achieved despite all the help from this world and the worlds beyond.

A hand gently touches my shoulder and with its strength I rise from my knees and move from the altar, my body burning with another wave of pain, my eyes stinging with tears. It is Seabhac. He stands, in his beautiful dignity, gazing out through the beeches to the western horizon. The sun has sunk low, a deep bronze that washes the sky with red. Filled with the smell of the soil and the richness of our abundance, filled with energy of the dark forest beginning to turn inwards, filled with the scent of the grass and the bread on the altar, the juice of the elderberries that stains my fingers like blood, I call within me through that swelling of my heart and the heat in my spine. *My Lord, my Lord of the highest light, my Lord of the Sun, O ancient father, I give you such thanks for all you have given me! Your inspiration and your deepest warmth…But what is this pain?*

I sink back to my knees, surrendering to Seabhac as I am drawn up as if I were breathing in. Another stab takes my breath away and I fall to the earth, aware that a part of me is holding on, my hands tense as if clenched, and I consciously let go, not knowing what will happen next. I am suddenly hurled forward, leaving my body as if thrown – and pulled. The speed makes me dizzy, getting quickly worse, the pressure inside and from outside taking me to the edge of my endurance. I feel the need to scream and the stars under my eyelids are now flickering lights, warning me how close I am to blacking out completely. I thing I'm going to throw up and I want to cry for help but have no idea how, no time to think. Seabhac's voice is steady, *Go through, go on...* And in the very moment when I am sure that I will lose consciousness, the pain in my head like a fighter jet engine, melting my spine like an oil-spill fire, I manage to shift, to move just a finger, push against the clenching. Instantly I crash dive through a wall of flaming light, spinning out into a void of endless darkness, and I am held. I lift my face and feel the touch of a soft and wizened hand. *You made it,* he whispers.

In my head, in my blood, there is a new sensation: a bright clarity, even and rich with oxygen. The pain is gone – just the memory remains, like an old schoolbook, dogeared, once discarded into a dusty corner, now somehow a precious reminder of what no longer exists. I am filled with an extraordinary calm. Tears flow down my cheeks like cool mountain streams and, opening my eyes, I watch them fall into the grass, splashing on the pink edges of daisies closed for the night. For a moment I am overwhelmingly thankful that this is a circle of elders, that nobody in their *naïveté* has run to check that I'm OK. I have simply slid to the ground and the rite has carried on. I look up and find the sun has caught hold of the others in the circle, too, and without a word they are drifting towards the western edges of the sacred circle. Someone turns to me and smiles gently.

Seabhac lifts me to my feet and though I stumble, exhausted, my body is amazingly light. I almost float as we walk to join them.

Did I really do that? Break through the pain? Dan I do it again?
Yes, priestess.

For a long time we gaze in silence at the beauty that is painted wide across the sky, touching the flat horizon of the sea between the hills. There is powerful sense of a long day experiencing its own ending.

Then, with the gentlest of notes, our priestess begins to sing. I cannot understand her words, clipped and strong in the Gaelic tongue, but her voice is like honey. After a while a priest joins her, following her melodies with his flute, then another picks up his old bodhran and skips then strides the rhythm so my feet start to tap and my hips slowly move. The sound seems to ricochet through my bones and my eyes meet those of the other priestess. She is holding her heart, her face streaked with tears, and between us there pours an ocean of knowing. A woman in spirit is dancing beside us, moving over the grass like a seagull above the waves, and the rising and falling of the harmonies curl their way through me like smoke from a taper. The energy that throbs in my head slowly tumbles and rolls and forms itself into sound.

As the golden disc sinks into the mist of the horizon, out on that hill, five folk of the old Craft and a dozen from the spirit worlds are swaying and softly singing, dancing and watching and stamping the rhythms of the earth, calling out their love, their grief and their relief, preparing to travel on into the emptiness beyond the dusk, when the heart is poised between night and day, the magical twilight, invoking the devas and the ancient ones to make the journey with them, enchanting their gods, held within the arms of the grove of old beech trees.

* * *

Finding a way through pain is the motivation for so much of life. The whole business uses up incredible amounts of our global resources in terms of energy and time and human potential, reaching from the world of science across into religion. The Druid philosophy is no exception. While a Druid is perhaps less likely to reach for a bottle of pills or illegal drugs, the focus in Druidcraft is clearly on the way in which we can reach beyond.

Pain calls for two responses: tools which allow us to cope with it in the immediate moment and tools which guide us to understand the cause and how to release it. The former is a process of knowing our own bodies, knowing how to stretch and relax key muscles, knowing how to access the body's own endorphins, while the latter is the longer work of finding the block which is holding the energy under pressure. The level on which a Druid works (from the intellectual through the psychotherapeutic to the shamanistic) will determine how deeply he can travel into the pain, be it his own or that of the person he is guiding, or how long he can carry it within his own system.

While people who have acute sensitivity are often able to help and guide others, relieving through their vision and their clarity of sensing the problems that are triggering emotional and/or physical pain in others, very often these sensitive people experience a great deal of pain themselves. A sensitivity which offers the ability to sense earth energy, auric imbalances, past lives and spirit presences can bring with it a sensitivity to food, pollution, barometric pressure and emotional disturbance that makes living in a busy world difficult to sustain. A great many highly sensitive Craft people, some of whom work actively in healing, are thrown by the tides of emotion around them, retaining their clarity but needing to cope with the effects their interactions are having on their own health. Those who have worked with death and the dying process, who can still slide through into the spirit worlds, are also susceptible to the wash of pain that exists where souls are stuck between life and death. Learning how to live with pain, how to process what is picked up from the collective unconsciousness and from those who come in search of help is an important part of the training for the Druid (and any priesthood).

While not an inevitability, pain is common for those whose work requires the journey between the world of the spirit and the world of agreed reality. For some it is possible to learn how to close down or cut off from various levels of sensory input, working either in one world or in the other. This is easier on the whole for those who have consciously worked at opening up their abilities. For others, the act of cutting off is a painful process in itself, provoking a stressful tension in the same way that temporary blindness might in someone who has always been sighted. These people tend to live in a sensitive and precarious balance, existing with a foot in both worlds, acting always as a bridge between the two.

When a Druid works with pain as a part of the shamanic toolkit, using it to dance deeper into the realm between the worlds, it is the edge that is important. Like the razor-sharp blade of a sacred knife, the intensity of pain takes the priest to the edge of her endurance, to the edge of sanity, and it is work that can be extraordinarily potent. It draws the priest into the critical experience of the shift where joy is lost to suffering, peace is lost to war, creativity plays with chaos, purpose with insanity. To make changes on this blade edge and then move into the spirit world or into the physical, holding the threads of those changes pulls them tight into manifestation.

So it is that in Druidcraft profound understanding is needed about the nature of pain. We begin by acknowledging that the natural state of the spirit is one of bliss. This is our goal – it is our communication with the earth, it is the touch of the gods, the divine inspiration of perfect freedom and existence beyond the need for trust where there is perfect relationship. Anything less than bliss is the ache of the journey, with all the colours of its emotional experience.

To clarify our understanding, the wide spectrum of emotion

is divided into seven levels. Six of these are the 'negative' (the crises of the journey), while the other is 'positive', the goal achieved, the bliss which stretches up into infinite potential. While each one of these seven is a distinct primary emotion, it's the transition points between them that are the most interesting places.

At the bottom of the spectrum, the vibration is so low it is often missed entirely, passed right by. This is the realm of the dark unknown, the unconscious, inhabited by the monsters that lurk in the shadows. In Christian terminology it is the place of the Devil. In Druidcraft, where no embodiment of evil exists and where the darkness is known to be a place of nourishment and source energy, this part of our world is seen simply as that which we deny exists, consciously or subconsciously. It is a place of stupor, of non-action.

If we are able to move at all, then out of this denial we rise up to the next level, which is that of apathy. Here we've come to understand that an issue or belief does exist, but the energy is barely enough to activate a response. We can sink under its weight back into denial or, where there is sufficient energy to shrug or even throw it off, we can let its density fall onto us again and again. Apathy is the place of depression, where we keep giving up.

If we are able in some way to stir the energy from there, we find ourselves crawling into the realms of grief. Grief is not the pain of having lost, but the struggle of keeping hold of something which we know we must let go. If the vibration sinks, we lose hope again and continue to allow the abuse of our passivity to batter us.

When the vitality rises to a degree which enables us to stretch out of the grief, we come to the level of fear. We have let go and now we're scared. There's nothing to hold on to. We feel alone.

From fear we can either slip and grab back on, or else we can allow the energy to rise up to where it shifts into the next emotion: anger, anger at our weakness and our lack of directed progress, anger at the vulnerability that we see within ourselves or witness around us. But the expression of our anger can be frightening and our energy can fall again, back into fear. Most people are more aware of this transition, between anger and fear, than of any other. It's at this level that many relationships exist, as it is the place that holds the balance between victim and aggressor.

When anger rises, the vibration quickening, what kicks in is the sixth level, which is pain. Pain isn't often referred to as an emotion, yet as energy that is patterned by our thoughts (and our subconscious belief systems) it can be seen as emotion and addressed in the same way.

Most of us have known how pain can evoke anger. Expressing the anger can relieve the pain, yet at the same time it slows our energy, lowers the vibration. On the other hand, moving the other way and rising, being able to walk through the pain, to dive clear through the wall, we reach bliss, ecstasy. We're released into the worlds of pure potential.

Anyone who has known extreme pain has experience of either controlling the nightmare with sheer aggression, or surrendering to it in a wild craze of exhilaration. Where the pain is not well managed and is only one part of a catalogue of difficult emotions which need addressing, there is also the option of slipping down through fear into the death wish of apathy, or suppressing it with denial or drugs, but this cut out is not so easily available at the highest levels of pain. Many women who have been through childbirth without drugs have experience of this first hand. Warriors train to use pain as a source of energy which can be accessed and used to counter attack. People who live with chronic pain, because of disease or disability or hypersensitivity, learn ways of working with its high energy too. This is the difference between feeling the pain and suffering it. We learn to deserve our emotional energy, feel it, use it, flow through it.

Indeed, our movement between the levels is like a game of snakes and ladders, our excitement to reach that last little box being the craving for the state of peace and joy.

If denial is the darkness of the unknown, then joy is the pure light of knowing. It can of course be overwhelming and kick us right back to fear – where there is the brightest light we have no place to hide from ourselves or from anybody else and furthermore the shadows can be alarmingly distinct. Beneath the limelight is a daunting place to stand. In religious terms, we could say that this is the place of grace, the realm of God, heaven.

Druids don't accept that such exquisite bliss is inaccessible while still on Earth and in body. Most people have experienced at least glimpses of this joy, the ecstasy which is their perfect freedom. But while we struggle through our negative and self-negating beliefs, it tends to come spontaneously and be out of our control. Yet the more we experience it, the more addicted we become, the more we want – and on demand. The Druid smiles at his apprentice, saying, 'If you learn with dedication and commitment, you'll be able to walk into that space whensoever you wish.' It could be said that the paths of Druidcraft all lead to that one place.

* * *

Magic is not a great concern within Druidcraft, in terms of the wizardry of raising power in order to effect change. The focus – on the joy that is the touch of the gods, on the *awen* of divine inspiration – steers the practice towards personal transformation, with the understanding that the clarity that comes with healing allows us to create our world more effectively.

Every day with our every action we are creating the reality in which we live, forming and colouring it through our perspectives, with the freedoms and limitations that are our own belief systems. Yet with paradigms that drain our energy, redirecting our actions with their own quiet agendas, what we are creating appears to us both far from our control and not what we consciously want.

A rather simplistic example might be that in the belief that I am overweight, I go on a diet. But if my attitude towards myself is a sure belief that I am fat, however much I diet, even if I lose a little weight, I shall still – according to me – be 'fat'. Either I put the weight right back on or I starve myself to skin and bone – unless that paradigm shifts. Similarly, if I believe that my father doesn't love me, even though I may compromise my true self to the very limit in trying to please him and gain his positive acknowledgement, I will never see that love. He could absolutely adore me and I would simply not believe or feel it.

Our belief systems colour the energy through which we live and create, giving the energy its level of vibration, its quality of emotion. Though it can be hard to see clearly what is being made with the very low levels of apathetic emotion (except the swamp of inertia), by the time we reach the pitch of fear it is clear what we're creating. Many create vast tracts of their lives with the fuel of anger. It could be said that using any vibration of energy is viable and that all one must focus on is the distinction between self-pity (with its integral self-destruction) and the peace of self-confidence. There is a distinct difference, none the less, between something which is created with low vibrational energy and something created with high energy. It is a difference which is so obvious in the manifestation that it can easily be perceived by anyone who has made something through love and freedom.

In Druidcraft there are many ways in which we raise the level of emotion, some of which have been described in these pages. Through the deeply healing journey of the Druidcraft circle, through self-discovery, honesty and clarity, we come to a point where it is possible to climb with ease into the ecstatic, and after a while that state is sustainable for longer and longer periods of time. At first it burns extraordinary amounts of calories until nourishment can be absorbed more effectively at high levels.

Physiologically we know that it's impossible to remain angry or scared, or in any negative emotional state, if the body is relaxed. Pain is also released when the body relaxes. I'm not declaring that this is a simple action – it can be extremely difficult to achieve. None the less any vibration of energy which is lower than joyful is held in the body in a way which is restricting. By relaxing the muscles, relaxing the nervous system, we allow our energy to flow in its natural inclination and so the vibration rises.

Many of the ways in which we actively lift energy in Druidcraft are purposefully and definitively designed to raise confidence and personal empowerment, working through the beauty and imagery of ritual, through visualization, through the expression of love and reverence, in poetry and song, in dance and prayer. They begin by affirming our safety in the caring arms of the spirit of the sacred grove, then gently take us to a place where we feel sufficiently assured to trust in the process. From that point we can surrender, we can relax. Our energy rises and we are taken on the currents of natural law, fast and clear, perfectly attuned to our highest intention.

It must be said that some ceremonies don't work specifically on raising high-level energy, but simply on accumulating energy. Rituals working magic on this basis are either best avoided at all costs or else need extremely cautious handling, as essentially they run the risk of being entirely erratic. If someone is raising a force of low-level energy, such as anger, and knows what they are doing, they could well be extremely dangerous. If someone is doing it without understanding what they are doing, the same is true. Sadly this is often the case, with magic being worked by those who don't have the clarity to see that the energy being used is not sufficiently clear. Energy can, however, be neutralized with careful handling, its pattern shattered and specifically reworked. These things are easier when only one or two souls and their complex psyches are involved. Evoking low-vibrational energy on purpose might be done reasonably only in a healing situation, with as much clarity and guidance as is available, with full knowledge of who is present, the collective motivation and intention, and most probably alone in a well secured and consecrated circle.

Raising low energy is easy, after all. It is simply a case of provoking the emotion. Any good orator knows that – and can wind up an audience in just the way he chooses. It is because so much damage can be done by someone who understands the human psyche and is clear in their own motivations and goals that the magical arts have found their way into serious disrepute – as has politics. It is also the reason why training in these ways needs to be so rigorous, woven with the need for respect and the understanding of equality, reverence and natural law.

In a beautiful grove, bathing in the exquisite light of joyful energy, filled with awe and the songs of love and wonder, clear and certain, committed to a path and surrendering to the flow, the energy that we have raised, energy which is both the impetus of our inspiration and the fuel of our journeying, radiates from deep within us. As we take our creative control and steer through the ever-dividing waterways and tributaries, it is our intention that guides us – and not only our conscious intention.

* * *

It is quiet. An empty beach is early October. I walk along the sand, watching the pools of my footfalls darken then shimmer with water and disappear. Coming over the ridge, the last rays of the setting sun were playing on the horizon, sparkling on the water, and now the air is changing, becoming emptier yet thicker, as if turning inside out. Responding to the twilight, my body too seems to open, to invert. I walk with my spirit, my body held safe and deep within its core, leaving no footprints upon the sand.

I watch the rippling surge of the tide, the gentle waves slipping up towards me then receding, the little water sprites and faeries scampering up to touch my boots, then running away giggling. I smile and reach down as if to tease them, cool water splashing around my fingers. I breathe in the salty dampness of the wind then shake like a cat coming out of the rain, releasing my hair from my coat and scarf, shaking out into the wind my head, shoulders, spine and hips, and I breathe in again. Breathing out, the tension of a long day slips away down the sand with the tittering sea undines, disappearing beneath the breaking of another wave. My body receding, I am back within my spirit form. Again I breathe, letting go, letting go more and more, and again, until I start to feel the freedom in my limbs and in the brittle-baked edges of my soul that I am sweetly aware of in the lightness of my spirit.

I gaze out over the water and feel its rising and falling, its breathing rhythm that draws me in, calling me, enchanting me. And I hear the songs of a distant part of me moving with that rhythm, as if spinning in slow motion, taking me in. I remember as a child watching the spirit of the water as she rose up from the ocean floor in the form of a woman, lifting with her arms the towering waves like a robe that fell around her, her hair wild and white, her eyes a vivid blue. I watched those 20-foot breakers come crashing down on the sand like divine fists of thunder, heard her laugh at her own power and laugh at the little men that ran to drag in the fishing boats, and saw her smile at my awe before she sank beneath the waves.

As a child in the Caribbean I learnt to love her and to fear her. Her name was Yemaya and I saw both her wealth, the rich and colourful abundance she held within her dark womb, and her lack of compassion for humanity. As a student of the old ways, my love shifted the fear into respect as she taught me how to bathe in her beauty.

As I breathe with her now, my soul lulled into an exquisite

calm, bubbles of sweet vitality start to rise and I cannot resist. I slip from my body and into the chilling water, and then I am running, chasing after the tide, little paws splattering over the wet sand. When it turns and a wave comes for me I stretch up my long neck to avoid it, shake the splashes from my whiskers and dive. In that beautiful fluid motion, my body ripples and weaves, undulating like the currents, as I swim out far and strong. Twisting and rolling, I play and come up for air and lie floating on my back, watching the sky getting darker, the first stars blinking light. Then, heading back, I dive and brush against something quickly slipping past, turning to chase in the dim light, exhilarated and free.

Bad time to hunt, sister otter.

Who said that? I whirl around, looking for the source of that voice, up through the water surface, heart racing. But up here it is so still, so incredibly calm, I forget the chase. Yes, it is late. A distant chill shudders through me, drawing me out of the moment. In the slow blink of my eyes, I am suddenly back in my human form, shivering on the shore.

Bobcat, you must look after yourself!

The shimmering spirit of Silverwolf stands beside me, holding me.

Yes, I concede. *I am sorry.*

Move, my love. Your body is frozen. Move, physically.

It takes me a minute to get my thought processes to connect with my nervous system. *Was I gone so very long? It only seemed like a minute.*

It was around 25. But the wind is cold, your feet are wet and you are tired.

I walk, a little awkwardly, up beyond the reach of the tide. My legs are wobbly and my neck stiff. He watches me go, then disappears into the darkening air. I wonder at how badly I seem to balance the different worlds I live in, confusing realities, forgetting to care for the body I work in.

Balance. I look up at the sea, the breaking waves, the water racing up the shore and slipping back. There is so much water inside me, it is as if it were a more natural home, a place of my source, a place of my ancestors. I remember my childhood on the warm beaches of the tropics, sleeping in hammocks to the sound of the ocean's breathing, the laughing of the undines playing with tumbling shells and pebbles. I look towards the cliff, the track a way back down the beach that would take me up to my car, to my life, my future and all that is expected of me, all that I long to achieve. For a moment I wonder if I ought to get back, curl up in the warmth, face my pile of correspondence or the half-written article that overwhelms my desk, snarling for attention.

If a suggestion contains the word 'ought', I have learned to disregard it.

I bend down and undo the laces of my boots, taking them and my sodden socks off. I start to walk down to the dark wet sand where the sea meets the land and the games are played of kiss and turn away; where the past and the future push and pull, give and take; where my footsteps disappear.

It is the end of a hard day. A new cycle is ready to begin in the quiet of the darkness that is settling around me and I stand in the gap, the intangible moment that is now, in the stillness, yet where it is ever changing. In that place I cast a sacred circle, dancing with a fluid grace my invocations and my reverence to the elementals and the spirits of place, letting my mind, which throughout the day has been organizing, concentrating, formulating, be free to dream and play, free to find a place of silence, letting my emotions release, stretching the energy through my body and out, as I reach out, swirl and kick, tense and glide, feeling the extremes of my reasonings and my instinct, the instants of compromise throughout my self-justifications, and letting them go. Through my movement, I balance the flows and tides within my soul, dancing the pathways of the sacred circle that run from the winds of the east, where high in the clear air our minds are caught up with thoughts, over to the swell of the ocean in the west, where our power is held by the strength of our feelings. I play with the balance over the pivot of the centre, now embraced by my temple, encircled with the light. My voice rises smoothly, like a cormorant from the ocean, hardly seen in the twilight, as I sing to my Lady of the energy that surges through my body, filling the space that is the gap between who I was and who I could be.

The wind rises and the waves break more substantially, the water splashing around me as I move and sway, half entranced, lifting into the air in flight and diving down into the water in joy and certainty. *O Lady of the Deep Sea, feel me as I feel you! Fill me as I fill you! O Lady of the Deep Sea!*

My heart pounding, I stop still, breathing hard, somehow held, and through my trance I open my eyes to see the moon, its waning crescent rising over the hills down the coast. The sky is dark and mapped with stars. Automatically I follow the lines to find Vega and open my heart to honour some strange knowing. Then I turn to the moon and bow to the beauty, closing my eyes. I sink down and touch the sand.

Through the mists that lead into the otherworld, I hear that extraordinary sound that is almost music but can barely be heard, though it fills my soul just as if a harp were being played in the depths of my womb. I wait, desperately wanting to open my eyes and my anticipation builds so that I am sure I shall explode. The softest touch of a finger runs down my cheek, like a tear.

Blessed with love, he whispers.

A part of me knows that my perceiving his being depends upon the extent to which I can hold that state of deep surrender. So, through my exhilaration, I breathe deeply and relax, letting my energy rise further, and open my eyes.

My Lord. I bow.

Priestess of beauty, priestess of the night.

His energy is almost androgynous – such beauty and dignity, every movement leaving silvery colours in the darkness. He walks around me, awakening every nerve in my body as if his hands were caressing me. He whispers, *You are asking to be left alone.*

That is not what I truly want.

Then do not ask, for your loneliness will freeze you from the core.

I want to say 'I'm sorry' or 'I didn't mean to' or explain that I just get so tired and my body hurts. But I manage to avoid the crap and ask aloud, 'What is it I want?'

What is it you want?

He lifts my face with a finger, so that I am looking into his black eyes that are sparkling with starlight. I can hardly speak and the words I manage are a mash of feelings.

He whispers again, *What is it you want, priestess?*

I don't want to feel abandoned any more, I want to feel cared for.

His gaze is like a knife slipping slowly into my solar plexus.

Do I care for you?

I want to blank out, to shake my head and know that he will disappear, but Seabhac is behind me. Somehow I know I have gone too far this time. I wouldn't be able to forget this time, to kid myself I'd got somewhere. It's time to face the truth.

No, I say. *Well, yes.*

A massive pain stabs into my kidneys, making me flinch, all too aware of my physical body now. I feel a cool breeze around my face and, suddenly disoriented, I open my eyes wide, breathing fast.

He is standing at a distance, light shimmering, his form vague, drifting, his eyes pinning me to the sand. He moves a hand, leaving streaks in the air, and his words slide into my head again.

Do I care for you? Do I?

No! I scream. *No!*

I close my eyes and suddenly feel his breath on my cheek, his fingers touching my lips.

Who am I?
You are love.
I am.
You reflect me.
I do.
So what is this I feel? This sense ... this beautiful sense of you?
And who is caring for you?
Every nerve in my body is tingling, aching for release.
I have known you for so long. Teach me who you are, now that I can listen –
I am within you and I am existent without you. I am Myestia, to whom you call through the light of the moon.
You are such inspiration. I honour you with all that I am.
Then dance, my priestess. For me. Dance.

I bow to him and start to circle, to spin and weave, then glide, turning, stretching, balancing, balancing, as he holds my hand and his smile plays with my limbs like a length of fine silver silk. My dance is alive with every twist and turn of my every existence, and it shines with my love for him and I move my body so that every knot of confusion and tie of longing is broken through into joy and sweet exhilaration as he whispers in the breeze, *You are free, you are free.*

My dance gets faster as I circle him and lose myself, feeling myself, hearing the pulse of the earth and my heart pounding, and he shouts to me, *What do you want?* And in my trance I cry, Freedom! and he pulls me towards him.

For an instant I feel the impact of my body against his and in that instant I am overwhelmed with such a flood of release that when I come to a moment later my first thought is that I've wet myself.

I'm not sure if I have. I'm sitting where I landed in the sand just above the lap of the tide. It's very dark and I am alone. I am so acutely wide awake that I start to laugh. For a moment I don't move, then gently I get to my feet. I feel stiff, then suddenly cold, though my head is burning up.

In a deep silence, I move around my circle. The tide has obviously risen right over it and is now receding. There is no trace of my working. In whispers I call aloud my thanks, my farewells to the spirits, to the elementals, uncasting the sacred space almost in slow motion, as if in a state of deep thought, though no thoughts are present in my conscious mind.

When I look up and feel again the world all around me, my circle open, I feel the wind that is whistling down the beach, blowing through my clothes. Seabhac is waiting for me with a look that is a mixture of disapproval and satisfaction, and I grin. I don't know if I've ever been quite so wide awake.

Picking up my boots from where the tide had scattered them, I make my way through the darkness back to the path that winds though the heather and up to the road. Out of somewhere words are sliding together: I have found exactly what I need to finish that bloody article.

IX

EXQUISITE RELEASE

SAMHAIN: IN THE DARKNESS THE CYCLE ENDS TO BEGIN AGAIN

I do nothing. Having set up the circle, with blood red roses and springs of berried yew, three candles burning in the cauldron in the centre, calling to the spirits and the guardians of the directions, I stand back to let her do as she wishes. The rain pours down around us, thundering on the corrugated iron roof of the barn, splashing into the puddles I can see through the broken slats of the door. The bank of straw bales behind me keeps the wind from chasing its tail right through us, but its howls make me shiver and, though the sacred space is warm with energy and spirit, there's a loneliness of the world out there in the midst of the storm. I am glad to be who I am.

At first she moves about the circle, feeling her way, tiptoeing, unsure of what to do with her hands, her fingers touching the air, stopping as if listening to her own heartbeat. From here on my role is to be that of witness to her rite while holding the sanctity of the sacred space. I empty myself so that my presence is minimal and chant internally the spells of my invisibility, drifting in my long black robe into the darkness of the circle's edge.

I have guided these rites with scripted precision, I have flowed and ad libbed right through the whole thing. When we'd discussed it, Jude had frowned in horror. 'How can I pretend to be moving into a new era of my life if I have to have you telling me all the steps I should be taking? No, I'm gonna do this. And I have to bloody do it alone. My way.' She's slammed down her mug of coffee, spilling it over the table. 'Shit.'

Then she'd looked up, smiling so that the lines on her face accentuated every nuance of her expression, excited as a schoolgirl yet filled with so much of the world. She giggled, suddenly more the Jude that I was beginning to know. 'Is that OK? I mean by you? Is that allowed?'

I'd laughed so much my belly had ached. 'Screw what's allowed! Everything's allowed so long as it's wrapped around your intention! That's the whole point!'

She'd put her face in her hands and breathed in deeply, sighing from her toes, 'Oh God. Oh shit, this is wonderful.'

Now in her barn, a sanctuary within the storm, she starts to stretch, to reach out and feel the space around her, the lack of restrictions. I watch her as she moves, acting out her life, and so much of what she plays tugs at the cords of my own heart and womb, and her steps slide and jar and skip as she starts to dance, as if measuring who she is and who she can be, finding the freedom of exquisite flight. Suddenly, almost startled, she stops, looking up into thin air at the face of the man who takes her heart, who clips her wings and turns away, and like a duckling she paddles around after his shadow, devoted, imprinted, until her pride is given form as her belly swells. She dances, heavy with child after child, her body exploding with love and nourishment, then the chaos of time chasing time chasing time, around and around, busy and retorting, trying to keep order, trying to keep a sense of self. They are gone, so quick, the children grown. And where is he, the man who clipped her wings so long ago? As if blind she wanders the sacred circle, unaware of its beauty, seeming to stay within its bounds purely by chance. I close my eyes and affirm its casting, strengthening the ritual space, holding her state.

She stands absolutely still for a long, long time, the candle-light flickering in the twilight of the barn. She opens her mouth, stretched her mouth and her neck, and breathes, consciously breathes, then tries again, opening her mouth, this time making a sound. I realize that til now she has moved in utter silence. Again she makes a sound, freeing as if for the first time her ability to do so, and she starts to look around her, as if noticing the world clearly. Then she moves and starts to talk, just jabbering about anything.

'Yes, this is me, this is very definitely me, no, nobody else, this is certainly me, so that's about that, and whatever that is I don't really care, because this is me and I shall be that, which is me, uh-huh, certainly most definitely me.'

So she goes on, and I have to hold in my giggles, tears welling up in my eyes, and remain out of her space, but she notices me for the first time since she began and walks towards me and stands before me with the most beautiful smile. Briefly but so warmly we hug, and she catches me up in her energy and we dance together around the circle, around and spinning, laughing and whooping, like children happy children.

When we come to a stop, she breathes in her courage and turns to the centre, crouching down by the cauldron. I am about to move back again, but she gestures for me to join her, so I sit beside her on the concrete and hay of the floor and for a moment she holds my hand.

Now she speaks aloud, to herself, to the gods, to me, about what is happening, about the changes in her life, with the kids gone and her marriage uncertain, about her love for Mike and her need for freedom, about her pottery and her home, her dogs and her dying mother. She speaks, very clearly yet almost dreamily, of the ending of her bleeding tides, about what she feels it means and what she hopes it will bring.

'I am thankful for all I have,' she nods, quietly. 'But... there is little of what I have been that I would want to carry on being. I am ready for change. So I call to the gods,' and she cries out 'whoever the hell you are,' smiling at me broadly, 'I call... to the great universal life force. Hear me. Guide me. Help me to change. Help me to accept the changes in my body as being the balance of the changes in my soul, as signposts for my future, my different creative potential.' For a moment she closes her eyes. 'And so, in recognition of all of that, I have something which I think rather symbolizes the releasing process. Or a few things actually, if that's OK. Bobcat, can we..?' She gestures to the altar. I take more charcoal and replenish the incense, refilling the chalice with consecrated water. 'Thanks.'

From her bag she pulls out a wad of paper, perhaps 20 pages of typescript, which she lowers over the candles in the cauldron.

'Here is a story. It's a review of my life, with all its crap and lack of honesty.' She sighs deeply. 'Let it burn.'

'Spirits of fire,' I whisper, 'take the essence of these pages and by your art let there be transformation. In the name of the goddess, by the power of three, so may it be.'

Flames lick into the paper and suddenly it's alight. She holds it as long as she can then drops it to the concrete, where it continues to burn in a burst of light. Pieces lift off and up into the air, and we are both on our feet, catching glowing fragments, stamping out flames that land too near the dry hay, laughing and spinning, then relighting bits that haven't burnt, until all that is left is a shell of grey paper which she crushes with her hand.

In the quiet beneath the pounding of the rain, our laughter settling around us, we sit again beside that cauldron and from the bag she brings out a sculptured head. It's a self portrayal, rough in rich red clay, with wide eyes and lips pursed into a doubting smile, the hair a mess, as if she were in her own private storm. She sits for a while and looks at the piece. She runs a finger over the face, smooth, not yet wrinkled, touching the cheekbones, the mouth, with almost a caress, a parting touch of affection

'This I would like to return to the earth,' she whispers. 'Can we leave the circle?'

I nod. 'In a sacred manner.'

'Come on then.' She gets to her feet and waits for me to open a gateway in the circle cast, usher her through and close it behind us. Dragging the door open, the wind howls its greeting and she grins at me as I consider the rain that's pelting down, the track now a shallow river flowing down into the meadows. I am not dressed for this.

Go on priestess. You can sit by the fire later.

Thanks, Seabhac. Thoughtful as ever.

Out into the storm we run, splashing down the road and through a gate in the lodge into the orchard. Her Jacobs sheep are in the next field and the grass is over my knees. 'Over there,' she yells pointing to the far top corner where trees are silhouetted against the black tumbling clouds.

Through the long grass we run, me holding up my robes with one hand and keeping my hair out of my eyes with another. Jude, in her jeans, is across the field in no time.

It isn't like this being a priest in the Church of England.

Shut up, Seabhac. I'm with it. Sodden wet to my knickers, but with it.

When I reach her, she is kneeling on the ground beneath an old apple tree. The energy is quite beautiful and I lift my face to the skies, letting the vibrancy soak into me as I reach for my centre, catching my breath.

'This is where Robert was conceived,' she yells through the rain.

'Your eldest? I didn't realize you've been here that long. How old is he?'

'Twenty-five. It was my uncle's place then. I brought Mike up here, the first time, not long after we were married. We made love in the moonlight, under this tree.'

Beautiful. Calm. So distant from this storm. The last of the apples on the tree are heavy, shimmering with the rain. Into a crook at its base Jude places her clay head. 'It's not fired,' she yells. 'It'll just... gradually dissolve, break up.'"

I'm about to say something, to whisper to the dryad, to ask that great magic be done by this action, when I am flooded by a warmth and a voice whispers through the rain, *No more is needed. It is done.*

Thank you.

Jude's hand reaches for mine and holds it tight.

'OK?' I ask.

'Shit. Yes.' She closes her eyes for a moment and I sense her tears falling but they are mixed with the rain that is streaming down our faces. 'OK.'

'Ready?'

'Yup. Next?'

'Let's go and close the circle.'

'Yup. Back to the barn.'

In the haven of its shelter, with the rain thundering down on the corrugated iron roof, there's a strong feeling that something important has been achieved. We are both absolutely drenched and my bobcat instinct is to shake, head to tail. Jude's expression when she sees the state of me is quite wonderful.

'Oh Christmas!' She's giggling, then she laughs and laughs. 'I'm so sorry!'

'Hey, it's all part of the job -' *Not a word, Seabhac!*

'Oh no, oh hell, here comes another rush!' She's pulling off her sodden jumper, her face beetroot red and shiny wet as the hot flush rises, and now I can't stop laughing too as, struggling to get it off, her muffled voice yells through the bulk of wet wool, 'What am I supposed to do with these damn things? Direct the energy? Follow it, didn't you say? Oh shit!'

* * *

The Rite of the Elder, which for women is often called the Croning Rite, is another important one which in our culture is all too often suffocated with taboos and concepts of weakness. Women are offered hormone replacements so as to delay the natural process instead of being honoured and guided through the turmoil of change. A man's transition into the third phase of life is often felt to be less specific: he has no evidence in the form of bleeding that comes to an end. For a man conscious of his own being, though, the transition is not so vague. His moving from the warrior status to that of elder is equally important, establishing and affirming his continuing value in society even after the younger men are beginning to oust him in the hunting grounds. Feelings of competition are naturally calmed when the changes are acknowledged, by the young and the old, openly or personally, and new values affirmed, new relationships nurtured.

In the same way that menstruation is considered to be a curse, its beginning not celebrated, its magic no longer learnt, the menopause is also dreaded, barely tolerated or denied. Yet we lose so very much in rejecting these gifts and the spiritual teachings that are integral to both the bleeding and its ending, separating ourselves from the natural world once again. And this time we are turning away not from an external world but nature as it exists within our own bodies, as the tides of our hormones reflect the tides of the moon – in both women and men. In our denial, not only do we lose opportunities for spiritual growth, but also the ways in which such turbulent changes can be managed.

The hot flushes a woman experiences through the menopause are a good example – they can be very alarming. Yet this is energy that can be accessed. This isn't to say the flushes will always be entirely comfortable, but instead of being innerving or embarrassing they can become an exciting part of the process, giving a sense of riding the white water, guiding the raft, being at the front and directing the journey as the changes emerge in body and soul. As the woman learns just how to manage and steer the raft, the rushes no longer feel so harsh and destabilizing but become a source of increasing confidence. Relaxing into the current becomes a real possibility, knowing that it's taking us

SPIRITS OF THE SACRED GROVE

according to our own intent. Furthermore, in the action of relaxing, the energy can rise higher.

While understanding the many levels and stimuli of our emotions does allow us a different kind of creative control and potential for release within that control, getting to grips with the deeper source of energy that flows directly from our spirit takes us to another level entirely.

Without the provocation of a significant physical or spiritual change – such as the menopause, an accident or a religious initiation – the essential life energy pulses within us, half-sleeping, alert for danger yet not motivated into the fullness of its expression. The Sanskrit word for this energy, which has been adopted by our culture is *kundalini,* and in some mixtures of Western Paganism and in Indian healing techniques, Kundalini is revered as a goddess. In Druidcraft, it is referred to simply as 'the serpent within'. Curled up at the base of the spine, it tastes the air but doesn't stir, waiting.

The Druids of our ancestors were, according to folklore, called *naddred,* or adders – the most potent snake of the British islands. Though we have few sources to explain why this was so, it is linked with the egg-shaped amulets called in Gaelic *glain naddair,* meaning 'serpent stones', which were also called *glain na droid,* 'Druid stones'. (My guide, Nathair, uses the same name, though my spelling is the phonetic – how I heard it when we first met.) These *glain* were noted by Pliny the Elder as being prized possessions of the Druids, holding within them some extraordinary power. Although to speculate in retrospect has its shortcomings, my sense is that this power was the ability of the Druids to use the deep serpent energy within themselves and, where appropriate, to provoke it to rise in others.

The tale of St Patrick throwing the snakes out of Ireland, first recorded in the twelfth century, is often assumed to be a reference to his getting rid of the Druids. Indeed in many religions and cultures, in many individuals, the snake is seen as dangerous, if not downright evil, even in lands where there are no native snakes or very few that are dangerous. We can make connections between the myths and reputation of the snake and the force of male energy, the penis sleeping, rising and thrusting forward, or we can connect it with the eternal energy that wakes and uncurls, rising up the spine, bringing with it the heat and strength of our very being. Whichever we use, what is potentially dangerous is not the power itself but the way in which it is used.

In Druidcraft the serpent energy is something deep and mysterious which needs to be treated with particular caution. The eye and the mouth of the serpent are the doorway to our fundamental power, the source of our life energy, and its body is the flow of that power, where it is solid enough to feel physically.

Dragons are understood to have the same power within the land. They hold the energy, directing it with their movement, shifting according to what attracts them, burning up or destroying what they don't like, shaking or withdrawing, holding safe and strong or snarling with rage. Areas of specific power are often referred to as the heads of dragons and the bodies of dragons can be mapped across the landscape.

These dragons of the land have no compassion for humanity, existing for their own perfect expression, interacting on a global level. At best they treat us as curiosities, moving to peer at the sacred work we do. On the whole we are regarded as insignificant or irritating, like buzzing flies. In the same way, the serpent that lies within has no attachment to life. It will offer us opportunities to survive (by fighting a virus or giving us supernatural strength in a crisis), but essentially it exists on the level of spirit, and will listen to the guidance that comes from our eternal spirit, for whom the temporal nature of a particular body and its personality are comparatively irrelevant. Both dragon and serpent will, if we are quiet, ignore us. If we aren't – and we don't want them to destroy us – they demand a profound and very conscious respect. Their potential power is beyond what the human mind can conceive.

There are many reasons why we would not wish to attract the serpent's attention – such as wanting to avoid insanity... Yet if it is done well, it reveals an experience of living which nothing can match. While the most perfect power will flow when we open purposefully and in joy, the energy can rise even with the body wracked in pain. Strong emotion, a flash of anger, shock, or extra-ordinary fear can lead the creature to strike out of its own accord or through some unconscious bidding. Yet it has to be remem-bered that this energy is not emotion but spirit. When it rises quickly, the mind usually manages to grasp what has happened in retrospect, then the serpent recedes, back into the darkness, as fast as it emerged.

When it lifts its head with staring eyes and starts slowly to move, slowly enough for each coil to be felt, sliding up and around the spinal column like a weight of bright light, bringing its uncompromising power through the centre of the nervous system, the centre of the energy body, the pain can be excruci-ating. I thought that childbirth was the very limit of human pain endurance until I went through a week of initiation into the power of the serpent energy. My temperature burned at well over 100° throughout, my skin softening into blisters from the het inside, my brain melting, leaving me in pools of utter stupor. Every nerve was alive and taking in information, to the extent that my sense of smell sated any need for food. I could barely open my eyes to the searing light of a cloudy day.

In my experience the pain of the serpent rising doesn't disappear completely, for as long as we are in the body we still have blocks and resistance to the perfect flow of spirit. The more it happens, though, the easier it is. The body becomes more flexible as the heat breaks down calcification and other build ups, and the fear that is provoked by the force of the process dimin-ishes. The Druidcraft teachings which guide us to awaken the serpent consciously, and to work with the energy for healing and for clarity, encourage us to find a state of high energy beforehand. To feel the serpent rise from that place of joy is a very different experience. There is no instant transcendence, such as when we lift out of the apparent chains of the physical body reaching for the deity of the stars and beyond matter – when we do that the serpent has nothing significant to hold on to and the process loses most of its powerful potential. Instead there is a perfect balance of total freedom of the spirit with an absolute wakefulness of the body unconstrained.

This is the essence of *awen*. It is a doorway within to the gods of creation.

* * *

The path is thick mud. My boots are weighed down with it. I want to take them off but there are too many fallen holly leaves and brambles to make it viable to walk barefoot in the moonlight. I'm sweating and shivering with the cold. I want to rest but the need to get to the mound is overwhelming. The energy of the forest brushes past and through me, caressing, but I'm enraged and half-blinded by my humanity.

Why? I scream inside myself, not wanting to see, not wanting to understand.

Yet as the image slips through it brings with it that strange calm, the calm of my sacred room which pervades and holds every action, every thought and prayer that happens within it. I want to swipe it from my head. I want to get stoned on vodka and cocaine like I did in my teens and just *forget!* But at the same time I gaze at the scene without a thought in my mind. I gaze at where she lay on the couch, her face taunt with agony, bathed in the soft light of the painted bulb, the burning oils soothing, colouring the air. Her fingers were white, clasped in rigid tension, her breathing staggered, and she gasped for air as she half told me, barely conscious of my presence, what it was that her memory was holding before her. Her fingers shook and twitched as her arms came up around herself, holding the baby, holding herself, the baby that was dead, and though she was lying on the couch she started to curl and rock. She knew the baby was dead. It hadn't died in her arms. It was given to her dead, taken from its birthing between her legs, when she had lost consciousness.

There was a moment of stillness. Though a part of me had wanted to shake her awake, I also knew it was not my right and I'd waited, holding back, holding the sanctity of the space, clearing the air of negativity and centring again, emptying myself of any judgement as to what was happening.

Then suddenly she was screaming, shaking the house, 'Bastard! You took my baby! You bastard!' and then whimpering, as if realizing her hands were empty. The baby was not there. Did she know it was not his fault? With her shaking hands she clutched at her womb. Reliving the bleeding, the dreadful endless bleeding, and I closed my eyes as if in doing so I could give her a little more dignity. I closed my eyes to cope with the energy that was sliding, knowing that she was sliding with it, that she was letting go, yet listening to each word that she was mumbling as her memories got mixed with the drugs, blurring into hallucination. I didn't know what she had taken but as I shifted my hands across her solar plexus and through her aura I could taste the bitterness drying my tongue.

I looked up and saw Aktinia, her eyes closed and watched for a moment her hands hovering over Jenny's forehead. I wanted to ask, *Are we doing the right thing?* But before I could find the words she had answered, looking into my eyes with that strangely detached certainty only a spirit seems to have. I wanted to check again that she was OK – she was Jenny's teacher, not mine, and perhaps I'd misjudged – but at that moment Nathair appeared beside me. Her hand moved over mine and the heat intensified.

Carry on, priestess. Know now your doubts are your own.

Saliva was dribbling out of Jenny's mouth. She coughed. So clearly I could feel her spiralling, downwards, inwards, letting go. Nathair's presence had pulled me back into my centre and again I had stilled and cleared the air for the inevitable. The room was prepared. I was prepared. I had called to my goddess to be with us.

The mound of the long barrow emerges through the trees, a the darkness in the moon's glow, and I stumble over my boots, falling to its slope, my head in my hands, the memory hits me of those moments just after she stopped breathing. *No, no! Help me, please help me!* I had been so calm. All the faith I had needed had been there, all the guidance. But now it is too much to bear, as the pain of her grief balanced on fingertips above me, crashes down through my body. And it is not only her pain, but the rage at the cruelty of nature that allows so much love and caring to be fed into a child that dies. Onto that pain, a weight that is strapped to the nerves of my spine, comes the crumbling wall of desolation, brick by brick, of brutality and famine, of torture and disease, of the distortion and exhaustion, all the faces of those who have died and cried calling to me, drifting through me, watching me as if waiting for some bloody gift of relief, salvation.

I can't do it anymore! My hands, now muddy, crush the brown leaves that cover the grassy mound, hurling them back into the dark air at the trees from which they'd fallen. *No more!* Gravity has doubled, the world is spinning too fast, and I cling to the earth, with tears too big to fall, till I cry aloud, 'No more! It makes no sense!'

The noise stuns me. The forest is silent.

Who am I calling to? Why am I still fooling myself that anyone is listening? How could I live so long with such an illusion, such a pathetic search for purpose when there is none, such a sad craving for friendship that I have to create invisible people? Isn't it time right now to admit the reality, that all this is no more than the stench of bile vomited out of my twisted psyche, somehow made into art...?

Stupefied, I stare at the mud and grass, the little twigs, and slowly I curl into the smallest heap of insignificance I can manage with a human form.

It isn't as if, were I to call, there would be no answer. Cataleptic, I gaze out into the shimmering trees, the energy of the dryads talking, swaying with their own rhythm. It isn't as if that image will go away. At the head of the mound a big puddle of still black water is like a mirror to the elder and the oak against the sky.

I didn't ask to do this job! You gave it to me! I didn't want to be a fucking priestess. I just wanted to be me. What do I have, what am I, that I have to do this job? So much pain. And it was you who gave that to me too, with this vision of the world!

Who? More people of my imagination.

My doubt sneers and spits on everything I am, everything I respect, everything I hold on to. Seabhac, yes Seabhac would laugh at me now, or watch and wait and chat with the spirit that resides in his staff.

What kind of insanity created him as a guide? Ha.

Thoughts seem to land in my mind one by one, like dry dead leaves drifting through the night to the forest floor.

He would guide me to go through this, contain it and dive in. But I stare, utterly blank, quite unable to move. There is no fear, no expectation. I simply stare *But I've lost it*: Through the darkness, the shadows that thicken the air all around me, gold and copper leaves are floating down like feathers. I watch, barely moving, until panic rises, too intense, and I look up, knowing that these leaves are falling from absolutely nowhere, fighting the tension in my neck that is my need *not* to see.

There's a movement within the branches of the yew or somewhere beyond which ripples right through me. I wait for it to settle, but when it moves again I shift my eyes. It feels like deer. Then I'm aware of the form of a woman. And in that very instant I am hurled off the mound as if the earth had been pulled from under my feet. I'm not sure if it's my dream or dense reality until, slamming into my body, I hit the ground. For a moment I lie there in utter horror. My hand is in some water and the cold forces me up. I stagger to my feet, breaking through the shock and breathing hard, fear tight around my chest, waiting for the next movement.

'I can't see you,' I snarl.

I can feel my claws as I'm stuck half way between cat and human, then through the trees I see it again and spinning round I am *thwacked*, reeling backwards into the mud, holding onto my stomach and choking as if I've been kicked. I am very wide awake. I get back to my feet, very human now, standing firm, breathing fast. I stamp a foot on the muddy ground, my teeth clenched, determining it to be real. And the woman emerges out of the shadows.

'I am real,' I snarl again, not quite sure why I've said it. My heart is pounding.

Oh yes, she nods.

Why did she have to die?

Why do you doubt? Does someone else's view so affect your own?

Through the forest, I hear the sound again, that beautiful sound, the baby downstairs. I had shifted my hands to ease her choking cough and my words had rolled out of me, soothing her, guiding her. She struggled to return to the moment, to the present, and when she'd opened her eyes they were full of love and tears and sweet relief.

'I can hear him', she'd murmured.

Then we'd gently talked about what had hurled her back into some vision of her own fear and loss and she'd shone, so much of that energy having left, that fear released, as if she'd confronted the image of grief, fatal grief, and her own death. As we'd closed the session, I'd laughed. 'You see, it wasn't so bad, not being with him for just an hour or so. Mick has done a fine job daddying.'

'Yes,' she'd smiled shyly. 'He does sound happy enough.'

My lady, I breathe deeply, *am I fit to do this work?*

Lie down and we will show you.

I lie on the old burial mound, 5,000 years old, and close my eyes in the darkness, aware of Nathair beside me.

* * *

Doubt is always there. Perhaps if it weren't we would not be so very wide awake, nor so open in our senses, listening, watching. In Druidcraft, as we search for where we belong, in time and in space, we respond to the songs and the calls of every spirit around us, nurturing relationships, learning to hear and to truly communicate, knowing that only by doing this will we find true responsibility.

Samhain is not just the ending of the year, the ending of the day, the ending of a life, but also an opportunity to die a little to ourselves. Through doubt the world emerges in colours of our lowest energy, rationalized through our intellect as much as is possible, through those protective belief systems, and stamping with their emotion. Yet in allowing it to express itself, we awake to ourselves a little more. We question, we clarify, we make our choices.

Just as in times past, with the winter ahead, all but the breeding stock of the flock or herd would be slaughtered, at Samhain we let go of the past that will burden us and drain our resources. The harvest is in and for a short while we sit and look at what we have. We have walked the whole circle, from the moment when inspiration reached into the womb of our souls, through the first light of dawn, through its acknowledgements and clarification, the times of interaction with others and the sourcing of the power which would fuel its needs, the leap of commitment and the moment of release into its own natural flow, so the tides that take it and return our energy as manifest creation. Now, with our inspiration held in form in our hands, we must let it go, give way to the chaos once more of total potential. If we stop now, we will drown. The water at Samhain is still and deep.

The past does not exist, except in how it is affecting our present. The things we carry in our pack or grasp in our fists, things that drag us down, the traumas and the triumphs which should be soft and malleable memories, become distorted aspects of the present, battered from being carried too far. In letting go, we also release future expectations that are based upon the past and we start to find an objectivity that allows us the freedom of pure expression.

So it is that at Samhain, through respect and tenderness we honour the spirits of those who have died within our community, our family, our spiritual heritage and our inner world. We give thanks for what we have gained through the year's cycle of creation and creativity. And with joy we once again open out to our potential, breaking out of our constraints in a festival of glorious laughter and chaos.

When the whole circle is known and each point reflects its opposite along the paths within, the understanding that we exist naturally and peacefully in the centre becomes more and more real. From that place of perfect balance, any burden or redundant weight, any crisis of energy or emotion, will be felt and found with ease and the balance restored.

It is said that to find divine inspiration for their work the Bards of old would seek out those places where the energy of the earth was strong and the spirits beyond the mists were more than usually active. There they would stay for an allotted period of time. A Bard would emerge from this meditation (if he survived) in one of two states: madman or poet. As we slide, in Druidcraft, between the worlds of nature and spirit, reaching for our source of inspiration, the chalice that is filled with *awen*, the only liquid which will quench the thirst of our spirit, it's easy to wonder if we didn't make it to be the poet.

Yet we have a language in Druidry we, have the tools of our Craft, which are always there, sharp and clear, to ease the doubt. And these words and tools create a product which has such a brilliance its value cannot be questioned.

It is a perspective of beauty, an understanding of pain, truth, and freedom of self and creativity. It is a centrepoint within the ever changing spirals of life that shines with the most exquisite serenity.

* * *

Five hours ago this place was filled with people. It was black dark, a stormy night, the rain coming sideways through the trees in bursts, thrown by gusts of the westerly wind. Thirty people were laughing and shivering around the grove, trying their best to find shelter for their lanterns, which kept blowing out. But not long into the rite, with the fire ablaze, the energy had changed and with wild music and dancing the old year had been honoured, and all that was crass and redundant, all that would compromise through the cold moons, was cast into the flames. Accolon, with his mandolin slung over his shoulder had caught me up in his arms and we'd spun round the circle, and Silverwolf had watched me with that beautiful smile. The drums had danced their driving rhythms and the chants had risen and found their peak when with a shout the year was brought to its end.

Into the silence had crept the spirits of confusion, into the gap between the old and the new, between the past and the paths of the future, when the darkness is at its most pervasive. With masks and veils, talking rubbish walking backwards, half a dozen of the Grove started to spread the confusion, the Bards joining in with a cacophony of nonsense, the drummers now entirely out of sync.

It's an onslaught to the mind unless you're willing to get involved, and last night I had watched as people got lost and found their place in the chaos and I had watched the spirits of the forest, who in turn were watching us bemused, and I had watched the spirits of our ancestors, who'd gathered to be a part of the celebration. I had watched this hidden company as it grew and smiled as even the most grounded of the Grove began to feel the presence.

I had called out into the grove for silence to be restored, for the spirits to be honoured, our offerings given and the first steps of the new cycle to be put into motion.

That was five hours ago.

It is a little before dawn. After taking them back to the house, after coffee and teas and blessings, after seeing them all off, yawning and warm inside, I had tried to sleep but quite in vain. My body was buzzing and my mind so alive it was jumping at any vague thoughts which might pass by. So I'd come back to the grove. The wind had moved off, taking the rain clouds with it, and making my way across the fields I had chanted to the moon that hung low in the indigo blue of the western sky. The grove felt wonderfully empty, offering a quietness within my whirling energy.

The fire, little more than glowing embers that cast hardly a shadow, is now licking up the wood, flames flickering around the trees, glancing off the leaves which are fluttering down around me. The floor of the grove is awash with their gold and copper and palest yellow. Acorns and hairy beech nuts lie scattered about, and by the glow of the fire I wander around the circle, slowly feeling every footfall as it lands upon the earth and gently singing to myself.

I reach into my pocket and bring out a sticky wodge of bread spread thick with honey. A vixen barks close by amongst the trees and I look up to see a face peeking through the hazel under-growth. Then it's gone. Breaking the bread in two, I leave half

SPIRITS OF THE SACRED GROVE

beneath the tree.

'Blessings of joy, spirits and little people of this place.'

When I return to the fire, I kneel and say my prayers of thanksgiving, calling to my ancestors, to all whose paths have brought me to this moment in time, to all whose energy has helped create this reality, this beauty. Breaking off a piece of the bread, I put it into my mouth and let it melt, its sweetness flooding through me. Then, offering it in the name of my Lady Nemetona, I put it into the fire so that its essence might be joyfully shared with all those souls.

For all that you are so am I. And all that we will be.

Hello beautiful lady

I look up. 'Hello'.

He stands at the edge of the clearing in his big coat and smiles that smile that makes me melt inside. Not taking my eyes from his, I walk to the gateway in the west and open the circle, bidding him enter my sacred space. He bows as he walks in and goes to make his greetings to the spirits of the place.

By the fire he takes me in his arms and I curl myself around him inside his coat.

'You left a cold space in the bed.'

'I was too bouncy to sleep.'

'Forest pixie.'

We hold each other for a while, embraced by the circle and the dryads around us, and as our souls open out, our bodies, as if of their own accord, begin to sway to some pulse that we share. He buries his face in my hair, nuzzling into my neck, and sings softly. I breathe him in, feeling our bodies in perfect rhythm and, letting him go into his strength I feel his energy start to find its freedom. His body is hard yet so fluid, and I feel his hips and his muscles as he moves. As my own body responds, the heat builds, the energy rising, in its rich silence expanding, spreading through my being, lightness and pressure. He puts back his head and his smile spreads across his face, his eyes staring wolf. When he looks into mine, he whispers, 'Who are you?'

I laugh. 'Forest pixie.'

'You awaken my energy.'

'You awaken my mind.'

He whispers, gazing into my eyes, 'My priestess of the night'.

'My Lord of the Light, in your sweet innocence, you guide me.'

'In your darkness I find such inspiration.'

'*Awen,*' I whisper. 'Let it flow!'

We dance and swirl, our spirits weaving, and the magic of the grove slips into my perception, and the man in my arms is my Lord of the Wild, and the sensations within every nerve of my body are suddenly magnified, forcing me to breathe through the tension, to let go into a new high, my love for a man now entwined with my love for my god. When we kiss I taste life on his lips, for he is the breath of the sky and the roll of the sea, and he is rich with the scent of the stag, and I am the hind. And with every move I make, he shimmers like the leaves of summer in the sunlight. By the fire we make love, our love for each other so beautifully woven, strand upon strand, with our love for the land which lies beneath us.

'You smell of the falling rain,' he murmurs.

My fingers play through his hair, taking out the leaves and the bark. Every move that we make shifts the circle, making me dizzy. I close my eyes and lay my head upon his chest, just bathing in the energy that is held within the grove, floating in the silence. Perhaps for a moment we sleep. I don't know. As dawn's pale light starts to slip into our consciousness I move, stretching and breathing in the clarity of the air.

'Silverwolf?'

He looks up. *Bobcat.*

'Do you feel it? This energy. Us'

'A new cycle beginning.'

'Fed by this.'

I close my eyes affirming the intention, and with hardly a word spoken aloud we get up and make our offerings into the last of the fire. Walking the paths of the circle in that gentle stillness of dawn we give our thanks to the spirits of the place. I bow to Tyroshai and look to the dryads, their leaves fallen to the ground with the last of the nuts, their energy slowing, turning in. And the forest in its serenity seems richer than ever.

My Lady Nemetona...

But no words come. All I feel the need to say rests calm within me, in a part of my soul that seems now to hold my soul, and I know that she knows, for she too is within me.

As I open the circle, a rush of cold air moves through us and we laugh and move to share each other's warmth. It's hard to leave the grove. Yet I also know now that I never do.

The world is calling, my son in his warm bed is just starting to wake.

'Come on Bobcat. I'll make you your favourite breakfast.'

'Avocado, chilli pepper and raspberries?'

'Are you pregnant?'

'With some new crazy plan.'

We walk through the forest, glowing with its confidence, sensing how in this perfect moment the bounds of the *nemeton* have spread wide, out of the holy sanctuary and clear across the world, ecstasy of the body and soul spreading into ecstasy of perception.

We walk down the road and past the pub. There is a glorious stillness, silence.

'What a beautiful world.'

It's your world you're seeing, says Seabhac, standing at the end of our drive as if he'd been waiting. *You made it, priestess.*

A light goes on in a downstairs window. People are just starting to wake up. Me too.

Blessed be as blessed is.

Appendix

Glossary and Terms

Nathair:	From Gaelic naddair, pron. 'nathair'. An adder. One of my spirit guides.
Nemeton:	pron. phonetically (Gaelic). A sanctuary.
Nemetona:	The goddess of the sanctuary or holy place.
Seabhac:	pron. 'she'vac' (Gaelic). A hawk. One of my spirit guides.
Tyroshai:	pron. 'Ti'roshay'. No idea of its meaning - Tyr is a northern war god. My grove guardian.
awen:	pron. 'ah'oo'wen' (Welsh). Flowing spirit, inspiration. In Druidry it is used as a chant that opens us to the flow of inspiration and the energy of spirit.
eisteddfod:	pron. 'ice'teth'fod' (Welsh). A session or sitting, and the time during a gorsedd (qv) for story-telling, poetry and music.
gorsedd:	pron. 'gor'seth' (Welsh). High seat, originally referring to the sacred mounds where tribes gathered for special occasions, but now meaning a gathering of Bards.
Grove:	A group of people come together for a ritual or to celebrate in the Druid tradition, as opposed to a
grove:	(not capitalized). A circle of trees or woodland clearing used as a temple site in the Druid tradition.
little people:	A term used to denote the original or first people of the Pretannic Isles who are said to have partly disappeared into the mists at the first invasions, to dwell between the human world and that of the faerie.
lloegwar:	pron. 'chthloy-gor' (Welsh). A stranger. This is

the word I heard that day but I can't find it in
modern Welsh, though gw^r means 'man' and
Lloegr is 'England'. He was a Saxon.

sain: pron. 'sa'hn' (Scots Gaelic). Similar to the
Native American word translated as 'smudge'.
Saining is a process of burning incense, particularly herbs, to cleanse, lift or alter the atmosphere or energy of a place or person.

shamanic: Shaman is Siberian word for the priests and
healers of the indigenous people. It is now used
to describe any Pagan practice which walks in
the spirit worlds.

skyclad: Naked; first used to describe the naked fakirs of
India and imported into British Paganism by
Gerald Gardner.

The Solar Festivals

Midwinter: The winter solstice festival, celebrated on the
astronomical solstice, around 21 or on 24
December, also called Yule, Alban Arthan. The
meaning of Alban is unknown, although it is
thought to derive from an early Brythonic word
meaning 'white, bright, light'. Arthan (Welsh) is
thought to refer to the constellation of the Great
Bear, though some consider it to refer to Arthur,
the king, spelling it Arthuan.

Spring Equinox: Celebrated between 20 and 23 March, also
called Alban Eilir (Welsh), meaning 'regeneration' or 'spring', or Eiler. Some give its
meaning poetically as 'earth'.

Midsummer: The summer solstice festival, celebrated around
21 or on 24 June, also called Alban Hefin
(Welsh), meaning 'summer', or Heruin, with
the poetic meaning of 'shore'.

Autumn Equinox:	Celebrated between 20 and 23 September, also called Alban Elfed (Welsh), meaning 'autumn', or Elued, with the poetic meaning of 'water'.

The Pastoral/Agricultural Festivals

Imbolc:	pron. 'im'olk' (Irish Gaelic), with a debated meaning, either referring to ewe's milk or swelling of the womb. The festival of spring, celebrated on the full moon of Aquarius or 2 February; also Gwyl Fair (Welsh/Brythonic), meaning 'Feast of Mary', Candlemas.
Beltane:	pron. 'bel'tain' (Irish Gaelic), meaning 'the Fires of Bel'. The festivial of summer, celebrated on the full moon of Taurus or 1 May, also called Calan Mai (Welsh/Brythonic), meaning 'the calends of May', May Day.
Lughnasadh:	pron. 'loo'nass'ah' (Irish Gaelic), meaning 'the Festival of [the sun god] Lugh'. The second festival of summer, celebrated on the full moon of Leo or 1 August; also called Gwyl Awst (Welsh/Brythonic), meaning 'the Feast of August', Lammas (Saxon), meaning 'Loaf mass', Bron Trogain (Irish), meaning 'Earth's sorrowing in autumn'.
Samhain:	pron. 'sow'inn' (Irish Gaelic), with probable meaning of 'Summer's end', possibly related to the word samhaim, meaning 'to quiet down or become silent'. The festival of the beginning of winter, considered by many modern Pagans as the end of the year/beginning of the next, celebrated on the full moon of Scorpio or 31 October; also called Nos Galan Gaeaf (welsh/ Brythonic), meaning 'Night of the winter calends', Hallowe'en.

The Universal Gorsedd Prayer

as written by Iolo Morgannwg

Grant, O God, thy protection
And in protection, strength
And in strength, understanding
And in understanding, knowledge
And in knowledge, the knowledge of justice
And in the knowledge of justice, the love if it
And in the love of it, the love of all existences
And in the love of existences, the love of God
and all goodness.

The Druid Prayer

re-written by myself and Sandra Guy

Awaken within us, O God and Goddess, your
inspiration
Your inspiration of true strength
Your strength of true understanding
Your understanding of true knowledge
Your knowledge of natural law
Your love of natural law
And in the love of natural law, the love of all
existences
And in the love of all existences, the love of our
God and Goddess and all creation.

Moon Books invites you to begin or deepen your encounter with
Paganism, in all its rich, creative, flourishing forms.